A MIGHTY PURPOSE

A MIGHTY PURPOSE

How Jim Grant Sold the World on Saving Its Children

Adam Fifield

Other Press
New York

Frontispiece: James P. Grant holding a small child at a UNICEF-assisted center for unaccompanied children in Nyamata, Rwanda, while a worker looks on. Photograph © UNICEF/NYHQ1994-0481/PressRWANDA, 1994

Production editor: Yvonne E. Cárdenas
Text designer: Julie Fry
This book was set in Minion and Alternate Gothic.

10 9 8 7 6 5 4 3 2 1

Library of Congress Cataloging-in-Publication Data

Fifield, Adam, author.
    A mighty purpose : how Jim Grant sold the world on saving its children / Adam Fifield.
        p. ; cm.
    ISBN 978-1-59051-603-4 (hardcover) — ISBN 978-1-59051-604-1 (e-book)
        1. Grant, James P.   2. UNICEF—History.   3. United Nations—Officials and employees.   4. Child welfare—History.   I. Title.
        [DNLM: 1. Grant, James P.   2. UNICEF.   3.   Administrative Personnel—Biography.   4. International Agencies—history.
5. Child Advocacy—history.   6. Child Health Services—history.
7. Child Welfare—history.   8. History, 20th Century.]
    HV703.F54 2015
    362.7092—dc23
    [B]   2014050069

To my wife, Kathy, and my children, Will & Audrey

"*This is the true joy in life, the being used for a purpose recognized by yourself as a mighty one; the being thoroughly worn out before you are thrown on the scrap heap; the being a force of Nature instead of a feverish selfish little clod of ailments and grievances complaining that the world will not devote itself to making you happy.*"

— George Bernard Shaw, *Man and Superman*,
"Epistle Dedicatory to Arthur Bingham Walkley"

I had never heard of Jim Grant until about a year before I decided to write a book about him. I was aware of the organization he led, the United Nations Children's Fund, or UNICEF, mostly from its popular Trick-or-Treat for UNICEF fund-raising campaign on Halloween. In late 2007, as a journalist who recognized how precarious my profession was becoming, I decided to try something different — at least for a while. I answered a job ad for a writer and editor at the US Fund for UNICEF, a nonprofit that raises funds and awareness for the UN agency in the United States. I ended up staying for more than five years, leaving in 2013. In my second or third year there, while rummaging through a filing cabinet, I found a tattered copy of an anthology of essays about Grant that was entitled *Jim Grant: UNICEF Visionary*. It had been published by UNICEF and was out of print; Grant had been dead for more than thirteen years. I thumbed through the pages and was transfixed — how was it, I wondered, that I was just now learning about someone who had so profoundly altered the course of recent history, who had shattered the idea of what was possible and impossible in the fight against poverty?

I was a new father at the time — I now have a son and a daughter — and felt an immediate, palpable admiration for what he had done for so many other parents around the world. Who was this man? How and why did he do this? I wanted to find out.

The following account is not a comprehensive history of UNICEF. Nor is it a thorough chronicle of Jim Grant's life. It is a narrative that selectively focuses on key moments during his tumultuous fifteen-year tenure at UNICEF and on several relationships that were pivotal to his unprecedented achievements. Many important episodes, issues, and individuals are not included in these pages or are mentioned only briefly. This is ultimately a personal story that I hope will inspire and enlighten and perhaps trigger some contemplation of the possibilities for progress and of one person's ability to truly change the world.

A MIGHTY PURPOSE

Introduction
YOUR CHILD WILL LIVE

The baby was almost gone. Eyes dull, skin pulled taut over tiny bones, mouth gaping silently, he lay slack in his mother's arms. She had wrapped him in a towel. At only a few months, his brief life was receding. Malnutrition and dehydration had staked their claims on his brittle body. It was no surprise to anyone here on the outskirts of the City of Death.

In September 1992, Baidoa, Somalia, was the epicenter of a raging famine kindled by a drought and vicious fighting. The mother and her baby had come to a medical tent in a camp teeming with sick, displaced people. About twenty other mothers and children waited there for help, though they did not look like they hoped for, or expected, much. Their despair was quiet and stifling.

A thin, white, slightly stooped, seventy-year-old American man walked into the tent. He wore an untucked blue short-sleeved shirt with a bulging chest pocket. He glanced around and then asked, "Can someone get me a cup of water?" His voice was crisp, his words clipped. After someone handed him the water, he reached into his stuffed chest pocket and pulled out a plastic packet. He then produced a spoon. He tore open the packet, spilled some of its powdery contents into the cup of water, and stirred it. The solution he had made was a mix of salts and sugars that can quickly halt the deadly effects of severe dehydration. He walked over to the mother and baby and cupped the child's head in one of his hands. He set the cup down and began to spoon the solution into the baby's mouth. The mother's eyes widened.

"Everything is all right," he told her gently as he fed the baby. "He will live. Your child will live." A man standing nearby translated the words. After about ten minutes, he stopped. He said aloud: "I want the same thing done for all the children here." Then he left.

Jim Grant was the head of UNICEF, the United Nations Children's Fund, and he was in Somalia to see how his agency was faring in an almost impossible situation. Accompanying him was UN official and former UNICEF Somalia representative David Bassiouni, who relayed this story.

A few days later, an inquiry into the child's condition showed that Grant's promise had been kept. The child had recovered.

Grant visited many such places over the years, places where the death of a child was nothing out of the ordinary, where it was so commonplace that it was numbly, quietly endured. Countries racked by war and disasters, but also peaceful regions devastated by a sinister force even deadlier — poverty.

In refugee camps, slums, run-down rural health centers, thatch-walled classrooms, remote mountain villages, Jim Grant

was an incongruous sight. Unrelentingly upbeat with seemingly no inhibitions, he would traipse through scenes of jubilant
celebration and those of paralyzing despair. He would cheerfully join troupes of singing children. He would dance and clap
his hands and laugh out loud. He would throw his arm around
the shoulder of a local village chief or a reserved government
minister. He would lift up babies and hold them to his cheek.
Squatting amidst a throng of children, he would work the tiny
crowd: "Can I get a smile? Can you give me a smile?" Himself
the father of three boys, he became the most powerful champion for impoverished children the world has ever seen. They
were his warrant and gave him the license to push every edge of
every envelope.

And push he did. His controversial tenure would upend
this venerable UN agency and forever alter the face of global
health and international development. The death of millions
of children every year from malnutrition and disease had been
seen by many in the international community as inevitable and
was even tacitly accepted. Grant changed that. As a result, the
issue of children's well-being would soar to a position of unprecedented political and social prominence. During a grievous
global recession, he spearheaded a historic surge in worldwide
childhood immunization rates — an astonishing achievement
that many had considered simply inconceivable. He convened
the largest-ever gathering of world leaders, placing the needs
of the world's youngest inhabitants squarely on the world stage
for the first time. But the most important legacy of Grant's leadership is the children themselves. His child survival revolution,

as he called it, is estimated to have saved the lives of tens of millions of children during his tenure and many millions more after his death in 1995.

By the time Grant took the helm in 1980, UNICEF was already widely respected for its independence, decentralized structure, and hands-on effectiveness. Created as a temporary agency to aid children suffering the after-effects of World War II, the United Nations International Children's Emergency Fund had provided clothing, health care, and powdered milk throughout postwar Europe and Asia (it had also bolstered milk production by equipping dairies in Europe and, later, Latin America). Becoming a permanent member of the UN system in 1953, UNICEF shortened its full name (losing "International" and "Emergency") but kept its acronym. It started to outgrow its original mandate, evolving from an emergency relief operation into a broader development organization that helped the most disadvantaged children all over the world — whether they were in the crosshairs of a natural disaster or enduring the quiet horror of sickness and malnutrition. This included providing vaccines and medicines (and in the case of malaria, the insecticide DDT) for mass antidisease campaigns; supporting feeding and nutrition programs; drilling wells, building latrines, and promoting sanitation; delivering basic medical supplies and equipment to support child and maternal health; and funding the training of health workers, midwives, and volunteers. In the early 1960s, UNICEF strove to find a place for children in the emerging international development movement and in countries' national development plans, and its programs began to encompass other issues, including education and family planning. It has always been voluntarily funded — by governments, corporations, foundations, individuals, and others — and operates at the invitation of governments. Its assistance is designed to strengthen countries' and communities' services for children and is primarily funneled through partnerships with government ministries, other aid agencies, nongovernmental organizations (NGOs), and local groups. For instance, while UNICEF provides vaccines and helps train immunizers, it does not actually administer immunizations; this is done by government health workers and volunteers.

Grant believed that UNICEF's annual income — $313 million in 1980 — was too small to make a lasting difference worldwide. UNICEF could be and do far more. By cultivating the agency's considerable but largely untapped political and social influence, he turned the children's organization into a propulsive global advocate — unlike anything the UN or the international community had ever experienced. Leader by leader, country by country, donor by donor — Grant supplied a moral spark that jolted governments and communities and contributors to spend more and do more to take care of children and to combat poverty. UNICEF soon went from cruising speed into hyperspace. Not only was it providing aid, it was sweeping away hulking bureaucratic obstacles, beefing up government budgets, setting concrete targets for advancing children's programs, and spurring an ethical shift in the developing and developed worlds.

For all his energy and obvious compassion, Grant was not an emotional or sentimental man — he did not tend to get misty-eyed at the sight of suffering children. That was not what truly motivated him. The children were the end, but they were also the means — a Trojan horse, as he would say. He would use them to prove a point — to show that it was possible to bring the benefits of progress to all people.

Though still revered in many countries around the world, Grant is virtually unknown in his own country. This may be a reflection of the population he and UNICEF set out to help — mostly nonwhite children from Africa, Asia, Latin America, and the Middle East, from forgotten corners of the world that many Americans couldn't find on a map. Boys and girls whose suffering and death hardly ever make the headlines, except maybe when they find themselves caught in a newsworthy crisis — or what Grant called a "loud emergency" (like the Ethiopian famine of 1984).

His triumphs did not come without a price. He drove UNICEF to its limits, and it cracked under the stress. He fostered a culture of risk-taking that turned red tape into ribbons and undoubtedly saved many lives, but also may have contributed to numerous lapses. A major financial scandal in the UNICEF Kenya office during his watch scarred the agency's reputation. He ruthlessly batted aside many things not central to his mission of advancing children's survival, and in so doing ignored unpleasant realities and dismissed some important issues. He punted difficult personnel decisions and refused to take action against staff members accused of serious wrongdoing. His management skills were both brilliant and reckless. As he strove more and more rapidly toward his unassailable goal, he was willing to do almost anything to reach it. Throughout it all, he never looked back — he was simply moving too fast. So fast, in fact, that he made no plan for a post-Grant UNICEF — after all, he *was* UNICEF.

A US World War II veteran who was born and raised in China and who would become a premier international aid expert, he remains an enigma to many who knew him. Colleagues and friends alike marveled at his extraordinary energy (one staffer called him a "metabolic freak"), his childlike optimism, and his prodigious ability to persuade just about anybody to do just about anything.

"Mr. Grant, he could conquer you," says former UNICEF Central America representative Agop Kayayan. "Convince you very easily, sometimes just by the eyes that would be shining."

Known to some on his staff as "the mesmerizer," Grant talked combatants into dropping their guns so kids could get vaccines and medicines; he cajoled taciturn presidents and prime ministers into setting aside big portions of their budgets for child health programs; he coaxed priests and imams into providing armies of volunteers to help immunize millions of children.

Lanky and thin-lipped with big, protuberant ears and often wearing a wrinkle-free Brooks Brothers suit, Grant had an old-fashioned, almost priestly bearing. Some were surprised to learn that he was nonreligious, because he radiated a messianic zeal — he was, after all, an apostle of sorts, a crusader for children. Part of his persuasive power stemmed from his undeniable moral urgency. You quickly learned that you could not oppose him — doing so, one staff member suggested, was like wrestling with an angel.

Some former UNICEF staff members get choked up talking about Grant — he still exerts an ineffable pull on them. Others roll their eyes and groan in annoyance. Sure, he was inspiring, but boy, could he be a pain in the ass. Holding meetings on the weekends. Keeping people in the office until one in the morning. Repeating the same thing over and over and over again, in meeting after meeting, as though he suffered from short-term memory loss. Dispatching staff to remote corners of the globe sometimes with little more than a day's notice. His unadulterated enthusiasm could chafe even his most loyal supporters. And his willingness to ignore major problems in order to maintain a locked-in focus on child survival was off-putting to many.

Some people feel his influence is overstated — don't get wrapped up in the mysticism and magnetism of this one man, they warn. The story is more complicated than a single person's blazing influence — and surely that's true. There was a vast network of allies, some of whom risked and lost their lives to advance the child survival revolution. It was not just Jim Grant's mission — it was the world's. But without him, would any of it have happened?

"Jim cleared all the brush away," says Richard Reid, former UNICEF regional director for the Middle East and North Africa and a close Grant adviser. "He went ahead despite tremendous drag from old-timers and naysayers, and he steadily collected allies and believers. He put people together in such catalytic perfection."

The UN had never really seen anyone like Jim Grant before. His kinetic "can-do" style clashed with the bureaucratic, consensus-driven culture of the world body. "His name and the UN in the same sentence are still jolting to me," says Grant's former chief of communications John Williams. "He was so adventurous and so free — in many ways, the epitome of what the UN is not."

He pushed political and diplomatic boundaries, and he also pushed the clock, wringing every encounter for every minute he could, wreaking havoc on every calendar he came across. He was perennially late to meetings, meals, and flights. He and his deputy executive director Richard Jolly even had a running competition to see who could leave last for the airport and still make the plane. Several staff members who accompanied Grant to the airport recall high-speed, white-knuckle rides during which Grant himself was perfectly calm, even relaxed. After a visit to the Philippines in the early 1980s, Grant and his chief of health, Dr. Steve Joseph, went on a "screaming ride through the traffic of Manila," as a driver raced them to the airport at the very last minute. "I've had a number of hair-raising experiences," says Joseph, "but this was the most hair-raising experience of my life. Jim, of course, was quite cool. He knew we were going to make that airplane...But it was insane. I was sure we were going to be killed." Even more shocking than the ride itself, adds Joseph, was Grant's "inability to accept the rest of the physical world around him."

In September 1994, then noticeably wasted and withered by cancer, Grant asked for a private meeting with Pakistan's prime minister Benazir Bhutto. He had been invited to a high-level education conference at Bhutto's residence with other UN agency leaders and major donors, and she had agreed to see him ten minutes before the meeting started. The glamorous forty-one-year-old heir to a political dynasty and the first woman elected to lead a Muslim nation, Bhutto had already acceded to many of Grant's wishes on child survival. But there were a few outstanding issues, according to former UNICEF Pakistan representative Jim Mayrides. Grant may have wanted Pakistan to improve on immunization gains it had already achieved and may have asked that it iodize its salt (iodine deficiency disorders were then the leading global cause of preventable mental impairment in children). In Bhutto's home office, Grant sat on one end of a long sofa and she sat on the other. Mayrides sat in a side chair. An armed guard hovered nearby.

Grant began his pitch, and as he spoke, started sliding across the couch closer to Bhutto. Like a magician, he began pulling items out of his pocket — a polio dropper, a packet of oral rehydration salts, an iodized salt testing dropper — and waving them at her. She smiled politely and nodded. Ten minutes became twenty, then thirty, then forty-five. Through her interior windows, Bhutto could see the shadows of her other guests, milling around in the hall. At this point, Grant had scooted a full two yards down the couch, like a prom date moving in for the kiss. He was now sitting right next to Bhutto. The armed guard was looking anxious. Sitting nearby, Mayrides nervously thought, *Jim, don't get too close.* Out of Grant's sunken, gaunt, wizened face, his eyes sparkled and pleaded.

Bhutto said she would consider his requests. Then she tried to end the meeting.

"I think it's time now," she said firmly. "You said ten minutes, and it's been more than double that. It's been charming." She then reached for an intercom button to tell the other guests to come in. But before her finger touched the button, Grant reached out and grabbed her hand.

"Madame Prime Minister," Grant said. "I have one more thing."

He told her that her presence at a major, yet controversial, population meeting in Cairo in a few days would be critical to the meeting's success; Grant believed that slowing population growth would advance child survival (and vice versa). Bhutto had already indicated she might not attend. Another UN official had asked Grant to try to convince her, says Mayrides. "You would make a stunning presentation," Grant told her, smiling brightly.

Bhutto laughed. "Everybody says if I go to the conference, they're going to kill me, they'll assassinate me," she said. This was not an idle concern; Bhutto had received death threats and would be assassinated thirteen years later. She told Grant, "I will consider what you say, my dear James."

A few days later, Prime Minister Bhutto attended the meeting with Grant.

Many of his former staff wondered aloud what kind of a businessman Grant would have been, had he chosen a career in the private sector. He was a masterful salesman. In his office at UNICEF headquarters, he kept a carefully filed collection of more than two hundred packets of oral rehydration salts, the "miracle" mixture of salts and sugars that he had dissolved in water and given out at the Somali refugee camp. Each packet had been manufactured in a different part of the world. The salts were central to Grant's crusade, and he carried packets with him everywhere; when visiting a village, he would often stop mothers and health workers on the street so he could show them how to use the solution. The packets were also a key marketing tool.

When an Italian official visited Grant in his office, recalls Sir Richard Jolly, Grant produced a packet of oral rehydration salts. "Do you realize that for ten cents, one can save a child's life if we have enough oral rehydration salts?" Grant said. He selected one of the packets from his collection, held it up, and said, "This is the packet." He then tossed it on his meeting table, but made sure that it landed upside down, so that its manufacturing location label was visible. Grant had chosen this particular packet because it had been made in Italy. The Italian aid minister picked up the packet, looked at it, and chuckled. "Do you realize, Mr. Grant, this packet is actually manufactured in a town ten miles from where I live?" At this point, says Jolly, Grant suddenly wore a look of surprise — as if to exclaim, *You don't say?*

If official channels were not available or accommodating, he would use unofficial ones. He had been doing these so-called end runs throughout his lifelong career in international development. In the mid-1960s, as the head of the US Agency for International Development (USAID) mission in Turkey, Grant nurtured the Green Revolution, helping provide farmers with high-yield wheat seeds developed by American agronomist Norman Borlaug — seeds that would eventually help to avert starvation for up to one billion people worldwide. But the Turkish agricultural research establishment didn't want the high-yield seeds brought in, because they feared they might make their own work irrelevant, according to environmental analyst Lester Brown, who then worked for the US Department of Agriculture. So Grant collaborated with a group, including Brown, to secretly smuggle the seeds into the country. "We did get the high-yielding wheat [seeds] in," says Brown. The Turkish Green Revolution went on, and wheat production went up.

A decade earlier, at the age of thirty-five, Grant had led the American aid mission in Sri Lanka (then called Ceylon) when floods paralyzed the country, stranding scores of people without food, water, or medicine. In the wee hours, he secured the help of a US military helicopter squadron, stationed on an aircraft carrier in the South China Sea. But they would not deliver the aid without an invitation from the Sri Lankan government. Instead of waiting for the sun to rise and following proper protocol — according to a close friend to whom Grant had relayed the story — Grant went to the prime minister's home in the middle of the night. He threw stones at his window. He roused his wife first, and she woke the prime minister, who gave Grant the emergency approval he needed. The helicopters apparently arrived shortly thereafter.

An obsessive quality fed his determination. During his rare vacations, he loved to snorkel. His senior communications adviser, Peter Adamson, remembers snorkeling with Grant in the waters off Montserrat when Grant noticed an old fishing trap on the sea floor. Several fish were stuck inside, and Grant decided he would free them. The trap was about twenty feet deep — "deeper than I could go," Adamson said. Grant dove down but could not release the fish. Eventually, after several attempts that left him gasping for air, he was able to let them out. "He could not stand the thought of these beautiful fish caught in this trap," says Adamson.

Despite his optimism and his cheerful exhortations and luminous smiles, "there was something lonesome about Jim," says Joseph. "There were times you would sense he had this crushing weight on him." Whatever success he had, it would never be enough. The more he pushed, the more children would live. With that knowledge, how could he rest?

Chapter 1
THE AMERICAN IS CRAZY

The American made them uneasy.

In a venerated international organization with a gravely important purpose, his enthusiasm was a little too incandescent, his banter a little too bold, his back slaps a little too brisk. Didn't he have any idea where he was? What this was all about? That this was not some think tank or law firm? That the decisions made here could mean the difference between life and death for millions of children? It was not a place for recklessness or bravado — mistakes and missteps could simply not be afforded. Was he naive? Clueless? Out of his depth? Or just bullheaded?

James Pineo Grant took over as the executive director of the United Nations Children's Fund on January 1, 1980, its third leader since the organization's founding in 1946. He was not a total stranger to UNICEF — he had represented the United States on the organization's board for two years, and his kinetic ambition was well known. He had, in fact, had his eye on the job and had lobbied hard for it. Nonetheless, his appointment arched many an eyebrow among UNICEF staff and others at the UN. *Jim Grant? Really? That American think tank guy?*

The man he was replacing, a respected diplomat and statesman named Henry Labouisse Jr., was also an American. (UNICEF has never had a non-American at the helm — tacit recognition of the fact that the US government has long been a major financial contributor.) But Labouisse was a cultured, genteel Southerner from New Orleans. He spoke French. He kept a neatly folded handkerchief in the breast pocket of his suit. He was understated in almost every respect and was essentially considered an honorary European. The word most often used by former UNICEF staff to describe him is "patrician." He was married to Eve Curie, the daughter of Nobel Prize–winning French scientists Marie and Pierre Curie. Labouisse himself had accepted the Nobel Prize on UNICEF's behalf in 1965.

In contrast, Jim Grant was a "cowboy" — a blunt, buoyant, sometimes uncouth, very "American" American. He was a World War II veteran who employed frequent military analogies, drank black coffee out of Styrofoam cups, whistled while strolling into his office, jogged in place to psych himself up for meetings, used words like "yesable" and "doable" and ate peanut butter and jelly sandwiches his wife had packed for him.

Ostensibly lacking any pretense, he at first seemed devoid of another quality: finesse. Some Europeans on the board and staff "felt he was not right for the position," recalls Mary Racelis, UNICEF's former regional director for eastern and southern Africa. "There was a feeling that he is too much of a maverick…that he doesn't know how to operate as a UN diplomat in these rarefied circles." It didn't help that Grant told some people that President Jimmy Carter had "appointed" him to the job. Carter had nominated him, but it was UN secretary general Kurt Waldheim who had officially appointed him (though everyone knew that the American president's choice would likely not be disregarded, which made Grant's phrasing all the more impolitic). He often invoked Carter's instruction to him that his job was not only to make UNICEF run well, but to improve the image of the UN as a whole within the United States. "He kept making references to the mandate he had from the president of the United States, over and over and over again," says Margaret Catley-Carlson, who represented Canada on the UNICEF board and who was later recruited by Grant to work for UNICEF. "There are several of us who said, 'Jim, you're working for an international organization.'"

Many staff members bristled at his frequent references to Carter and his old employer, USAID, where he had led several foreign missions. R. Padmini, an Indian woman who served as UNICEF's Ethiopia representative, recalls some reactions by staff: "'Does he think he's an agent of the US Government?'... 'He thinks he's still in USAID!'... 'This is the United Nations, not the United States!'" (In a testament to the smallness of the international development world, Henry Labouisse had previously run the International Cooperation Administration, the predecessor to USAID, in 1961, and had been Grant's boss.)

One rumor that would eventually leak into the corridors: Grant worked for the CIA. While this carried the sharp whiff of delusional paranoia, he had, decades earlier, briefly worked for an American college student group that would later be exposed as a notorious CIA front organization. According to his résumé, from August to October 1950 — after enrolling in Harvard Law School — Grant conducted surveys of student movements in Southeast Asia for the National Student Association "for the purpose of initiating program[s] to offset increasing Communist domination of SEA student movements." Grant may well not have been aware of any possible links with the CIA at the time, though "offsetting Communist domination" does not sound like a typical extracurricular activity.

Despite the taint of his Americanness, everyone at UNICEF would soon learn that Grant was far more sophisticated and worldly than he first seemed. His idealism was matched by his shrewdness, and in some ways he knew the peaks and pitfalls of international aid better than anyone else in the building. Still, the label of "American Dilettante" clung to him like old gum to a shoe.

His deeply lined face — a filigree of grooves earned from a life packed with intense and harrowing experiences — suggested an age beyond his fifty-seven years. So did his occasional tendency to stoop slightly, as though ducking under a low doorframe.

But what struck people more than anything else was that he was in a hurry. The jaunty lawyer moved fast and never let up on the gas. Except, that is, when he locked his gaze on you — his luminous blue eyes fixing you like tractor beams. In that moment, something in those eyes told you that the rest of the world did not matter. It was just you and him. "He really did burn with this fierce light," Catley-Carlson says. To fire up staff, he would sometimes cheerfully exult, "Onwards and upwards!" Or he would wish someone well by hollering, "Godspeed!" (though he was not religious). People would learn that it was only when you challenged him or shunted away from something he wanted to discuss that those iridescent eyes could dim or go glassy.

He insisted everyone call him "Jim," and, in a place of rigid hierarchy, gave little, if any, regard to rank or station. He stopped to talk to everyone, from secretaries to doormen to janitors to drivers to mail room employees. Unlike many other high-ranking UN officials, he did not seem to care about pomp or protocol. On visits to countries where UNICEF worked, he eschewed government limos; he'd rather ride in a van packed with his staff members. He traveled with only one small bag, a carry-on, and washed his own clothes in the hotel bathroom sink. He scribbled copious notes on tiny steno pads, napkins, envelopes, Post-its, and scraps of paper, and his swollen wallet, by one estimate, was more than three inches thick. He collected Chinese cookie fortunes (affixing them to his notebooks with Scotch tape) and had a fondness for historical quotes and inspirational aphorisms. One of his favorites: "The greatest pleasure in life is doing what other people say you cannot do."

Personal space, it seemed, was not a concept he understood or appreciated. Like a gregarious grandpa at a family gathering, he gripped wrists, pecked cheeks, wrapped his arms around shoulders. He behaved this way with everyone, from staff members to heads of state. His rapturous energy became a topic of water cooler speculation: Where did it come from? How can it not run out? And what is he going to do with it?

In his first communiqué to staff, Grant wrote of the need to accelerate UNICEF's work, equating the preventable deaths of as many as fourteen million children each year to "more than 100 Hiroshimas annually." He exhorted, "if more of us care" and "if more of us start acting now," the deadliest aspects of poverty could be defeated. You can excuse UNICEF staff for rolling their eyes a little after reading this. They were certainly aware of the dire odds facing impoverished children, and there was no doubt that they cared. Even so, could they do more and do it faster? Grant was priming them for something big.

If he annoyed or irked or simply confused staff members, Grant also disarmed them. Part of it was his anomalous even temper — many people said he was simply incapable of becoming upset, even in maddening circumstances. On one of his first field visits, to Pakistan, his humorous reaction to a freakish incident stunned the man who considered himself responsible.

Steve Woodhouse, a chipper Briton who was then a program officer in UNICEF's Pakistan office, took Grant to slums in Karachi to see some "soak pits" — big, sandy holes excavated to collect sewage from nearby homes. In a place where plumbing was nonexistent and drinking water could become contaminated with open sewage ("It was like Boston around 1650," says Woodhouse), the pits were critical to halting the spread of deadly waterborne diseases. Grant walked up to inspect one of the fifteen-foot-deep holes, and Woodhouse began to describe the program. Then, suddenly the edge of the pit gave way, crumbling down. It was the exact spot where Jim Grant stood. He tumbled in and fell, by Woodhouse's estimation, at least ten feet. "If he'd fallen any more, he would have been buried in the sand," he says.

Fortunately, the pit was not yet in use. Woodhouse and others quickly leaned over the side and reached down to pull him out. Coated with sand, Grant grabbed their hands and clambered back to the surface. Relieved his boss was alive and apparently uninjured, Woodhouse braced himself for a lashing. But he did not get one. Grant dusted himself off and remarked, "That was an interesting experience." Then he quipped, "Did you plan that, Steve?"

Reflecting later, Woodhouse still marvels at the reaction. "Any normal person would have been shaken up and angry," he says. "But he wasn't. He took it as a joke."

What also surprised Woodhouse during that same trip was Grant's rapport with children. In the slums of Karachi, Grant stooped down to pick up children and tried to get a laugh or giggle out of them. Most were malnourished and wearing tattered clothes or rags. "A lot of kids picked up by strangers would cry," says Woodhouse. "But I didn't see that happen with Jim. He felt very much at home with the kids, and the kids understood that, so they didn't cry... He was absolutely brilliant with children."

Former American UNICEF staffer Carl Tinstman witnessed Grant's soft spot for kids on numerous field visits in Africa. "Suddenly, you're looking around for the executive

director, and there he is, surrounded by forty or fifty children."
The father of three would wade into throngs of children and
squat down to reach their level. If a child carried a notebook or a
schoolbook — often his or her most prized possession — Grant
would ask to see it. Then he would crack it open and inquire
about the contents. "He had this sparkle in his eye," says Tinstman. And the kids could see it. They crowded around him as if
he was Santa Claus.

Maybe it was because Grant was, in many ways, like a kid
himself — giddy, hyper, implausibly hopeful. That youthful exu-
berance would serve him well in his first year, as he encountered
his biggest test yet: the calamitous aftermath of Cambodia's Killing Fields.

Pol Pot's Khmer Rouge had murdered as many as two million
people in a countrywide paroxysm of brutality. UNICEF and
other aid agencies had been kicked out when the ultra-Maoist
regime took over in April 1975. They completely sealed off
Cambodia from the outside world, emptied cities, forced most
of the country into spartan work collectives, and unleashed a
reign of terror that lasted for nearly four years. They employed
a particularly vicious, primitive form of oppression, beating
captives with clubs, pulling out fingernails, cutting off fingers,
slashing throats with serrated palm tree branches, impaling
victims on bamboo stakes, smashing babies against trees. They
forced children to kill their own parents and then turned them
into child soldiers. They made family members watch as loved

ones were raped and hacked to death and forbade witnesses to show emotion.

The genocide finally ended in January 1979, shortly after Vietnam invaded Cambodia. During the Vietnam War and before, the North Vietnamese had supported the Khmer Rouge, their fellow Communist insurgents. But after the deranged Cambodian Maoists decided to launch military incursions against their former patron, Vietnam responded with a full-scale offensive in December 1978. It quickly toppled Pol Pot's regime and began occupying the country. The nightmare was over, but its nasty residue stubbornly clung to the country. Much of the landscape was ravaged and desolate. Sick, starving and frail, survivors searched desperately for food and for lost family members. Children wandered alone through decimated villages, looking for their parents or siblings or aunts or uncles — or anybody they knew. To escape ongoing fighting, hundreds of thousands fled toward Thailand. Some were barely alive as they staggered across the border. They had already beaten death once, and UNICEF and the International Committee of the Red Cross (ICRC) were trying to make sure death did not get a second chance. One unsettling reality: mingled with the victims were many of the killers. Khmer Rouge cadres joined the groups of refugees spilling over the border. Some Khmer Rouge leaders would eventually, in essence, run their own refugee camps. Their presence would become a monstrous quandary.

The international relief effort, which began before Grant took office, had become one of the biggest humanitarian operations in the world and the most complex one UNICEF had ever undertaken. Because of its mandate (to help all children regardless of politics) and reputation for neutrality during times of conflict, UNICEF had been designated the lead UN agency in 1979. This responsibility required circumnavigating treacherous political hazards.

Cambodia had become a pawn in a tortuous Cold War rivalry. Since it was still reeling from the Vietnam War, the United States had supported the enemy of its enemy: the Khmer Rouge. Not only had America failed to stop the mass killers, it actively backed the pernicious group after it had been routed by the Vietnamese. In 1979, the Carter administration voted in favor of a Khmer Rouge bid to represent Cambodia at the UN General Assembly. This was a kick to the stomach for Khmer Rouge victims — the murderers, it seemed, were being rewarded for their crimes.

The US government went even further, subsidizing a political coalition that included the Khmer Rouge. The Americans also enforced a trade embargo against the new Vietnam-backed government that had been set up in Cambodia's capital, Phnom Penh. The hope was that Pol Pot's forces could be strengthened enough to dislodge the Vietnamese from Cambodia. And if successful, what if the Khmer Rouge resumed their bloodbath? As far as the United States was concerned, that possibility was ostensibly worth the risk.

US culpability in Cambodia actually predates the genocide: in the late 1960s and early 1970s, in an attempt to destroy North Vietnamese bases inside the country, the Johnson and Nixon administrations dropped a total of 2.7 million tons of bombs on eastern Cambodia. The massive and, at times, indiscriminate devastation claimed hundreds of thousands of innocent Cambodian lives and may have emboldened the Khmer Rouge. The United States also backed incompetent Cambodian general Lon Nol, who had ousted the country's influential leader Prince Norodom Sihanouk in March 1970. The coup — followed shortly thereafter by a US ground invasion of Cambodia in April that was ordered by President Nixon to flush out the North Vietnamese — drew neutral Cambodia further into the Vietnam War. Sihanouk responded by lending his legitimacy to the ragtag Khmer Rouge rebels, who were then allied with the North Vietnamese. All of these developments strengthened Pol Pot's forces and helped them to defeat Lon Nol in 1975. The worst, of course, was yet to come.

China was Pol Pot's biggest and most loyal sponsor, while the Soviets threw their weight behind Vietnam. Following the genocide and overthrow of the murderous regime in 1979, the Vietnamese apparatus in Cambodia emerged as a patently corrupt puppet state that included several Khmer Rouge defectors. Its primary agenda was its own political survival, not the well-being of millions of suffering Cambodians. Even so, it was obviously better than what it had replaced. Thailand also aided Pol Pot and treated the refugees with violent disdain; in one appalling incident, Thai soldiers forced 42,000 Cambodians over a steep mountainside at gun point, and as many as several thousand perished in the heavily land-mined terrain below. Vietnam, in turn, was angry that Thailand was allowing the Khmer Rouge to operate from its territory and purposefully hindered the delivery of relief.

As a result of these schisms, the humanitarian response split into two different aid operations: one inside Cambodia (allied with Vietnam and the Soviets) and one on the border (allied with Thailand, China, and the West). UNICEF and the ICRC worked on both sides, in a gloomy, disorienting fog of suspicion and mistrust. It was in the midst of this bloody diplomatic briar patch that Jim Grant found himself.

Southeast Asia was not new to him. From 1967 to 1969, Grant had served as the USAID assistant administrator for Vietnam, helping to run "the other war" — nation building. This included the American "pacification" program, a campaign to win Vietnamese hearts and minds. In January 1969, Grant wrote a sanguine memo entitled "Vietnam — Progress Despite the War," proclaiming that the notoriously corrupt South Vietnamese government "is more effective and has more popular support than any government since the 1950s." The memo also stated that "the buildup of American troops saved the day," but added that it had also caused inflationary pressures and economic disruptions. He would later rarely speak publicly of his time in Vietnam, but would tell his close friend and UNICEF colleague Dr. Jon Rohde that sending men into harm's way had haunted him. Now, in Cambodia, the fallout from America's involvement in Vietnam cropped up as a boulder-sized obstacle in his path.

Grant's predecessor, Henry Labouisse, had already worked assiduously (along with the ICRC) to appease all sides in order to start delivering aid. The negotiating skills of UNICEF's intrepid envoy Jacques Beaumont had proved particularly critical in securing the grudging cooperation of the Vietnam-backed government.

But in early 1980, conditions remained acutely precarious, as the threat of famine grimly stalked those on both sides of the border. The Khmer Rouge used the camps to consolidate their power, and Vietnamese forces attacked their positions. The concussive sound of shelling was constant. Other armed groups sprouted among the refugees and started to steal aid and sell it for monetary gain.

Keeping the border operation from dissolving into outright mayhem was the job of a stocky, young, indefatigable Swedish man named Ulf Kristoffersson, who had been dispatched to the area by UNICEF in 1979 (he had worked for UNICEF in Phnom Penh in the early 1970s, before the Khmer Rouge had taken over). The challenge he had faced was stupefying. "People just came across the border and died," he says. "You didn't even know where to start."

The resourceful Swede became accustomed to extreme situations. A drunk, maniacal Thai colonel once put a gun to his head. Kristoffersson, himself a military veteran, patiently talked his way out of the standoff and then drank cognac with the colonel.

By the time Grant arrived, the effort Kristoffersson had put together was feeding more than a half million people. The ICRC supplied medical care; the UN's World Food Program provided some of the food. UNICEF delivered a variety of aid and ran the whole show. Dozens of NGOs also offered assistance. There was heroism and sacrifice, and there was also bickering and infighting, as agendas and personalities clashed like cars in a demolition derby.

Grant's first priority was to keep donors engaged and money coming in. He had already started doing this before joining UNICEF. As the president of the Overseas Development Council (ODC), a progressive international think tank, Grant had spearheaded an effort to pressure President Carter into dramatically increasing the US contribution to help Cambodia. On a Sunday night in October 1979, Grant had called the ODC's board chair, Father Ted Hesburgh. The idealistic, imperturbable president of Notre Dame University, Hesburgh was a respected voice on international affairs and a longtime friend of Grant's.

"We've got to do something," Grant had insisted.

The priest had demurred. "It's a big world, Jim."

Grant's reply: "Don't give me that."

He then had instructed Hesburgh to send a telegram to a group of several dozen religious and NGO leaders and ask them to come to the ODC offices the next day to draft a letter to President Carter. All but one showed up, according to Hesburgh, and the letter had gone immediately to the White House. It worked: within hours, Carter invited them to a meeting in the cabinet room. The president had previously pledged $7 million for Cambodian relief. Now they were asking him for $60 million. The survival of an entire country was at stake, they had told him. Grant had recognized that the source of the request was as important as the request itself. One of his signature strategies: demonstrate an overwhelming unanimity across a diverse spectrum of interests. Carter might have been able to say no to Hesburgh or even to the man he had recently nominated to run UNICEF. But saying no to a varied coalition of NGOs and clergy from several major faiths — representing tens of millions of constituents — would be more difficult.

After the meeting, the president had announced the US government would contribute $69 million to help stop a tragedy "of genocidal proportions." (Never mind that genocide had already taken place in Cambodia, and that the Carter administration was supporting the very people who had caused it.) Some of the money pledged by Carter went to support the effort Kristoffersson was building on the Thai-Cambodian border.

Grant saw that effort for himself shortly after taking the helm at UNICEF. He met with Kristoffersson at the operational headquarters in Aranyaprathet, Thailand, and was immediately impressed by the alacrity of UNICEF staff, who were working around the clock in austere conditions and ceaseless, smothering heat. Grant asked to visit the camps, but Kristoffersson warned him it was unsafe.

"Are you going?" Grant said.

"Yes," Kristoffersson replied.

"Then I'm going."

Grant threaded his way into dense crowds of Cambodian refugees. They barraged him with stories and complaints and pleas. As an interpreter relayed it all, he assiduously took notes.

Buoyed by the visit, Grant started putting pressure on governments all over the world to contribute. Often accompanied by the secretary general's representative, a formidable Aussie and esteemed UN veteran named Sir Robert Jackson, he canvassed the globe. The two men drummed up money and awareness and studiously avoided taking sides. As accusations swooped from every direction about corruption and misappropriation of aid, Grant made a point to praise everyone. He thanked Thailand for hosting the refugees, commended the Russians for their support of efforts inside Cambodia, and extolled a decision by the Vietnam-backed government to allow peasants to keep rice they had grown.

As of mid-February, it looked as though they had won a reprieve from further devastation. "Disaster has been averted," Grant told the UNICEF executive board on February 14. He also noted that the Cambodia effort had drained UNICEF's resources and had taken up "well over a third of my own time." This concern would nibble, and then gnaw, at him over the next year, especially as new emergencies proliferated in Africa.

New famine fears in Cambodia unfurled in March, after harvest failures, and the case for even more money had to be made. In *The Quality of Mercy: Cambodia, Holocaust and Modern Conscience* — a detailed and critical look at the relief effort — William Shawcross contends that the threat of famine had earlier (in 1979) been "overestimated" by the Vietnamese government and others. Grant may have himself overstated the severity of the situation when he warned in March, according to the *New York Times*, that Cambodia was facing "the equivalent of a Holocaust." A master of messaging, Grant would not hesitate to use hyperbole (though, as Shawcross points out, the Holocaust analogy was used by many "with as much imprecision as passion"). Exaggeration or not, Cambodians were still badly malnourished — as Ulf Kristoffersson saw firsthand, day in and day out. And Grant had to spark attention, especially as the world's gaze drifted to other news: the Iran hostage crisis, the assassination of Archbishop Oscar Romero in El Salvador, and, not least, the Soviet invasion of Afghanistan.

Cold War bias ultimately skewed the relief effort disproportionately toward the border operation. Shawcross notes the "obvious preference" of Western donors to fund relief inside Thailand and cites funding estimates indicating that as much as eight times more was spent on each refugee on the border compared to what was spent on Cambodians inside Cambodia (though he cautions that these figures "are at best imprecise, at worst tendentious"). Kristoffersson and others were able to minimize the stark Cold War aid disparity by supporting an unofficial relief system known as the "land bridge" that funneled aid from Thailand into Cambodia and that may have made a crucial difference. Cambodians would cross the Thai border, get food and rice seed from UNICEF and the World Food Program, and bring the supplies back into Cambodia via oxcart. "Jim was convinced that [the land bridge] saved Cambodia," says Kristoffersson.

Grant had always believed that the United Nations high commissioner for refugees (UNHCR) should be running the border camps. After Thailand announced an "open door" policy in January 1979, welcoming Cambodian refugees across its border, the UN refugee agency was allowed to set up officially sanctioned refugee "holding centers" inside Thailand proper. But after a scant three months, Thailand reversed course and abruptly shut its border and announced that the holding centers were now closed to new arrivals. The refugees kept coming, with nowhere to go. The UNHCR washed its hands of the growing crisis at the border. UNICEF and the Red Cross were left holding the bag — and that included the morally vexing question of what to do about the Khmer Rouge.

Kristoffersson was rattled after his first encounter with Pol Pot's henchmen. "It's very difficult to explain the turbulence that you went on emotionally when you drove back from meeting with these bastards," he says. "They're standing there, smiling at you, and you knew what [crimes] they had committed. It was horrible."

The nauseating prospect of "feeding the butchers" tormented many at UNICEF.

The United States and China had a vested interest in keeping the killers well fed: they wanted to maintain a robust resistance to Vietnam's occupation. Grant's relationships extended deep within both the US and Chinese governments — how he felt about helping them to sustain one of the most evil regimes of the latter twentieth century was not a topic he openly discussed. He seems to have alluded to the brewing controversy in his February speech to the UNICEF board, noting that there was "an element of risk to UNICEF's good name . . . we are obviously caught in the pocket of geopolitical pressures."

Whatever he felt, he and UNICEF had little choice in the matter. On a diplomatic level, the Khmer Rouge regime was a recognized member state of the United Nations. How can a member state be refused assistance? At the same time, according to Shawcross, the UN legal department had ruled that feeding the Khmer Rouge was unacceptable. An effort was temporarily made to halt food deliveries to "Pol Pot areas" — one immediate consequence, says Kristoffersson, was a sharp uptick in reports of malnutrition among refugees. There were innocent children in these camps. Starving the butchers, Kristoffersson and others realized, would also starve their victims. The conscientious Swede recommended that food deliveries to Khmer Rouge camps resume.

In late July, Grant told the Associated Press that "Cambodia remains one step ahead in its race with disaster." UNICEF, the ICRC, and others kept that disaster at bay — but Grant was growing restless.

He had dubbed Cambodia a "loud emergency," in that it drew a consistent stream of news coverage. His first priority was, and would always be, the global "silent emergency": the deaths of tens of thousands of children every day from common illnesses, from malnutrition, from poverty. This quiet calamity did not make the news. The deaths took place far from cameras or headlines. He wanted to shine a light into the dark and dismal corners, to show the world that there were children there. As Cambodia continued to sap UNICEF's resources, he became determined to limit his agency's involvement in "loud" emergencies and big humanitarian endeavors. It would be a stubborn struggle.

The first real glimpse of Grant's stratospheric designs came at the secluded Sterling Forest conference center in Tuxedo, New York, in September 1980. The long, low-slung building with floor-to-ceiling windows and a big stone fireplace lay snug against a wall of tall evergreen trees. About one hundred yards away, the surface of a small lake shimmered softly. Inside, the mood was less tranquil.

Jim Grant invited around a hundred people — UNICEF staff members and outside experts — to a three-day retreat here. One goal was to stir dialogue about UNICEF's priorities and its strengths and weaknesses in a setting outside of the UN, but that was really secondary. What he really wanted to talk about was how to change the world for children everywhere. The people in this room, he believed, held the power to help him do just that. But first, they would need to be jolted and then convinced. They would need to see the big picture. No one knew what to expect from the new boss, and what they were about to hear would kindle inspiration in some and sow dread in others.

Though radiantly earnest, Grant was also awkward. He spoke in a halting, stilted way. His midsentence pauses were sometimes so pronounced that you might think he had forgotten what he was going to say. "His timing and rhythm were not good," says Grant's communications adviser Peter Adamson, who attended the Sterling Forest meeting and recalls what Grant told the audience.

He walked to the podium and welcomed everyone. Then he started to lay out his vision. What he planned for UNICEF, he said, was a "quantum leap." The organization needed to "shift gears." "We've been going along nicely in second...I want us to shift into third, and then fourth."

As he spoke, Grant projected an almost missionary ardor, like a preacher whipping up a revival crowd. But many in this crowd did not react accordingly. Worried glances ricocheted around the room, and smiles morphed into winces.

"I'm not interested in incremental increase," Grant went on. UNICEF's impact on the world must increase tenfold, a hundredfold even. "How do we do this?" he asked. "We're a handful of people with a pocketful of coins," he added, noting that UNICEF's budget was a few hundred million dollars. "We can't change the world with that."

So, he asked, how can we? His emphatic answer: "A major shift in thinking."

It sounded to some like Grant intended not to wipe the slate clean, but to discard it entirely. A few younger staffers were excited by his bold proclamations — what is this guy going to come up with? — but many others were uneasy.

After Grant's speech, some people clustered in a corridor, shaking their heads, rolling their eyes, and whispering to each other, recalls Adamson. Some were "carrying on — 'What the hell is happening,'" he says. "Including me, I was wondering what the hell was happening."

UNICEF veteran David Haxton muttered to a colleague, "Holy shit. What does he think we do every day?"

Gravelly-voiced, with a keen intellect and acid wit, Haxton was an American who served as UNICEF's regional director for South Asia and would later openly challenge Grant on several occasions. That evening, after a drink at the hotel bar, he asked

Grant to go for a walk with him. Like other UNICEF old-timers, he was frustrated that the new boss did not seem to appreciate everything the agency was already doing. The two sat outside in the hotel garden.

"Jim, I have to say," Haxton told him, "you need three or four people in that room to be your legionnaires and your lance people to get this thing moving." But what he had done, Haxton added, was "piss off the people who should be working with you." Haxton then invited his new boss to India, so he could get a better feel for what UNICEF was already doing.

Grant was receptive, though Haxton doesn't recall his exact response. Sometimes, the new executive director simply wouldn't respond to an adverse comment; sometimes he would just look at you wordlessly, maybe cock his head.

The next morning, when Grant went out for his morning jog, a bevy of UNICEF people joined him. Some were runners, some not. Some had brought sneakers, some had not. They ran in whatever shoes they had. If the boss went jogging, you went jogging, too.

Over the next few weeks, Grant's Sterling Forest speech unleashed a torrent of speculation. Decades of progress could be undermined, a carefully crafted reputation indelibly sullied, and future operations jeopardized. Many felt his big talk was rash and certain to backfire — and that when it did, the scar left behind would be a nasty blemish, the kind that can't be covered up or scrubbed away. Didn't he know that UNICEF had already won the Nobel Peace Prize? That it had helped spare millions of children from tuberculosis and the misery of yaws? That it had valiantly delivered lifesaving aid during the Nigerian civil war in the late 1960s? And didn't he see what was now at stake? That the organization's ability to raise money and provide basic services — to function on a fundamental level — could be compromised?

The meeting was "quite shaking — almost a shattering experience for some," says Racelis, then a junior staff member.

Word rapidly traveled in conference rooms, the cafeteria, and after-hours bars: Jim Grant is crazy.

Chapter 2
THE QUANTUM LEAP

In the summer and fall of 1981, the scuttlebutt flitting around the corridors of UNICEF, alighting on one tongue after another, was grim: A year and a half after taking the job, just as he was starting to establish himself, Jim Grant was in trouble. He was so out of touch, his ambitions so fanciful, his thinking so divorced from UNICEF's programs, that the board had decided to get rid of him before he could do real damage. The new boss would be fired — that was the rumor, anyway.

It started with Grant's first "big idea," his plan for making his quantum leap. One way to take UNICEF to the next level, he had decided, was to hire a group of experts to foster a "marketplace of ideas," to cook up a robust medley of game-changing strategies that would enable the organization to far exceed its existing capacity. The message heard by some existing staff members was: You are subpar, insufficient, unremarkable. We need superior individuals, intellectual pioneers, and we have to go outside the organization to find them. Some sarcastically described Grant's proposal as "giving UNICEF a brain."

The children's organization had long been known as the "doer" agency of the UN. An oft-told joke that has circulated for years among the disparate constellation of organizations under the world body's umbrella goes like this: The World Health Organization knows everything, but does nothing. UNICEF knows nothing, but does everything. The United Nations Development Program (UNDP) knows nothing and does nothing.

Apparently, Grant felt UNICEF should do everything and know everything.

The board did not agree.

At a May 1981 meeting, in addition to proposing the creation of a team of experts, he also asked the board to approve a dramatic staff expansion — a total of 384 new positions (some were temporary slots he wanted to make permanent). This request coincided with the dawn of the conservative Reagan era, an emerging global recession, and austerity measures throughout the UN system. Many members were taken aback. Who did this guy think he was, suggesting such a big increase when everyone else was counting pennies?

The UNICEF board was composed of thirty members (soon to be expanded to forty-one) who represented a mix of developing and industrialized countries; Grant would eventually garner far more sympathy from the developing country delegations. At the May meeting, he was roundly admonished. Your ideas could take UNICEF away from its core functions, isolate it from other agencies, and make it too top-heavy, they told him. Your income estimates are too ambitious, as are your budgetary requests. The Swedish delegate said that Grant's "far-reaching policies" could change the "policies and structures of UNICEF." The discussion eventually became so heated that a special, closed-door session was called.

To show the quixotic executive director that it meant business, the board referred his ambitious, unwieldy proposal to the UN budget committee for review. This was a bitter pill, particularly for someone who had once served on the governing body.

Go back to the drawing board, Grant was told. Start over.

"It was a slap in the face," says Fouad Kronfol, a Lebanese man who then ran UNICEF's Vietnam office and was the organization's longest-serving employee at the time. Staff were shocked, he adds, and their doubts about Grant mushroomed. "People were saying, 'What do we have here? This is someone who does not have the confidence of the board.' We had never in our history had any serious issues with the board."

This rancorous atmosphere was Richard Jolly's introduction to UNICEF. Grant had recruited the gracious, erudite British economist to serve as his deputy executive director for programs and had invited him to a later board meeting in October 1981, so he could get a feel for what the job was all about. During breaks in the proceedings, Jolly chatted with board members in the corridor. Several told him Jim Grant might have to step down. "I was amazed," he says.

Grant's stepmother, a voluble Frenchwoman named Denise, wrote him on May 19 — after the first board session — presumably to cheer him up. She reminded him that his own father — a widely revered public health doctor, whom Jim idolized and who had died in 1962 — had also faced ridicule and resistance. She wrote that after reading a copy of Jim's response to the board, "my heart sank"; she equated the tone of Jim's statement to "that of a rebuttal to the prosecutor's indictment." She continued: "If you are any good, and you are very good, you will be pilloried for the rest of your life. To my question to your father if it had bothered him to be attacked and criticized all his life, he answered: 'No, because, in the long run, I always proved right.' So will you."

In this instance, Grant had proven woefully wrong. He had misjudged where UNICEF's primary strength lay. It was not at headquarters. It was not in its intellectual fecundity. It was in the field. It was in the programs, people, and on-the-ground presence in more than 110 countries. And it was in the good name that had been scrupulously forged over the years in nearly every corner of the world.

Says Jolly: "Jim came in wanting to change gears, wanting to give new objectives to UNICEF, and not showing enough understanding, let alone respect, for UNICEF's existing structure...So there was a need for change there."

And Grant did change. But he still needed a strategy — a springboard from which to make his quantum leap.

The man who would provide it had first met Grant in June 1979 at the Narita International Airport in Tokyo. Frank, fervent, and impelled by a potent mix of optimism and indignation over the preventable deaths of children, Dr. Jon Rohde was an American pediatrician and graduate of Harvard Medical School. He had helped set up clinics for refugees fleeing war in East Pakistan (now Bangladesh) in 1971 and later ran a clinical practice at a rural hospital in Haiti. A sailing enthusiast who grew up in Rhode Island, he savored adventure and a physical challenge. There was a blunt toughness to Jon Rohde and an overall air of no-nonsense pragmatism. Though a formidable intellectual who was then amassing several scholarly works to his name, the young doctor was, and still is, impatient with ponderous academics. "There are too damn many experts in the world," he says now.

One of Rohde's most trying experiences as a doctor happened not in an impoverished village or a refugee camp but at Children's Hospital in Boston, where he did his residency. He was caring for a twelve-year-old girl named Debbie who had a congenital heart disease. She had a rough home life — Rohde didn't know the details — and had come to view him as a father figure. One night she had started vomiting blood. Rohde rushed to her side. She threw her arms around his neck, hugged him tight, and told him, "I know you'll save me." Then she said, "I love you." She died in his arms, as he feverishly tried to resuscitate her. He kept trying to bring her back for what seemed like hours, tears flowing down his face, until hospital staff finally pulled him off. They told him she was gone. "I failed Debbie," he says, his eyes growing moist at the memory. But there were many other children he did not fail, many who were alive because of Jon Rohde.

In June 1979, he was working in Indonesia for the Rockefeller Foundation. Grant was then serving on the Rockefeller Foundation's board; both men had been invited on a trip to China sponsored by the foundation. The day before the flight from Tokyo, Rohde and his wife, Candy, had put their five-and seven-year-old daughters on a plane by themselves for the first time (they had all gone to Tokyo together). The girls were now flying back to the United States to stay with relatives. The parents got little sleep that night, "chewing our fingernails," as Rohde recalls. The next day, after they knew the girls had arrived safely, they checked in for the flight to China. Milling around the waiting area was a group of people on the same flight. A gregarious middle-aged man with a kind, lined face walked up and introduced himself. He was with his wife. When he said his name, recognition flared in Rohde's mind: *Oh, the son of John Grant.*

A major pioneer in global health — known to some as "the father of primary health care" — John Black Grant was born in China to medical missionaries who had come from Canada. He became the first head of the Department of Hygiene and Public Health at Peking Union Medical College (where his son James was born in 1922). He believed that health care should be made available to all for a negligible cost and created a program by which health workers were recruited from their own communities — this would later become the basis of China's barefoot doctor initiative in the 1960s. Like Rohde, John Grant had long worked for the Rockefeller Foundation.

"I saw myself as the heir to John Grant of the Rockefeller Foundation," Rohde says, adding that he had never met the great health guru.

But now, here he was in the Tokyo airport, face-to-face with John Grant's son. Grant and his wife, Ethel, were convivial, and the two couples fell into a companionable rhythm over the next month as they traveled through China. Grant, who had lived in Beijing until age fifteen and spoke fluent Mandarin, served as a de facto interpreter and tour guide.

During a boat trip on the Yangtze River, Grant and Rohde stood together, taking in the imposing rock gorge walls that towered over them, and discussed Grant's nascent plans for UNICEF. "Jim was looking for ideas," Rohde says. "He was looking around for what was possible." Pulsing in both men's minds at that moment was a simple phrase that was then echoing in the zeitgeist: "health for all." Less than a year earlier, UNICEF and the World Health Organization had sponsored a seminal international conference on health in Alma Ata (now Almaty), Kazakhstan, that was attended by government representatives from around the world. The conference had set a daring new goal: "health for all by the year 2000." The laudable aim — to provide every citizen with comprehensive, quality, locally sensitized, and affordable health care within the next two decades — had excited many in international health. But it had flummoxed others. Whether startlingly utopian or boldly idealistic, there did not seem to be much of a plan to make it a reality.

As the broad Yangtze slid beneath them, Rohde shared his two cents with Grant: instead of trying to solve all the health and social problems of the developing world, focus on a few specific things. At some point, as they spoke, they drifted by an astonishing sight that ultimately reinforced Rohde's point. It was an old mining town on the riverbank, almost completely coated in black soot.

"Can you even imagine comprehensive health care in this community?" Rohde asked. "Where would you start?"

This small moment on the Yangtze would reverberate with great force over the next few years.

If Jim Grant was depressed or shaken after his drubbing by the board, he did not show it — not to staff, anyway. He projected a visceral enthusiasm; so much so that you'd think he was riding the high of a great victory. His optimism was obdurate, as if Teflon-coated. At a staff meeting shortly after the board showdown, Grant framed the setback not as an inconvenience but as an opportunity. We have six months, he jauntily told those in attendance, to reorient ourselves and refocus our priorities.

"He exuded positivity in that meeting," recalls Alan Court, a Briton who worked in the Indonesia office but was visiting New York at the time. "I remember other people saying, 'Oh my God, he's gone out of his head. He doesn't understand this board. Things aren't done that way.'"

Grant didn't let on there were any problems. He also did not have the luxury of wallowing or pausing to take stock.

Drought and civil conflict had spawned new emergencies in several African countries, and Grant began to ramp up assistance. The Cambodia crisis continued, though by the spring of 1981 the worst was definitely over — "that patient is off the critical list," he had told donors in December. The Cambodia operation, despite the taint of Cold War rivalry and the Khmer Rouge quandary, would be lauded as one of the greatest international aid efforts in history. In spring 1981, it looked as though UNICEF would be able to extricate itself from Cambodia by the end of the year.

The same diplomatic dexterity he had used in Cambodia came in handy as UNICEF was drawn into a controversy involving infant formula. Grant was a vociferous advocate of breastfeeding and would routinely tell anyone who would listen that it could save a million babies' lives each year. He would explain that breast milk boosts young immune systems and wards off deadly diseases — this was especially critical for babies without decent nutrition or basic medical care. The advertising of infant formula in developing countries was therefore a matter of life and death. Babies in impoverished communities who drank formula were at a double disadvantage: they were denied the protection of breast milk and they were also ingesting powder that was often mixed with contaminated water (which was, in many cases, the only water available). This, in turn, could lead to fatal bouts of diarrhea.

After a major global campaign was launched against the makers of infant formula, including Nestlé, the World Health Assembly (the governing body of the World Health

Organization) passed a measure in late May 1981 banning the advertising of formula to hospitals and health clinics. It was up to individual countries to implement the code on the marketing of infant formula, as it was called. The Reagan administration was dead set against the code, siding with the formula companies; the United States had, in fact, been the lone dissenting vote. UNICEF had backed the code, but Grant was cognizant of the need to appease the American government, UNICEF's biggest donor.

He was careful not to appear too vigilant. In one instance, while the code was still being negotiated, he had resorted to sleight of hand. Kathleen Cravero, then a young American UNICEF staffer, was asked by Grant to represent the organization at a World Health Assembly meeting where language within the code would be discussed. "We were down to words," says Cravero, "and these words were either going to give the code teeth or no teeth." Representatives of the US government would be there, and Grant was worried that if UNICEF came out too strongly against the companies, the consequences would be severe. "UNICEF was getting some pretty direct threats from USAID and the American government," says Cravero. Nonetheless, Grant instructed Cravero "to do what's right."

She went to the meeting with another junior colleague and spoke forcefully in favor of strong restrictions against the companies, taking a position "contrary to what WHO, the corporations, and the US government would have wanted UNICEF to take." At first, Cravero did not understand why Grant had sent her instead of a more senior person. But after the meeting, when

complaints started tumbling in about her unequivocal comments, she realized why Grant had picked her.

"Jim Grant had a reasonable level of deniability that we were
young people who didn't understand or were out of control," says
Cravero. But at the same time, she adds, he "was able to ensure
that UNICEF took the positions UNICEF had to take."

In so doing, Grant managed to keep the US contribution
intact, as well as UNICEF's integrity. "He handled it master-
fully," says Cravero.

Quietly advising Grant on many of his decisions and serving as his moral cornerstone was his wife of thirty-eight years.
Ethel Grant was a thin, unassuming, quietly magnanimous
woman with short hair and a quick smile. She would sit in the
back of the room during meetings, so she could later give her
husband her take on the proceedings. On evenings when Jim
worked late, she would sometimes sit quietly in his office, knit-
ting, as he beavered away. One senior staff member told her that
Jim was working too hard and wondered if she could get him to
slow down. She politely declined. "He's a spinning top," she said.
"If I slow him down, he'll fall over."

Over the last four decades, she had found ways to be there
for her husband, even in daunting circumstances; when Jim
had served in the Burmese theater of World War II in the
US Army, she had sent him fruitcakes with bottles of whis-
key baked into the middle. After the war, when he worked in
China for the UN Relief and Rehabilitation Administration,
she surprised him one day by showing up on his doorstep
unannounced. A social worker for the Washington, DC, public

school system and a Democratic Party volunteer, she continued to work in Washington during Jim's first year at UNICEF. But she would eventually give up her career entirely to bolster his. Their three sons, John, Jamie, and Bill, were all grown when their father took the UNICEF job.

Ethel became his emissary to UNICEF staff, holding cocktail parties and dinners and formal teas. She created a welcoming committee for new hires or those new to New York and made a special effort to get to know employees' spouses. Even those who found Jim overbearing loved Ethel; she tempered his intensity and pulled him back when he went too far. She was also a pivotal go-between: often the fastest way to get to Jim was through Ethel.

Grant did a lot of entertaining, but almost all of the work — the cooking, baking, inviting, and organizing — fell to Ethel. Celebrities, presidents, ambassadors, high-ranking UN officials — Ethel hosted them all. Her "Hostess Book" for Jim's first few years at UNICEF is packed with the names of UN luminaries. Jim was perennially last-minute, and he would sometimes call Ethel late in the morning and tell her he had invited an ambassador over for lunch — could she throw together some soup and sandwiches? With a chuckle, Grant's youngest son Bill recalls his mother's reaction: "He thinks it's so simple. You can't just bring over these senior-level people... You can't just make soup and a sandwich. You've got to set the table! You've got to get out the good china!"

As he built alliances and drummed up funds and rallied staff and traveled to Paris and Tokyo and Riyadh and Geneva and

Cairo and dozens of other places, Grant was constantly casting around for his next scheme for remaking UNICEF. This quest became more urgent as the gloom of recession closed in, growing murkier and more foreboding. He needed to find something transformative but not grandiose, something big but not too expensive, something easy to sell, with built-in PR appeal — in essence, something "doable."

He used every opportunity to spread word of the "silent emergency." Smoking beneath his buoyant veneer were cinders of moral outrage — never too hot or too obvious, but they were there. On February 14, 1982, he delivered a guest sermon at the Cathedral of St. John the Divine in New York City. "About the seventeen million children who die each year, there is little more to be said," Grant told the congregants, according to his prepared remarks. "Whoever they once were, whatever religion they were growing up in, whatever language they were beginning to speak, and whatever potential lives they may have held, they were simply abandoned by the world into which they were born." He went on: "Have we not the obligation — to ourselves as well as to them — to bring an end to the needless waste of lives?" This language was likely a rhetorical alloy of Grant's ardor and the eloquence of his communications shaman Peter Adamson. Calm and considered, with eyes that could narrow to an intense, discerning squint, he was a respected British writer and expert on international development issues. Adamson would become the architect of Grant's messaging and one of his closest personal friends.

About a month after this speech, a package arrived in the mail. It was from Dr. Rohde. Inside was a copy of a lecture he had recently delivered in Birmingham, England, entitled "Why the Other Half Dies: The Science and Politics of Child Mortality in the Third World." The majority of deaths of young children, Rohde wrote, were due to a small "handful of conditions" — diarrhea, malnutrition, pneumonia, measles. Fully half of these deaths, he estimated, could be easily prevented — not with advanced medical technology and expensive hospitals — but with a few cheap, basic, and readily available interventions. Chief among these were immunization, oral rehydration salts, and a "colorful weight card" that could help mothers chart their children's growth and, therefore, identify and halt malnutrition. To put these remedies to use on a large scale, Rohde suggested, you have to "demedicalize" health care — put the means and power and training in the hands not of doctors, but of community health workers and parents. This was because the medical establishment was, in some cases, an obstacle. "Professionalism, international health bureaucracies and social power structures all combine in a strange mélange to ignore or even impede progress towards child health," he argued.

He recounted in the report how a professor of pediatrics had once told him that gastroenteritis is the "bread and butter" of the pediatrician in the developing world, "and that he could not afford to eliminate so radically his basic source of income by allowing oral rehydration technology to be disseminated."

Rohde's opinions were greatly influenced by his friend David Morley, a British pediatrician and expert on child epidemiology who had long supported simple and preventive treatments to tackle child mortality.

Rohde made his main message clear. "The road to health, I believe, does have short cuts," he wrote. In order to exploit those shortcuts, you have to home in on that "handful of conditions." And in order for the shortcuts to work, the consumer (in most cases, the mother) has to be involved, and "decision makers" (heads of state, officials, and donors) have to be engaged. This argument was classic John Grant: Jim Grant's father believed that health care could not be improved without social outreach and the buy-in of the local community. Finally, Rohde insisted, the message must be simple and easily conveyed.

The main problem, the biggest obstacle, Rohde claimed, was the absence of one key ingredient: political will.

Not all of this was news to Grant. He already knew about oral rehydration salts and immunization. And he knew, of course, that the majority of child deaths in the developing world were preventable — he had been bludgeoning people with this fact since he had started at UNICEF. But unlike Rohde or his father, Grant was not a doctor; he was a lawyer. He did not know the specifics. Though well versed in the labyrinthine annals of international aid and development, he did not understand the challenges of halting or staving off disease and malnutrition in impoverished communities. Despite his repeated exhortations to stop the "silent emergency," he did not have a workable blueprint for doing so. Rohde's paper provided one. It also gave shape and substance to a notion that had been turning over in his head since the two men spoke on the Yangtze River: Narrow your focus. Instead of trying to do everything, pick a few things, big things, bad things — the worst things. Pick them carefully, pin targets on them, and then unload on them with everything you've got. That was it, that was the quantum leap — marshal all of UNICEF's resources to launch a direct attack on child mortality. It was a fight that did not need to wait for new technologies or medicines or strategies, but could be waged right now with weapons already in hand.

Grant wanted to know more. Rohde invited him to Haiti, where he was then running a rural health program funded by USAID. The two men drove around in an old jeep on rutted roads (Rohde was at the wheel). Rohde thinks it was probably during one of these road trips, as they bounced along, that Grant told his friend what he planned to do. The conversation went something like this.

"Now look, I've read this thing," Grant said, referring to Rohde's paper. "You say that the science is there."

"Yes," Rohde replied.

"The epidemiology is there," Grant continued. "This is what they're dying of?"

"Yes."

"The science is there and the interventions are there."

"Yes."

Grant went on: "The organizational structure is there. We've got enough health workers who can do this. We don't need doctors to do this. We don't need ambulances. We could just do a mass campaign."

Rohde agreed.

"In other words, we have all these things and no political will?"

"That's right," Rohde said. "That's the problem."

"Well," Grant said. "I'm here to make the political will."

Rohde knew such a colossal task was not so facile. "How and where are we going to get that?"

Grant replied simply, "That's my job."

But before winning over prime ministers and presidents and generals and donors and journalists and UN bureaucrats, he had to win over his own staff.

It would be the most important meeting of his life. On the weekend of September 25 and 26, 1982, Grant asked a group of UNICEF staff and outside experts to join him for two days at UNICEF headquarters on Forty-eighth Street and First Avenue in Manhattan. It was an informal gathering and does not appear on an official list of his meetings and trips for 1982. There may have been a reason for that — he might not have wanted the meeting to attract the attention of too many people. It could have alarmed them. More importantly, he did not want to go through proper channels if he didn't have to. That would only invite interagency jealousy and a tussle for control.

What he needed to do was generate enough of a consensus to give him the legitimacy — or the appearance of legitimacy — to move forward. He also wanted to stoke a discussion about what worked and what didn't, what his next steps might be — though he was already probably fairly certain.

There were twenty-five people — ten from UNICEF and fifteen from outside organizations — who met in a stuffy, windowless conference room on the sixth floor, not far from

Grant's office. Everyone crammed around a large, oblong table. The space was not designed to hold this many people; some had to squeeze between the wall and the chair backs to get to their seats.

The stated theme of the meeting was nutrition, but the discussions veered from poverty reduction to primary health care to the need for community participation to curative versus preventive health care. Grant brought up the Green Revolution of the 1960s, when American plant scientist Norman Borlaug developed high-yield wheat seeds that averted starvation for up to one billion people. Borlaug is estimated to have saved more lives than any other person in history, and he was a big hero of Grant's. Grant wanted to do for child health what Borlaug had done for agriculture. He told attendees that a "global movement" was needed to spur a "revolution in child health."

Sometime that afternoon, Rohde gave a presentation based on his child mortality lecture. He used a flip chart and felt-tip markers and scrawled out big numbers. One was six million: the number of kids who died from diarrhea every year. "We can save six million lives from diarrhea alone," Rohde told the attendees. "And we're not doing it." He went through the interventions he believed would save the most lives.

The response was muted. Not everyone reacted the way Grant had.

As Dave Haxton listened to Rohde's presentation, an old Harry James tune ran through his head: *It seems to me I've heard that song before.* Haxton and Rohde had, in fact, both helped create a UNICEF-supported community health program in the 1970s in Indonesia, where much of what Rohde proposed was already taking place. (Rohde had worked for the Rockefeller Foundation at the time.)

Still, while the science was not new — Rohde never said it was — it was simply not in use in most of the rest of the world. Haxton eventually appreciated that that was what Rohde and Grant wanted to change, and he supported it.

Debate thumped around the room. Doubts and disagreements were lobbed across the table. Several people complained that Rohde's ideas were too narrow, too top-down — and they didn't place enough emphasis on family planning. Despite the discord, many participants did agree that four basic health interventions, if bundled together, could strike a convincing blow against child mortality. They were oral rehydration salts, immunization, the promotion of breast-feeding, and the use of growth charts to combat malnutrition.

As objections continued to flicker, Grant leaned forward and calmly listened. As he did in many similar settings, he may have folded his hands together and placed an index finger against his lips, just under his nose. This gesture seemed to signify intense attention. At one point, according to Rohde, he cocked his head and reiterated that Rohde's approach was "doable" and "yesable."

A turning point came during a particularly soporific lull, recalls Grant's former Overseas Development Council colleague Dave Gwatkin. Many people were slumped in their chairs, "brain dead" and "drowsing off." Then John Evans, a measured, sharp-featured Canadian doctor who ran the World Bank's health section, piped up. He had been scribbling notes and had scratched out a possible acronym for Grant's new program.

"What you've got here," he said, "is something you might call GOBI."

GOBI, he explained, stood for growth monitoring, oral rehydration, breast-feeding, and immunization.

Grant's eyes fixed on Evans, who passed him a scrap of paper. The UNICEF chief rose out of his chair, according to Gwatkin, visibly excited. "I could see Jim's eyes light up," he says. "I knew we were off and running."

Not everyone was so enthused.

"GOBI went over like a fart in church," recalls Haxton. "Only two or three or four of us were interested."

Haxton was one of them. "That's a terrific idea," he said. "Let's run with it."

Then came a loud, sardonic retort: "GOBI Shmoby!"

The source was Carl Taylor, a Johns Hopkins professor of international health. Taylor's background was similar to Grant's — he had been born in the Indian Himalayas to medical missionaries and had spent much of his life in developing countries. The two men were, in fact, longtime friends, who each shared a crusading spirit for improving the well-being of the world's most marginalized people. But Taylor was also a staunch proponent of the "community-based" approach to health care and had been a key contributor to the "health for all" declaration issued in Alma Ata. In the late 1960s, he had taught a husband-and-wife team of Indian doctors, Rajanikant and Mabelle Arole, who would go on to found a pioneering project in Jamkhed, India, that is widely regarded as a sterling example of effective, locally sustainable health care. Now Taylor was irate.

"GOBI is Hindi for cabbage!" he scoffed. (The Hindi word *gobi* can also refer to cauliflower.) The professor went on: "You can't codify all of health care, all of what people need, into these four things!"

Then, according to Rohde, Taylor stood up. He either angrily stomped out of the room or threatened to. "He was so pissed off," Rohde says.

The meeting resumed the next morning, and Jolly recalls that Taylor immediately begged Grant not to move forward with GOBI — at least not right away.

"Jim, I haven't been able to sleep," Taylor said. "I can see it in your eyes, Jim, you will take GOBI and run with it."

Then he added, "I warned you, Jim."

Taylor likely knew his plea was futile. UNICEF staff would soon discover that once Grant had chosen to do something, once he had "taken off," it was virtually impossible to change his mind. It was like trying to dissuade a charging bull. Either you got behind him or you got out of his way.

The GOBI meeting had not produced a uniform consensus, but it had given Grant the pretense of one. That was all he needed. The next step, quite literally, was to start a revolution.

Peter Adamson was one of the first people Grant went to see. The tall, methodical British communications expert had been at the GOBI meeting and knew what was coming. But that did nothing to soften the jolt of what Grant told him. It was the kind of comment that could knock a writer clear out of his chair.

"We need to redo *The State of the World's Children*," Grant said matter-of-factly.

The State of the World's Children was UNICEF's annual flagship report, created in 1980 by Adamson and Grant. It was a forceful advocacy tool to convey the plight of impoverished children and describe what could be done to help them. Also a superb promotional device, it chronicled UNICEF's recent accomplishments. Adamson had already written a draft of the *SOWC* for 1982. Heavily influenced by Rohde's paper, it focused on child mortality and invisible malnutrition — the first sentence estimated that if world leaders were walking through a village in a developing country, they would only be able to "recognize about 2 percent of the malnutrition around them."

But now, Grant wanted something bolder. He told Adamson he wanted the upcoming report to launch a "child survival revolution."

Adamson had about a week, maybe ten days, to sharpen his existing draft into Grant's manifesto, to fashion a document that would chart a wholly new course for a global agency. It would be translated into numerous languages and released to newspapers and radio and TV stations all over the globe. "I seem to remember that it was the only occasion when I ever worked through the night two nights running," Adamson recalls.

What vexed him most at the time was the "revolution" itself. Like Taylor and many others, Adamson had misgivings about a course that seemed to collide rudely with the predominant school of thought on international development at the time. A concept hatched by industrialized nations following World War II, "international development" was intended to spur economic growth and improve the well-being of people in former colonies and protectorates and other places considered to be badly lagging behind. But as the Cold War polarized the world, development also became an instrument for enhancing the political, economic, and strategic interests of donor countries on both sides of the divide. The first two "development decades" (from 1960 through 1979) had produced growth in some countries. But it would become increasingly clear that "development" was not all positive; in some ways it exacerbated poverty instead of lessening it. Part of this had to do with the stinginess of the industrialized countries, which gave far less than expected. It also stemmed from agendas that had been set by people who knew little about the realities on the ground, which differed greatly from one community to the next. The yardstick of success was usually a decent gross national product, and this did not take into account the actual health and well-being of people, especially the very poor.

Jim Grant had long been a proponent of "human development." Before coming to UNICEF, he had helped devise an alternate way of gauging success called the "physical quality of life index," which assessed infant mortality, literacy, and life expectancy of children at age one; these were more accurate measures of progress than gross national products. In the early 1970s, while at the Overseas Development Council, he had been an influential advocate of a major shift in US foreign aid policy away from economic growth and large infrastructure projects and toward "meeting the basic needs" of the world's poorest people.

As the third development decade began in the 1980s (one that would become known as the "lost development decade" because of the crippling burdens of debt and structural adjustment), a new line of thinking had already taken root: development should be driven not by the donors, but by the recipients, who knew best what their own needs were. This spawned the "bottom-up" approach, which emphasized community participation and was thought to be an antidote to Western arrogance and paternalism. The Alma Ata declaration on "health for all" had grown out of this vision.

Peter Adamson was a fervent believer in the "bottom-up" philosophy. The founding editor of a progressive, UK-based magazine called the *New Internationalist*, which chronicles issues of poverty and inequality, he was committed to social and economic justice. He felt that development was a long-term and nuanced process. It was not something you could tackle with a handful of health interventions prescribed from an office in New York.

"I was very doubtful that this was a viable or right thing to do," he says. "It faced everyone with a choice, and I was no exception. I found it very distressing."

At the very least, Adamson thought he would be able to persuade Grant to delay his revolution. Grant had not even reviewed the plan with the board. Except for the few people at the GOBI meeting, he had not run it by UNICEF staff. He had not officially vetted the idea with any other UN agencies, as would have been the custom. Why not take a few months and get some additional feedback? UNICEF's director of communications, John Williams, shared Adamson's concerns. Together, they asked to see Grant.

They met in Williams's office on the first floor, which was known as the "Chinese restaurant" (that's what had previously occupied the space). The three men started talking midmorning and did not finish until four or five hours later. Adamson and Williams tried to persuade Grant that he would have a very hard time pulling the organization behind him; it would be smoother and easier if he slowed down and built more support before going ahead with GOBI.

But Grant was impatient. "There was a sense of urgency and not brooking delay," Adamson says.

According to Williams, Grant eventually relented and "said something like, 'You've convinced me... We'll do this for next year.'" He adds, "Peter and I were so relieved, we met downstairs and had a few drinks."

The relief was short-lived. The next morning, Grant called Adamson and Williams. He had changed his mind. He was going ahead with GOBI and the child survival revolution after all.

Adamson kept trying to dissuade him. He remembers pleading with Grant late one night. They were sitting in the UNICEF chief's apartment, in his breakfast nook or living room. Grant was genial but unmoved. Desperate, Adamson deployed a big, blunt metaphor.

"This organization is a two-hundred-thousand-ton vessel," he said fervently. "It's an oil tanker, and you're driving it like a speed boat."

As soon as he said it, he realized he shouldn't have. The nautical image elicited a charge from Grant, a glint in his eyes. Grant "saw himself at the helm of an oil tanker, throwing the throttle, changing up a gear, watching the prow rise up in the water, taking off across the high seas," Adamson later wrote in an essay that was included in *Jim Grant: UNICEF Visionary*, published by UNICEF.

"I had pressed entirely the wrong button," Adamson says now.

Adamson and Williams lost their argument. Adamson set about rewriting the report. Grant quickly made preparations. It was as if, Williams offers, Grant was running a hurdle race by his own rules. "He would arrive at the end first," he says. "He might have knocked over most of the hurdles, but he could go back and put them up later, whereas everybody else was running a normal race."

Had Grant taken the advice to hold off and solicit more feedback, the child survival revolution might never have gotten off the ground, suggests Stephen Joseph. "Jim wasn't so stupid," he says. "Here, he was dealing with the UN bureaucracy... Imagine if he had called all UNICEF together, with representatives from the UNDP and [other agencies] and said, 'We're going to do this.'... He might never have gotten it done." Joseph adds:

"There are people who achieve things that could not be achieved by the traditional manner, because the traditional manner is part of the reason why they ain't being achieved. And that was Jim Grant."

As the word spread of Grant's designs, fears and confusion uncoiled. What was this revolution? How could such a preposterous plan possibly go anywhere? Would UNICEF survive Grant's reign? He soon earned a new nickname: the Mad American.

Adamson knew he had to take sides. Finally, he made his choice. No matter how ill-advised the timing, no matter how much it slashed against the grain, Grant's reasoning could not be dismissed. Some critics had charged that the eager new head of UNICEF was focusing only on the "symptoms" — mass child deaths, malnutrition, and pervasive ill health — and was therefore neglecting the fundamental causes of poverty and the complex, long-term, "bottom-up" solutions that were necessary to effectively combat it. But as Adamson came to appreciate, and would later write in a speech for his boss, these "symptoms of poverty help to crush the potential of the poor, to reduce their control over circumstance, to narrow choices available to them, and to undermine the long-term process of development."

He realized that, ultimately, what Grant was trying to do was "take up the slack."

That "slack" was an appalling daily toll of death and misery that didn't have to happen. At the time, an estimated fourteen million children were dying every year of causes that had long ago been banished to the medical history books in the industrialized world. The means to save these children existed; they were cheap, readily accessible — yet they were not being used. "It was as if a cure for cancer had been found, and no one was doing anything about it," Adamson says. "Because they were poor and had no voice."

Jim Grant had decided he would do something about it.

Adamson resolved that he would join the Mad American. "I decided this is worth a go," he says. "I threw myself in."

Chapter 3
TURNING OFF THE TAP

It was on his way to school on frigid winter mornings, peddling his bicycle through the kinetic, imperial labyrinth of Peking, that he would see the bodies. They lay in the street. What surprised him most was that passersby did not seem at all alarmed. They did not stop. They just stepped over the corpses or around them, as if they were heaps of snow or garbage. Whether these people had starved or frozen to death the night before, their bodies had simply become yet another part of the teeming, motley urban landscape. Peking (now Beijing) in the late 1920s and early 1930s was a city of opium dens and prostitution and commerce of all kinds, a dense metropolis surrounded by ancient walls and living under the crumbling legacy of two thousand years of dynastic rule (the last dynasty, the Qing, had fallen in 1912). The threat of invasion from Japan hung menacingly in the air. It was also a place where awesome grandeur mixed with pernicious poverty.

Commenting on the frozen bodies in the street years later, Grant would say that "it was virtually unthought of at that time that all these people would ultimately read and write and have access to health services." They were dispensable, insignificant — acceptable casualties for a society, not unlike many societies at the time, where the benefits of life and health and education were organized disproportionately for the few, and not the many. The visual imprint of these lifeless souls, and the morally vexing questions that came with them, would flicker in Grant's mind, on a continual loop, for the rest of his life.

But Peking was also a wondrous place for a young boy, a great domain to explore, which is something his parents apparently liberally allowed. "It was a boyhood of freedom," he would say years later. He bicycled everywhere, weaving between the rickshaws and street merchants. With his friends, he built tree houses and clambered aboard rooftops. Many of the roofs were connected, and the boys could roam above the city, from block to block, for up to half a mile, as occupants cursed them from below. Grant knew that, as a foreigner, he was not subject to the same laws as the Chinese, "so there was the additional element of freedom."

Curious and adventurous, he played tennis and basketball, collected stamps, and joined the local Boy Scout troop. He got into skirmishes. During one fight, a boy grabbed his arm and hoisted it roughly behind his back, until his elbow snapped. It was the third time he had broken it in the same place; the first was after rolling down a hill. He fell a lot, and, by his own estimation, his forehead was stitched up twenty times.

By far his favorite activity was reading. He read the entire *World Book Encyclopedia*, from A to Z. He claimed to have checked out *War and Peace* from the school library and to have read it in a few days. He liked *The Hardy Boys* series and *The Swiss Family Robinson*. The book that seems to have made the biggest impression on him as a young reader was *The Forty Days of Musa Dagh*, Franz Werfel's 1933 novel about the 1915 Armenian genocide. Based on real events, the book "powerfully affected" Grant.

He lived with his parents and sister, Betty, who was two years older, in a large, enclosed compound in the middle of the city that included the hospital and medical college where his father worked. His mother, Charlotte Hill Grant, was a "true homemaker" who looked after Jim and Betty attentively, with the help of a Chinese nanny. Her hobby was buying and collecting broad robes and pieces of art from the imperial court, which was selling off the items, and the Grant household became filled with elegant artifacts from ancient China. A perfectionist who "loved beautiful things," she also liked to sew and was often heard humming. Grant remembered "a light and happy atmosphere" permeating the home, seemingly due to his mother's warmth and positive aura; he credited her with largely forming his own upbeat and optimistic outlook. The family took weekend excursions together, venturing into the countryside to visit temples; over the summer, they sometimes spent several months at a resort. In one photo taken when he was six, he and his sister are standing with their nanny, who is holding their hands. They are both wearing shorts and long boots and are standing rigidly straight. Jim is staring into the camera, his eyes wide, looking surprised or perhaps bewildered. His ears protrude underneath neatly combed hair.

Like his son many years later, Grant's father worked long hours, traveled frequently, and "was gone half the time." When Grant was eleven, his parents divorced, and he and his sister lived with his mother.

He went to a school in the medical college compound, where he estimated that about half of the two hundred students were Chinese, a quarter were American, and a quarter were European and Japanese. Several of his closest friends were Chinese, and his first girlfriend was Scottish-Chinese. "I always grew up feeling that China was one of the greatest civilizations in the world," he recalled, "and that the disorder they were in was a temporary phenomena…, that the Chinese would regain their status as one of the world's leading civilizations during this century."

Growing up in China and regularly associating with Chinese, he later claimed, had spawned in him a "complete lack of race consciousness." Whether or not this was true or a rare burst of braggadocio, Grant's ability later in life to quickly establish a rapport with people from other cultures was undoubtedly influenced by spending his formative years as a minority resident in a developing country.

Grant's China roots began with his grandfather, a Baptist medical missionary from St. Stephen, New Brunswick, Canada, named James Skiffington Grant. After graduating from medical school at the University of Michigan, James S. Grant joined a university-sponsored volunteer program to open a health clinic in China. He was supported by the Baptist Foreign Mission Society. Dr. Grant went to the seaport town of Ningpo in 1889, and his son John Black Grant was born there on August 31, 1890. The clinic Jim Grant's grandfather helped found would become a major hospital. Dr. Grant was known for his deep personal commitment. He made house calls and skipped summer vacations to tend to patients. When hospital beds were filled up, he would sometimes invite patients into his home and reportedly even once offered one his own bed. He remained in China during the violent Boxer Rebellion in 1900, when foreigners and Christians were targeted and many fled. He knew the horror of disease intimately — he lost a brother to appendicitis and a son, John Grant's younger brother, apparently to dysentery.

Jim Grant was five or six years old the last time he saw his paternal grandfather. He recalled in his oral history that the elder Grant "had a stubbie" — he had lost part of his middle finger somehow.

John Black Grant left China to attend Acadia College in Nova Scotia. As World War I enveloped Europe, he tried to volunteer for the Canadian Army but was turned down because of poor vision. "One of his great regrets was that he didn't participate in the war at that time," Jim Grant remarked. His father chose Jim's middle name, Pineo, to honor one of his friends who died in the Great War.

After graduating from medical school at the University of Michigan in 1917, John Grant joined the Rockefeller Foundation's International Health Division. He briefly worked in North Carolina on a rural health project and was then sent back to

China to take part in a Rockefeller-funded program to combat hookworm disease. With some real-world experience under his fingernails, he enrolled at the Johns Hopkins School of Public Health in Baltimore before returning to China in 1921. He was sent again by the Rockefeller Foundation, this time to become the first-ever professor of public health at the medical educational facility Rockefeller had funded and built in Peking. The sprawling, state-of-the-art, twenty-five-acre Peking Union Medical College was intended to be China's answer to Johns Hopkins. It comprised a hospital, classrooms, laboratories, residences, and a school.

As a young man, John Grant found himself in a position of immense responsibility and influence. Thin and bespectacled, he eschewed small talk and projected an air of self-confidence "that could border on brashness," according to a 2005 profile in *Johns Hopkins Public Health* magazine. Though he aroused idealism in his students and inspired many to devote themselves to public service, he was not demonstratively warm or effusive. As Jim put it, "he was not a man to talk a lot." Several decades after his service in China, John Grant's then graduate student Conrad Seipp would characterize the legendary doctor in the preface of a book of Grant's collected writings: "Singleness of purpose is one of the outstanding characteristics of the man…There is in him a tenacity and a constancy, even an obsessive quality in the advocacy of his views on health care, but most of all there is a profound integrity."

John Grant's father had been wary of his son becoming a doctor. Practicing medicine in an impoverished community in a developing country with limited resources placed you at the mouth of an unceasing torrent of disease and death. It was overwhelming, dispiriting, crushing. The Canadian Baptist had imparted his reservations to his son with this metaphor: treating patients in this sort of environment is like "trying to mop the water overflowing the sink while the tap is still on."

This analogy resonated over several generations. John Black Grant and, later, his son Jim both resolved that they would try to turn off that tap.

For the elder Grant, this meant rethinking the way medicine was practiced and organized in the developing world. Exactly how to do this became clear through his social and medical experimentations in China and, later, India and Puerto Rico. But China was where most of this thinking crystallized. One of the first lessons was simple: Curative care and preventive care must be tied together. Doctors had to do more than simply treat disease; they needed to block it before it could strike. This sort of comprehensive health care should take place not just in urban hospitals, but also at health centers in remote rural villages. Grant believed that the government bore a responsibility to provide health care for all, but that the only way this could happen and be sustained was if members of local communities were trained and educated in basic health and hygiene techniques. Some doctors invariably felt threatened by this grassroots credo — it would take power away from the medical establishment and put it in the hands of the people. As he learned and evolved over the years, Grant came to the conclusion that public health was intrinsically linked to social and economic development — you could not pursue one without the other. These views earned him the moniker "Medical Bolshevik."

To begin putting his theories to the test, Grant teamed up with Peking's police force in 1923 to create a "demonstration health station" in an area of the city near the hospital; it was designed to give students experience outside the classroom and to offer police, midwives, and public health professionals basic health training. The center also provided medical care to area residents. Grant later took the demonstration model into the countryside, where he and his student C. C. Chen established a health station in a rural county more than 120 miles southwest of Peking; it would eventually serve four hundred thousand people and offer training courses and supplies for village health workers. This program was developed in concert with the Mass Education Movement, started by the Chinese literacy champion and John Grant's friend, Jimmy Yen; with better education comes better health, and vice versa. These novel approaches to extend medical care beyond the realm of urban and Western influence — and to equip local communities with the tools to stave off disease and malnutrition — inspired China's barefoot doctor movement several decades later.

According to an extensive article about John Grant by former World Health Organization scientist Socrates Litsios in the medical journal *Perspectives in Biology and Medicine*, the dogmatic doctor often struggled to persuade others to accept his ideas. Some at the Peking Union Medical College believed that the institution should be imparting "the best of Western science" to Chinese students; what the Chinese themselves thought was not so important. This directly contradicted Grant's underlying approach and likely fed the resistance against him — he felt that medical programs should ultimately be owned, conceived, and run by Chinese doctors, Chinese health experts, and Chinese political leaders.

Grant's growing clout and collaborative spirit ushered him into the corridors of power throughout the vast country, where he helped create health departments in Shanghai and Canton and the national Ministry of Health in Nanking. His breakneck pace prompted some reservations at the Rockefeller Foundation, according to Dr. Mary Brown Bullock's account of the foundation's work in China, *An American Transplant: The Rockefeller Foundation and Peking Union Medical College.* She cited a letter from Rockefeller Foundation president George Vincent to a Johns Hopkins official, in which he wrote: "We are a little disturbed at the eagerness with which Doctor Grant is undertaking his duties…and is going ahead more rapidly than we are prepared to follow." This sentiment would be echoed decades later by officials at UNICEF, when John Grant's son moved too quickly for their taste.

Many foreigners in Peking fraternized mostly with each other. In this, and in many other ways, John Grant was an anomaly: his close friends were almost entirely Chinese. As a boy in school in Ningpo, he had been forbidden to interact with his Chinese peers; the punishment for doing so was caning. But this cruel reprimand elicited the opposite result in John Grant. Jim Grant recalled that his father's Chinese "bosom buddies" were always visiting the house, and that "he traveled with them, drank with them, worked with them."

One notable non-Chinese visitor to the Grant household in Peking was a Jewish doctor from Poland named Ludwik Rajchman. A revered, outspoken international public health expert, Rajchman ran the League of Nations Health Organization and shared many of John Grant's views on social medicine, preventive care, and local collaboration. Like Grant, he was a left-leaning visionary whose sway over health policy and sometimes brusque demeanor stirred jealousies and stoked political suspicions; he was often accused of being a Communist. With a high forehead, thick mustache, and a deep, discerning gaze, he was said to have a captivating presence. John Grant had encouraged Rajchman to visit China to share his technical and medical expertise with the government.

The young Jim Grant listened in on "scintillating" conversations between his father and Rajchman. He did not know it then, of course, but his father's Polish friend — this intriguing houseguest from Europe — would go on to chart an astounding trajectory in the years ahead that would alter the course of global health, humanitarian activities, and Jim's own life and career. The League of Nations, created after World War I, would fail spectacularly in its primary goal: to prevent the next global conflict (though the league's health agency, thanks to Rajchman, was effective in promoting public health and containing disease epidemics). Even at the end of World War II, during which his own brother was believed to have been murdered in a Nazi concentration camp — according to a biography of Rajchman by his great-granddaughter, Marta Balinska — the indomitable Polish crusader did not relinquish his belief in the capacity of mankind to create a better world for everyone. A supporter of the Allies' nominal fledgling effort to do just that — the United Nations — he became the Polish representative of the United Nations Relief and Rehabilitation Administration (which was founded in 1943 and predated the actual UN). UNRRA, as it became known, provided food, medical care, and succor to survivors of an inferno of staggering violence and cruelty. Many of them were children. Jim Grant would later join UNRRA himself, after fighting for the American army in the Pacific theater of the war.

In 1946, as the Iron Curtain — so dubbed by Winston Churchill — began its icy descent, there was talk of disbanding UNRRA. Several leaders argued forcefully for a continuation of relief for the millions of people in Europe and Asia who were still gravely in need of help. Among them were former US president (and renowned World Wars I and II humanitarian) Herbert Hoover, former New York City mayor Fiorello La Guardia (who was tapped to run UNRRA), and, perhaps most effectively, Ludwik Rajchman. At UNRRA's final meeting in August 1946, plans were being made to close down operations and transfer some of its responsibilities to several nascent United Nations agencies. An UNRRA staff memo had recommended prolonging the agency's child-feeding programs; Rajchman argued that UNRRA's remaining funds be used to create an entirely new organization — an "international children's fund." Philip Noel-Baker, UNRRA's British representative, immediately seconded the idea. La Guardia voiced his approval. After a forceful speech by Rajchman in Polish, according to a UNICEF interview with

Noel-Baker, the vote was unanimous. A new international humanitarian effort was born.

Whether it would grow beyond a well-intentioned idea was not guaranteed. During several months of political wrangling, Rajchman lobbied for the children's agency and marshaled vital support. "In all these tortuous and bureaucratic procedures, Rajchman was the leading player," wrote Maggie Black in *The Children and the Nations: The Story of Unicef.* On December 11, 1946, the UN General Assembly adopted a resolution establishing UNICEF. Rajchman was elected as the first board chair and would use his authority to urge UN secretary general Trygve Lie to appoint Hoover's former protégé — a self-effacing Nebraskan and relief veteran named Maurice Pate — to run the new organization. Pate's quiet resolve would prove crucial in the years ahead in shaping UNICEF's programs and ensuring its survival. Considered by many to be the "founder of UNICEF," Rajchman is also credited with helping spawn the World Health Organization; it grew out of the League of Nations Health Organization he had built. In the expanding sphere of public health after World War II, it is hard to imagine any area or issue not somehow influenced by either Ludwik Rajchman or John Grant.

Jim Grant's father often included his preadolescent son in adult conversations and "treated me as a boy well beyond his years." He would bring Jim on cross-country train trips. "Wherever we went," Jim Grant recalled, "whoever we were talking to within a railroad car, I sat in and joined the conversation."

They were often talking of momentous things — of life and death on a grand scale; of so much happening all at once, in China and everywhere else; of the possibilities unleashed by new technologies and capabilities; of a global revolution under way that could make the fruits of progress available to everyone. Jim was transfixed. His father also gave Jim reading material well beyond his age level — a book on the Bolshevik revolution and articles on the New Deal — that seemed to carry the message that the world was a grossly unjust place, but that now, as never before, there was an opportunity to change that. From all of this, Jim gleaned a palpable sense of the great, vertiginous whorl of history — and of his own potential place in it. "This was where I got my first sense that the world could change, was really going through a very historic change, thanks to the Industrial Revolution," he said. "And that there was a major role to participate in this."

If Jim was to succeed in life, if he was to play a meaningful part in all that was going on, his father said, he had to go to graduate school. A bachelor's degree would not suffice. He did not tell him to become a doctor or suggest what line of study he should pursue. But he did advise that if he went into public service, he needed to secure his "economic independence," create a career fallback, in case he had to stand up to his boss or walk out. "So I always knew I would go to graduate school, but I never quite knew for what."

Aside from Chinese, there was no particular subject in grammar school that enthralled him; one he outright hated was Latin. He earned above-average grades but was never at the top of his class. "I never had the compulsion to be first in the class," Grant said. Every three years or so, he would leave China to visit his maternal grandparents in Michigan. Once, in 1933, he went to Princeton, New Jersey, for orthodontic work. Each trip was taken on an ocean liner.

On the evening of July 7, 1937, Grant and his fellow Boy Scouts went camping on the outskirts of Peking, near the Marco Polo Bridge. Built in 1192, the long, low stone bridge over the Yongding River featured eleven large arches and several hundred carved lions. The ancient structure, which had apparently earned the admiration of Venetian traveler Marco Polo, was a major point of connection between Peking and the rest of China. The boys had set up their pup tents about a half mile from the bridge.

Around midnight, a series of loud rumblings and explosions startled the Scouts awake. They got out of their tents and saw flashes of light blooming on the horizon. It was, Grant said, "like a giant thunderstorm was hitting us but without any rain."

Earlier that evening, unbeknownst to the Scouts, Japanese troops had been conducting maneuvers not far from the bridge. They claimed one of their soldiers had gone missing and had asked permission from Chinese authorities to search for him in the nearby town of Wanping. The Chinese refused, and fighting ensued. It quickly escalated from gunshots to shelling.

When the Scouts realized it was not a thunderstorm but a military clash, they quickly packed up the pup tents and rushed back to Peking. As they fled in the dark, Grant recalled, shells crashed down within a half mile of them.

The skirmish at the Marco Polo Bridge spread across Peking and marked the beginning of the second Sino-Japanese War. Some believe that the story of the missing soldier was a ruse by the Japanese to give them a reason to attack (Japan had already invaded and occupied a northeastern region of China then known as Manchuria starting in 1931). The incident was a prelude to the Pacific theater of World War II and eight appallingly barbaric years of Japanese occupation, during which as many as twenty million Chinese were killed. The infamous "Rape of Nanking," when Japanese troops attacked, sadistically tortured, and massacred hundreds of thousands of civilians and soldiers in China's capital city, would take place a few months later. In its resistance against Japan, China, led by Generalissimo Chiang Kai-shek, would be joined by Britain and the United States in fighting World War II.

For Jim Grant and his family, it was time to leave. Everyone was in a frenzy, trying to evacuate Peking. But one immediate problem stood in the way: Jim lacked travel documents. He was a Canadian citizen at the time, and since Canada was part of the British Commonwealth of Nations and there was no Canadian legation in Peking, he had a British passport. But he needed a visa. Then fifteen years old, he took a train by himself to the port town of Tianjin, sixty-nine miles from Peking, to get one.

The trip was memorable because of a parade of switching troop trains, some carrying Chinese soldiers and some Japanese, all passing through a rail junction south of Peking within minutes of each other. He noticed that "you could see a Japanese troop train and within five minutes, you would see a Chinese troop train, and just at the [Fengtai] switching, the Chinese switched into Beijing, and the Japanese switched towards the Marco Polo Bridge."

When he returned to the house, visa in hand, he and his mother packed "very quickly." The city was now under martial law, and banks of sandbags blocked many streets. On July 15, they left. Betty was already gone; she was by then a student at the University of California at Berkeley. They boarded the last train out of Peking. As the train crossed a bridge south of the city, Grant glanced back at the only home he had ever known. He was watching when, moments after they had cleared the bridge, it exploded and collapsed. It had been detonated. He never knew if it was the Japanese or Chinese who did it. In Tianjin, he and his mother boarded a ship bound for Shanghai and thence to New York via the Panama Canal. His father stayed behind.

Once they reached the States, Jim did not remain with his mother. She moved to Berkeley to be near Betty and find a house and sent Jim to stay with the family of his friend Ned Green in Worcester, Massachusetts. Ned's father had run the Peking Union Medical College. The Greens lived on the outskirts of town on a 170-acre farm with an apple orchard. Jim was given an attic suite and was, by his account, treated well by the Greens and welcomed into their family activities. A year later, after spending a summer with other family friends in Nova Scotia, he finally rejoined his mother in California.

She had bought a "New England style, white frame house" on the Oakland-Berkeley line. Jim had his own room. He attended an Oakland preparatory school, where an intellectually vigorous social studies teacher named Louis Swenson tapped into his appetite for history and sense of economic justice. Swenson taught his students about the New Deal, the idea of social responsibility, and the role of government in ensuring the well-being of its citizens. All of this echoed the musings of Jim's father and further stirred in him a yearning to make his own mark somehow. Grant's first paper tackled the Tennessee Valley Authority, the New Deal program to spur the revitalization of the Tennessee River Valley by dam and power production, electrification, farm revival, and reforestation. This sparked a debate among his fellow students. His classmates were intrigued by him, if only because of where he had come from and "the things I had seen." Swenson's class "opened up a whole new window" for Grant and nourished the conviction his father had seeded — the benefits of society must be made available to everyone.

Two years later, when he enrolled at the University of California at Berkeley, he quickly became one of those students who tried to do everything. In addition to his studies, he pledged at the Alpha Delta Phi fraternity, joined the US Army Reserve Officers' Training Corps (ROTC), headed the student association welfare council, ran a Coca-Cola franchise, joined the YMCA, and championed a minimum wage for student workers. During one final exam, he stumbled into the classroom, exhausted, and jotted in his exam booklet that he was too tired to write anything. Astonishingly, the professor handed the book back with a grade of B and thanked Grant for his honesty. A B average was his goal — that would get him to the next place he wanted to go. His report card from January 1940 is scattered with mostly B's and C's and an occasional A.

Earnest and polite, he did not blend in with his fraternity brothers. "I was different from most of the students who were much more rah-rah, beer drinking, women talking, and I was a different student." After he became the fraternity's business manager, someone suggested that he put Coca-Cola machines in the frat house and other buildings. He explored the idea and realized how profitable it could be. Each bottle of Coke cost five cents — Coca-Cola kept two cents and he would keep three. He bought and installed more than twelve machines, and they quickly paid for themselves. The proceeds covered a big portion of his tuition and expenses.

But the budding entrepreneur was also an activist. He became involved in the Fair Bear movement, which shamed local businesses into paying student workers a minimum wage and ensuring decent working conditions. The name of the campaign presumably alluded to California's state flag, which features a bear; the official mascot of the University of California was also the Golden Bear. Those establishments who obliged could affix a "Fair Bear" placard to their storefronts; those who refused were hit with boycotts and protests. Grant's involvement with Fair Bear earned him the nickname "Pinko."

The affable underclassman made friends quickly and fell in with a small group of students who shared his progressive views.

Their meeting place was often the YMCA off campus. One member of the gang was a young man named Doug North, who would go on to win the Nobel Prize in economics. Another was a vigorous, amiable woman, a few years older than Jim, named Catherine Henck. Catherine (who went by "Kaki"), Doug, and a few others decided that Jim would be a good match for Catherine's younger sister, Ethel, and conspired to bring them together by inviting them to the same events.

One of them was a Delta Delta Delta sorority party in September 1941. Ethel Henck was from the mountain town of Skyforest, California. The youngest of four, she was always known as the little sister. She and Kaki were both thin and liked to ski (Kaki was apparently close to the Olympic level). Sociable and cute, Ethel had bright eyes and a beaming smile. She was a freshman, two years younger than Jim; he was a junior. The matchmaking efforts worked splendidly, and within a few months she was wearing Jim's fraternity pin — a sign, Jim said, that "she's spoken for, hands off to others."

As Jim and Ethel's courtship became serious, the darkness and horror engulfing Europe cast an advancing shadow (despite the relative paucity of news coverage in American newspapers). Three months before they met, Germany had invaded the Soviet Union, expanding the war eastward. The widespread massacres of Jews by Nazi mobile death squads known as *Einsatzgruppen* were becoming more and more frequent. On December 7, 1941, Japan attacked Pearl Harbor, Hawaii; the next day, the United States declared war. As a member of the Army ROTC, Jim knew his own involvement was imminent.

Ethel was sweet, but Jim soon learned that she was also tough. A few months after they met, he went home with her for Christmas in Skyforest. She drove in her "little blue racer," an MG, up into the snow-clad mountains. At one point, they encountered a police officer, who cautioned them not to go farther; the roads were too bad. "Oh, officer," Ethel said, "we just live around the corner." And she drove on. Then Jim spoke up. "Aren't you worried about getting caught in the snow?" Ethel did not want to turn around. Her wordless reply was to gun the engine, stomp on the brakes and jerk the MG into a complete 360-degree spin in the snow. Then she kept driving up the mountain. Jim was completely, irreversibly taken with this pretty, scrappy mountain girl — within a few months they were engaged.

Ethel shared her beau's penchant for activism and standing up for a cause. After the US government began rounding up Japanese Americans and incarcerating them in internment camps following the attack on Pearl Harbor, she reportedly protested against the brutal and racist policy. According to Warren Unna, a friend of Jim and Ethel's from Berkeley, Ethel visited one of the camps to see the living conditions for herself.

On August 24, 1942, Jim became a naturalized American citizen, five years to the day after he arrived in the United States. A few months later, in December, he graduated from Berkeley. He stayed on campus for several months to take an intensive Chinese study program. To contribute to the war effort and make some extra money, he started working the swing shift as a welder at the Kaiser Shipyards in nearby Richmond. At the time, the facility employed many "Rosie the Riveters," women welders who were celebrated for filling the shoes of men who had gone to the battlefields of Europe and Asia. On Friday night, after his eight-hour shift, he would often walk out to the high-way and extend his thumb. He would then hitchhike all the way to Skyforest, a ten-hour trip. He would sometimes spend the time sleeping in the seat or chatting with the truckers or families who had picked him up.

Jim and Ethel were married on December 30, 1943, in Chi-cago, where his mother was then living. It was, they would both later joke, an arranged marriage, thanks to the machinations of Ethel's sister two years earlier.

Their wedding was made all the more meaningful by what immediately followed it. For the last two years, Jim had worn an army uniform around campus. This may have appeared incon-gruous for someone with left-leaning proclivities and a nick-name suggesting Communist sympathies. But Grant's activism was never fueled by antiestablishment fervor. On the contrary, he seemed proud of his ability and willingness, throughout his life, to "work with all groups." Joining ROTC was the begin-ning of a career with the US government that would span nearly three decades, with a few interruptions (including a two-and-a-half-year stint with the Washington, DC, law firm Covington and Burling).

That spiffy uniform also projected an obvious special sig-nificance in the early 1940s. The Axis powers were bent on exterminating an entire people and on unleashing a scourge of death and slavery upon the whole world. Those who wore an American army uniform were part of the essential (though long-delayed) effort to stop them. Grant did not talk in his oral history about his decision to serve in World War II, but his father's qualm about not being able to participate in World War I must have nudged him. He would not have that same regret.

In August 1943, he had enrolled in the US Army's Officer Candidate School (OCS) at Fort Benning, Georgia. The arduous, sixteen-week course included strategy and leadership training along with a punishing physical regimen: push-ups, hurdling walls, and crawling under barbed wire while live ammunition was fired above you, Grant claimed, so that "you really learned to keep your head down." The "washout rate" was steep: up to 60 percent of those who signed up did not pass muster. Those who did became second lieutenants; those who did not became corporals, a much lower rank. The graduation date was just two days before his wedding, and the two events entwined in a knot of panic. "I had enough vanity to fear being washed out and that our marriage would also be, and that I would be a corporal... I was on pins and needles all the way through."

But he did not wash out. He suspected that one particular skill put him over the top. It was not physical toughness or endurance or strategic acumen. It was his fluency in Chinese. An American army general named Boltner based in northern Burma specifically asked for Grant's services upon his graduation. He knew John Grant and had learned that his son was in OCS at Fort Benning and that he could speak Chinese. Grant said, "It's very clear I was helped" by General Boltner's request.

After their wedding in December, Jim and Ethel practiced married life for a few scant weeks in January at a one-room apartment in Fort Benning.

In February 1944, at the age of twenty-one, he shipped out of Norfolk, Virginia, in a twenty-seven-vessel convoy. He was crammed in the bow of a freighter with five hundred other young men, whose stomachs whirled as the bulky ship plowed across the jagged waters, seesawing over hill-sized swells, crashing up and down. It took twenty-one days to cross the Atlantic. Then the ship plied the Mediterranean Sea, wended through the Suez Canal, and eventually docked in the port of Bombay, India. The harbor was scorched and virtually leveled, after several munitions ships had apparently been accidentally blown up. The soldiers boarded a freight train, which took them across the baking country through days and days of 110-degree heat. They arrived in Calcutta on May 12, 1944, Jim Grant's twenty-second birthday. They would move on after a few days into Burma, to help repel Japanese forces.

But it was the brief stay in Calcutta that would haunt Jim Grant more than anything else he saw during World War II. In the waning days of the British Raj, an estimated three million people had died in the great Bengal famine — many of them starving on the streets of Calcutta. Indian economist and Nobel laureate Amartya Sen has written that the mass tragedy was not just due to a shortage of food or the disruption of food supplies by nearby fighting in Burma — it was about entitlement, or rather a lack thereof. Prices had soared, and many poor families simply could not afford to buy enough food to survive.

According to Madhusree Mukerjee's book *Churchill's Secret War*, Britain not only woefully failed to provide enough aid to those who were starving — it reduced its shipping of food to India and, as the famine set in, actually exported rice out of the country. Boatloads of Australian wheat, which drifted right past the famine-racked nation, were diverted to the Mediterranean region "not for consumption but for storage." Mukerjee describes a British "denial policy" to thwart Japanese forces, whereby boats and rice stocks in the Bengal region were intentionally destroyed. Britain also refused American and Canadian offers of food for starving people in Bengal, all the while continually building up the United Kingdom's own ample food stocks (some of which it apparently planned to use *after* the war). The effect of these policies, as detailed by Mukerjee, was calamitous.

Indian photojournalist Sunil Janah tried to chronicle the enormity of what was, in great part, a man-made disaster. His chilling pictures show a field littered with skeletons, a dog gnawing on what appears to be a child's corpse, and a small, naked, emaciated boy lying alone in the fetal position on a rough, stone street.

When alerted to the potentially catastrophic toll of the famine, British prime minister Winston Churchill's reported response was telling: if the shortage was so bad, Churchill asked, why hadn't Mahatma Gandhi died yet? A notorious racist, Churchill reportedly blamed the Indians themselves, saying that they breed "like rabbits." At one point he bluntly told the secretary of state for India: "I hate Indians...they are a beastly people with a beastly religion."

Jim Grant was stunned by what he saw. The bullish, rookie lieutenant was witnessing an atrocity that resulted, in part, from gross callousness — not of the Nazis or the Fascists, but of one of the Allies, one of the good guys. There were families staggering, suffering, dying in plain view on the streets, and no one was coming to their aid. He had heard that nearby warehouses groaned with lentils and rice and grain in big wicker baskets, yet their doors remained closed and under police guard. Decades later, he told a UNICEF colleague that he saw people going door to door, begging for the water left over from boiling rice, hoping it might carry some nutritional value. But Grant and his fellow GIs were instructed not to get involved, or as he put it, "to mind our Ps and Qs."

A vast feeling of helplessness — and anger — billowed in him. The British government "barely lifted a finger to help" and exhibited "quite a strong indifference to what happened to people," Grant later said. He drew a parallel with the Irish potato famine of the 1840s, when the British seized crops and exported them "while the peasants died."

For fifty years, the memory of Calcutta smoldered, an ember that never went out.

Chapter 4
THE REVOLUTION

Jim Mayrides was doodling.

At a large square table, ringed by about forty colleagues, he listened to Jim Grant speak. Then his pen started to shimmy. It drew a *G* with an upward-facing arrow, an *O* with eyes and a mouth, a *B* that looked like a pair of breasts with nipples, and finally, an *I* in the shape of a syringe.

Grant had summoned program staff to announce the new initiative called GOBI. He explained the elements that made up the acronym — growth monitoring, oral rehydration, breast-feeding, and immunization — but offered few other details, according to Mayrides.

After he was finished speaking, silence cocooned the table. For a few seconds no one seemed to know how to break it, what to say. Many did not appear to grasp what Grant was proposing. "He didn't really explain the technical issues of what all these things were," Mayrides recalls. "It was, 'Here are your marching orders. This is what I want everybody to get in line on.'" He adds, "Nobody really understood what the strategy was."

At some point, Mayrides passed his first take on GOBI, the product of his doodling, around the table. A jocular, bearded American who worked as a desk officer for eastern and southern Africa, Mayrides had a mischievous streak. In meetings with an unspoken but closely observed seating protocol — based on who got to sit closer to the head of the table — he would often try to stir things up by taking someone else's seat. He would then watch with delight as a coworker walked in a complete circle around the room to find somewhere else to sit.

This time, he thought his sketch would leaven the uncomfortable mood. It did elicit a few chuckles as it made its way around the table. But then it reached Grant. Glancing at the paper, the normally sanguine boss did not smile. Instead, he shook his head disapprovingly. The message Mayrides picked up was simple: *We don't need that!*

He says now: "It was not a very happy moment."

A few questions and skeptical comments trickled out. How will GOBI affect our work with the World Health Organization and the Pan American Health Organization? How will it affect our relations with other agencies? The underlying point was that UNICEF would be venturing into other agencies' territory and stepping on lots of toes.

Grant looked disappointed. "I got the sense he was not totally happy that this wasn't everybody jumping up and down and saying, 'Oh, you've discovered sliced cheese!'" says

Mayrides. "He was so convinced that this was going to happen and that we were going to do it."

But GOBI was not an easy sell. As Grant took the idea to his staff and tried to win their approval and stoke their excitement, the reaction was often muted. Some made fun of the term — "Isn't that a desert in Mongolia?" was an oft-repeated joke. Though he now backed the concept, Peter Adamson never liked the name. "I felt it was giving people a stick to beat us with," he says. The acronym grew even more unwieldy when Grant agreed to add three components to the program: food supplementation, female education, and family planning. "GOBI" sprouted an awkward offshoot, becoming "GOBI-FFF." A longtime veteran reportedly once made the wry suggestion that the "FFF" really stood for "Fuck, Fuck, Fuck."

Many also shared the reservation that had originally made Adamson uneasy — that GOBI clashed with the idea of bottom-up development and primary health care, the very sort of philosophy espoused by Jim Grant's father and that had shaped UNICEF's current "basic services" approach. But, as Adamson eventually recognized, this was really a false dichotomy — promoting the widespread use of simple, cost-effective measures to save children's lives and supporting community-based, bottom-up, grassroots heath care were not mutually exclusive. Even so, this belief continued to stubbornly tarnish GOBI.

But it was more than a philosophical disagreement. The premise of GOBI also seemed so *naive*, so laughably simplistic. And it seemed to ignore the most basic on-the-ground realities:

the infrastructure necessary to carry out such a campaign did not exist in most countries. What about the lack of roads? How could you develop a cold chain — the system of refrigeration for keeping vaccines cool — without basic electricity? Where would the money come from? How would you get everybody in these countries on board? And the stated scope of the program was astonishing — how could you possibly do something like this on a global scale with UNICEF's relatively meager resources? Nothing like it had ever been attempted. The risk of complete, unqualified failure loomed like a flashing neon billboard. And if GOBI did fail, if it sunk into the slippery sands that had consumed many of international development's grand ambitions, UNICEF's reputation would go down with it. And what about all of UNICEF's other existing programs — water, sanitation, education, child protection — what would happen to them?

The unanswered questions were crippling. And Grant was not doing a good enough job of answering them.

"At one point, nearly everyone was against him," says Adamson.

The details, the pesky hows and wheres and what-ifs — Grant would deal with those later. First, he had to summon momentum. If he could not do that among his own staff, he could do it elsewhere. He would go outside UNICEF. He would go to the media. He would go to political leaders. He would set in motion an inexorable public relations juggernaut that would flatten doubts as it steadily gained size and speed. That was the plan, anyway.

As he hastily tried to carry it out, the day-to-day exigencies of his job — including a major emergency in Lebanon and an important donor-pledging conference — chipped away at his time and attention.

The child survival revolution was officially launched on December 16, 1982, with the release of the 1982–83 *State of the World's Children* report. The lead-up to the event was a frenzied whir of last-minute, late-night scurrying — something everyone would soon learn to expect as a matter of course during the Grant era. According to an account in UNICEF's internal staff newsletter, the final report barely made it into Grant's hands before he unveiled it to reporters at a press conference in Paris. The day before the launch, as changes were still being made in New York, facsimile service to Paris broke down. Copies of the report would have to be delivered via courier, but the courier would need it by 3:00 p.m. As final graphic elements were composed and texts checked and French translations completed, 3:00 p.m. came and went. A harried call was made to Air France — maybe copies could be put on the last flight to Paris that night and still make it to the press conference on time the next morning. After a two-hour delay, an Air France official finally responded and arranged for a passenger, a young woman, Ms. Duchange, to take the package with her on the 7:00 p.m. flight. It was now well after five, changes were still being made, and UNICEF would have to somehow get the material from midtown Manhattan to John F. Kennedy International Airport in Queens. "Not even a Grand Prix driver could reach Kennedy airport through rush hour traffic in time," noted the author of the staff newsletter account, Tony Hewett. The only option was the 6:00 p.m. Pan Am helicopter at the Sixty-third

Street heliport. It was a long shot — getting to the helicopter and then to the plane — but an editorial consultant named Salim Lone volunteered to try. At 5:43 p.m., he finally got the parcel and ran out the door.

The package arrived in Paris just as the press conference was getting under way, and copies were promptly given to reporters. Grant then made a blunt, bold proclamation: the daily number of preventable child deaths around the world could be cut in half by the year 2000. Twenty thousand children's lives could be saved every single day — if governments around the world committed to using a few simple, inexpensive techniques, and if communities were organized and paraprofessional health workers trained to put them to use. Summing up the report's central theme, he insisted that these basic measures offered "new hope in dark times" — a reasonable, affordable way to reverse a grim backslide in children's health triggered by the global recession. At scale, it would cost about $6 billion a year, which, Grant would frequently note, was a hundred times less than what the world spent on weapons each year.

The announcement and stated goal were intentionally audacious — Grant's aim was to snag people's attention, make them do a double take. Cut child deaths in *half*? How the hell is he going to do that? Grant would show them how.

"At the start of one of the bleakest holiday seasons in a generation, this is one of the most powerfully hopeful news stories of a decade," he told the reporters, according to a United Press International account. His words often came out in quick staccato bursts, punctuated by swollen pauses, especially when he spoke publicly.

When concluding an emphatic point, he would clamp down hard on his final syllable, his mouth snapping shut like a trap. After describing the four tools in the GOBI arsenal, as reported by United Press International, Grant hoisted a wineglass filled with oral rehydration solution — as he would do at many future press events — and gleefully gulped it down.

Everything needed to make this happen, he went on, was already in hand. Just as important as vaccines and oral rehydration salts and recent medical advances, Grant claimed, was a technological item that had become ubiquitous in recent years: the radio. Even in the poorest, most remote places — even where there were no health centers or wells or schools — you could find radios. Combined with rising literacy rates, they enabled communities to connect with one another and created a critical conduit for lifesaving information. The burgeoning capacity to communicate in even the most isolated pockets of the world made great gains in child health possible.

The main obstacles, he would repeatedly explain, were a lack of awareness and commitment and resistance from the medical establishment. Opposition had also already sprouted out of ugly Malthusian reasoning — saving kids' lives in Africa and Asia could exacerbate population growth. These fears, Grant insisted, were unfounded — the more you can assure parents their children will live, the fewer children they will have. (He probably did not say that such fears, which essentially justified the death of African and Asian children, were also patently racist.) When making such points, he emanated a visceral elation and a certainty that all of these impediments could be overcome, knocked aside like balsa wood bowling pins.

He enticed the reporters, but he also chastened them. "Forty thousand small children in developing countries die every day," he said, according to the Associated Press. Likely hammering each syllable, he repeated: "Ev-a-ree day!" And then added: "And it goes unreported in the press."

The jibe worked. For a few weeks, the mass, preventable deaths of poor children were widely reported. Grant's "revolution" drew considerable coverage, landing in the pages of the *New York Times*, *Newsweek*, the Associated Press, the *Washington Post*, and a slew of other publications and outlets. UNICEF was not used to such intense media attention.

This was owed not just to Grant but also to Peter Adamson. Unlike most dry, dense, acronym-laden UN documents, *The State of the World's Children* pulsed with emotional fervor. Adamson's crisp, kinetic prose took the reader by the collar and would not release its grip. At the core was a searing moral question: How can a child be allowed to die of malnutrition or preventable infection when the means to save him readily exist? Adamson described such a tragedy in chilling detail:

> No statistic can express what it is to see even one child die in such a way, to see a mother sitting hour after anxious hour, leaning her child's body against her own; to see the child's head turn on limbs which are unnaturally still, stiller than in sleep, to want to stop even that small movement because it is obvious that there is so little energy left inside the child's life; to see the

living pink at the roof of the child's mouth in shocking contrast to the already dead-looking greyness of the skin, the colours of its life and death; to see the uncomprehending panic in eyes which are still the clear and lucid eyes of a child; and then to know, in one endless moment, that life has gone.

Adamson had witnessed this child's death himself in Upper Volta (now Burkina Faso). He was in a remote village, with a small group of people, none of them doctors. A woman nonetheless brought her limp baby to them, hoping someone could do something. The infant boy, maybe eight months old, was probably malnourished and badly dehydrated. "We didn't have anybody who could do anything for this child," Adamson says. "The child was almost dead."

For this child, it had been too late. But for hundreds of millions of others, it was not. Echoing Jon Rohde's paper, which had sparked all of this, Adamson wrote that making children's survival and health a worldwide priority required even more than technological know-how and community organization — it required political commitment. To pry the world free of its inertia, the wielders of power had to be mobilized.

And so Grant, a veteran government operative and former Kennedy administration official, wooed another class of people, even more important than journalists: heads of state. Grant quickly secured endorsements from prime ministers Indira Gandhi of India, Olof Palme of Sweden, and Pierre Mauroy of France. The day of the report's release, he snared a meeting with British prime minister Margaret Thatcher in London (where he had presided over a second press conference). She pronounced the findings "very exciting." Grant proudly later told people that after he had shown the Iron Lady one of his props, a growth chart in Haitian Creole, she had been so impressed with it she had asked to keep it. Soon, he would win the blessing of Pope John Paul II; Grant painstakingly cultivated the Vatican's support over the next several years. He even managed to coax a morsel of endorsement out of US president Ronald Reagan, despite Reagan's open antagonism toward the United Nations. "Literally hundreds of millions of young lives would be healthier," Reagan said in a statement, urging Americans to back the new UNICEF program.

Those within UNICEF who thought Grant naive or bombastic or profoundly irritating could not help but be dazzled by his marketing and political acumen. No previous executive director had so easily toured the corridors of power or so readily hobnobbed with presidents and prime ministers. Like him or not, he had propelled UNICEF's profile to a new level of notoriety.

Grant's whiplash-inducing marketing blitz signaled a monumental shift in UNICEF's approach: the role of advocacy and communications became central to everything the agency did. After all, this "handful of people with a pocketful of coins" had more than just money and manpower at its disposal — it had influence. It could pressure other entities to spend their money for children. It could prod governments forward. And it could shame those that lagged behind. It could be a potent catalyst, a peerless PR machine. But if Jim Grant had begun to bolster UNICEF, it bolstered him, too. It was his pulpit — from perhaps no other perch could his voice carry so soundly and so far.

For a while, that voice still came to a thudding halt in the halls of UNICEF itself. The enthusiasm wafting from the press and prime ministers' offices had still not done much to thaw the cynicism at his own agency. Grant's senior health adviser, Stephen Joseph, recalled sitting with a group of high-ranking old-timers one night during a staff retreat at Mohonk Mountain House in New Paltz, New York. At the time, he says, senior leadership at UNICEF comprised "a white men's club." Headquarters was an insular place dominated by a small group that had held power for a long time. They did not appreciate Grant's upheaval. That night they were playing poker — and trash-talking the executive director. Joseph, an incisive, principled American pediatrician who would go on to become New York City's health commissioner, just sat back and listened to the contempt clatter out amongst the cards:

What a ridiculous idea — a child survival revolution!

What kind of political bullshit is that?

We know what we're doing! We're plugging down wells! We're doing emergency feeding programs! We're handing out midwifery kits!

In other words, we're practical, clear-headed veterans, and this guy is a dangerous dreamer.

Says Joseph: "It was a dislike of the person, because he was disparaging of what they had accomplished" (or so they perceived). The old-timers also "disliked his methods."

Joseph, who started at UNICEF in 1983 after resigning in protest from USAID over the US government's failure to back a code curtailing infant formula marketing, was branded as an outsider. As a Grant hire, he felt the static crackling in the corridors. Walking down the hall, he would sometimes pass a small cluster of people whispering, and when they saw him, the whispering would suddenly stop.

"It was organizational warfare," says Joseph. "There was this stubborn, rearguard, step-by-step, hold-that-damn-bridge resistance to Grant...But he was not going to let that stop him."

Despite its previous battles with Grant, the UNICEF board went along with GOBI — even though Grant had hatched the ambitious program before formally consulting with the governing body.

The fiercest opposition came from another member of the UN family: the World Health Organization (WHO), the UN's health agency. Joseph was tasked with serving as the liaison between Grant and WHO's director general, Halfdan Mahler.

"The two agencies absolutely despised each other," says Joseph. "UNICEF people thought WHO was a bunch of old fogy physicians still living in the 1950s, and WHO saw UNICEF as a bunch of upstarts led by this guy who knew nothing about health care."

Though Grant only spoke glowingly about WHO in public — he needed to secure its cooperation — he privately grumbled about the agency's obstructionism. "He would tell me that a blockage point for public health was WHO," says Grant's son, Bill Grant, "because WHO was run by doctors, and many doctors felt that if a doctor wasn't doing it, it wasn't medicine."

Elitism no doubt tinged WHO's views, but it was not at all unreasonable to question what Grant and UNICEF were up to.

UNICEF was suddenly and brazenly traipsing around on its territory — health. WHO had every right to ask what the UN children's agency was doing there. There were also legitimate concerns about the sustainability of the program Grant was proposing — if GOBI worked, if all these measures were put into place and reached hundreds of millions of kids — how do you maintain it all? And how do you make sure other health priorities aren't shunted aside for what could be a grand, pyrotechnic, one-time performance?

Though WHO had earned a reputation as a stodgy know-it-all among UN agencies, it had recently presided over perhaps the greatest global health victory in history: the eradication of smallpox. Led by American epidemiologist D. A. Henderson, the campaign eliminated the cruel and often fatal disease once and for all (the only time a disease has ever been eradicated from the earth). The last reported case was in 1977 in Somalia. Grant would often hold up smallpox eradication as proof that amazing, seemingly impossible, triumphs in global health were worth pursuing.

Growing out of the smallpox initiative was the WHO's Expanded Program on Immunization (EPI), first unveiled in 1974. The primary goal, set in 1977, was to achieve universal childhood immunization by 1990. Coverage did start to edge up in the late 1970s and early 1980s, but progress was sluggish, particularly in the developing world; it became clear that the target was patently out of reach. There was a saying at the UN — before Jim Grant came along — that goals were "ever set and never met." Many felt the EPI, perhaps overshadowed by the "health for all" summit in 1978, was a typical example.

The gap between the need and the available remedy — and between poor countries and rich ones — was chasmal. In 1982, according to World Health Organization estimates, coverage for the third dose of the diphtheria, pertussis, and tetanus vaccine (DPT3) in the United States was 96 percent; in Europe it was an average of 74 percent. In Africa, it was a mere 12 percent; in Southeast Asia, also 12 percent. Some countries, like Indonesia (1 percent) and Sudan (2 percent) barely registered any coverage at all.

One person determined to get immunization rates up was Jonas Salk. The famous American inventor of the injectable polio vaccine, which had ended widespread epidemics of the crippling disease in the United States during the 1950s, wanted to see it put to wider use. French epidemiologist Philippe Stoeckel had been working with Salk to enhance the production of inactivated polio vaccine to make it more available in Africa. But even with more production, it did not mean the vaccine would be used. "We could see WHO...was not really making much effort into pushing the agenda of immunization," says Stoeckel.

So Salk reached out to someone well known for making things happen: Robert McNamara. The US secretary of defense during the Vietnam War, who was widely vilified for escalating America's involvement in a futile and catastrophic conflict, had since become known for his crusade against poverty. As the head of the World Bank for thirteen years, McNamara had completely transformed the institution, injecting it with progressive ideals. He had retired in 1981. The domineering, aggressively confident political virtuoso cut a sharp contrast with the shy, reserved Salk. He took up the scientist's challenge with alacrity. As for McNamara's motivation, Stoeckel suggests he may have been still seeking redemption. "McNamara had a great guilt complex when I met him," he says.

The two men had heard about Grant's child survival revolution — here, it seemed, was a way to finally close the scandalous chasm in immunization coverage. McNamara knew Grant from Vietnam, when Grant ran the USAID program there. They had also both worked for the Kennedy administration in the early 1960s. At the World Bank, McNamara had also emerged as a champion of the "meeting basic needs" shift at USAID in the 1970s, also then advocated by Grant. The two men had even more in common: both had served in World War II and both were UC Berkeley alums.

Ever since reading Jon Rohde's paper, Grant had thought the oral rehydration therapy would be the chief weapon in his revolution — the tip of the GOBI spear. Diarrhea was the biggest killer of kids, so why not go after it first and hardest? Ralph Henderson, who was involved in the WHO's smallpox campaign and headed up the organization's immunization efforts, remembers that Grant was "enthralled with ORS." When Henderson met with Grant, the head of UNICEF seemed "unimpressed with the difficulties of immunization... it was seen as a dead end."

Grant's obsession with oral rehydration salts also stemmed from the measure's "doability": ORS packets were cheap (a few cents), easy to use, and, unlike vaccines, did not need to be injected or kept cool. If the packets weren't on hand, you could even make ORS yourself — all you needed was salt, sugar, and clean water.

ORS and immunization would eventually become the "twin engines" of child survival; the other elements of GOBI — growth monitoring and promotion and the advancement of breast-feeding — had already taken a backseat (though they were never entirely ignored; Grant would support the provision of growth charts in numerous countries as well as a "baby friendly hospital" initiative in 1991 that encouraged new mothers to breast-feed). And as GOBI gained ground, one engine roared far louder than the other — immunization soon emerged as the polestar.

Part of this was PR: it was easier to promote vaccines, if only because you didn't have to talk about diarrhea to do so. But another part was likely Bob McNamara and Jonas Salk. The two men met with Grant numerous times, according to Stoeckel, and pressed him to make immunization a top priority. A proponent of rigorous analysis, McNamara may well have made the point that Grant should do something measurable, something that will show results. Whatever was said, Grant "embraced the idea," says Stoeckel.

The UNICEF chief reportedly even accepted a hundred-dollar bet from McNamara — the brusque, bespectacled former defense secretary wagered that immunization would become the leading tool in the fight to save children. Grant put his money on ORS — and lost. He told several UNICEF staff that he honored the deal and paid up.

The next step: win over WHO. Grant's child survival revolution and a new global push on immunization wouldn't get much traction without the health heavyweight. WHO's director general was a forceful, brilliant Danish doctor named Halfdan Mahler. The son of a preacher, he was one of the founders of "primary health care" and the "health for all" movement. Like Grant, he was often described as a visionary propelled by a missionary fervor.

In some ways, Mahler was even more of an idealist than Grant. His sweeping, radical dream of bringing quality and affordable health care to everyone on the planet — on their own terms — was courageous and laudable, though derided by some as hopelessly utopian. He believed in a world where "health is not manipulating people as objects but also making them subjects of their own kind of health development," as he once said in a video interview. Many of Grant's advisers and friends say he held a profound respect for Mahler, who was probably doing more than anyone at the time to carry out the legacy of his own father, John Grant.

Mahler's views on GOBI became disquietingly clear in May 1983, when he addressed the World Health Assembly, the governing body of the World Health Organization. The stentorian director general said he was alarmed by "people outside the developing countries" who had selected "a few isolated elements of primary health care for implementation in these countries; or the parachuting of foreign agents into those countries to immunize them from above; or the concentration on only one aspect of diarrheal disease control without thought for the others." He continued: "Initiatives such as these are the red herrings that can only divert us from the track that will lead us to our goal."

He did not name UNICEF, but everyone knew who and what he was talking about. The "red herrings" were the components of GOBI. The "parachuting of foreign agents" were presumably UNICEF staff (though UNICEF does not actually perform immunizations; this is usually done by government health workers). It was a jolting public rebuke.

How could they possibly convince Mahler to get on board now? McNamara, Salk, Grant, Stoeckel, and the Rockefeller Foundation's medical director Ken Warren met to discuss their options. Recalls Stoeckel: "There was a plan to corner Halfdan Mahler into agreeing to join UNICEF to do a WHO-UNICEF campaign to push immunization." Former Overseas Development Council analyst and Grant ally Dave Gwatkin said Grant and others "thought we were saving Mahler from himself." His ideas were seen as even more grandiose than Grant's. Those in Grant's camp believed GOBI was specific enough, narrow enough, that it could actually make a tangible difference.

But Mahler reportedly saw GOBI through the tarnished prism of the large antidisease campaigns carried out in the 1950s and 1960s. Before the triumph over smallpox in the 1970s, the model of big, frontal assaults on particular diseases had seen mixed results. The much-heralded battle against malaria, which began in 1955, had failed to stop the disease (in part, some believe, because it was imposed on local communities without much consultation). Mahler himself had led antituberculosis efforts in Ecuador and India in the 1950s, experiences that had apparently left him saturated in doubt.

But his concerns were graver than that. Mahler believed Grant's revolution reeked of the top-town paternalism that had dominated much of international development over the last few decades; people should not be told what to do — they should decide for themselves. GOBI would also fail without a robust primary health care infrastructure in place. That was the elementary first step, and without it, no health advances would be viable. Worse, he apparently saw GOBI as a fatal threat to his "health for all" movement. These mere "medical fixes" could shift resources and attention away from the basic mission of building a more equitable health system for all.

The qualms with GOBI, some of which were erroneous, nonetheless accrued into an abstract philosophical tangle that threatened to immobilize the whole endeavor. To Grant, Rohde, Adamson, and the growing army of GOBI adherents, the matter was now starkly simple: If you have the tools to save children's lives, you use them. You don't wait for an ideal environment that may never come. You do what you can do now. Plus, GOBI could actually help advance Mahler's vision of health for all by hewing a health path in remote places that could eventually be built into a road. It didn't preclude community participation; it encouraged it. How could people make decisions about their own health if they had no options to begin with? GOBI was a starting point.

As the confrontation with WHO intensified, Grant looked for places where he could bring GOBI to life. One was Haiti, the most destitute country in the western hemisphere, with high rates of malnutrition and diarrhea. It was "the poorest country closest to UNICEF headquarters," as he pointed out, and should receive more attention. The Caribbean nation had been branded a hopeless case, impervious to progress or international aid. It was also then ruled by one of the world's worst dictators, Jean-Claude "Baby Doc" Duvalier. Duvalier and his father, François "Papa Doc" Duvalier (who died in 1971), would reportedly pillage Haiti of a half billion dollars and, according to Human Rights Watch, order the deaths of as many as thirty thousand civilians. Hundreds of thousands of Haitians fled during their merciless rule. The pudgy thug with boot-shaped sideburns kept Haiti in a constant state of fear through the cruel, machete-wielding militia his father had started, the Tonton Macoutes. None of this fazed Grant. He wanted to show that change could happen, even in Haiti. He opened UNICEF's first full office there and decided he would persuade "Baby Doc" Duvalier to do something for children.

Recruiting despots became a Grant trademark, a practice that would rattle the scruples of many at UNICEF and elsewhere. He remarked to several staff members that he wouldn't hesitate to "make a deal with the Devil...if it helps kids." There was also a tactical consideration. "I asked him once, 'Why is it you seem to focus so much on dictatorships?'" recalls Urban Jonsson, a Swede who served as UNICEF's Tanzania representative during the Grant era. "He said, 'Dictators are dictators. We don't like them, but they're bloody good at scaling up programs. Because if you get them — it's just one, two, three, and the country's covered.'" Jonsson found Grant's assessment to be true in his own dealings with various leaders. "It is much easier to work through a dictatorship. Things just get done. In a democracy, there must be a committee and a committee to supervise the committee."

UNICEF's former director of programs, Nyi Nyi, says that he and Grant noticed that "there were lots of coups taking place in Africa" and that the newly installed leaders were "looking for ideas to make them popular." He adds that "saving children's lives naturally is a very popular thing" and then admits: "We took advantage of that."

In the case of Duvalier, Kul Gautam, who was UNICEF's representative in Haiti at the time, recalls that "some of us, after shaking hands with him, felt like washing our hands."

Grant was candidly practical about the moral conundrum of dealing with thugs such as Duvalier. Gautam recalls his boss reminding staff that "we have to live with the leadership we've got and get the best out of them" and that "even the dictators want something good to happen in their image."

Gautam recalls wondering whether Grant would even consider collaborating with the infamous Tonton Macoute terror squads. Named after a bogeyman that kidnapped children in the night, the Macoutes mutilated, hacked, burned, and viciously tortured their victims, killing whole families and reportedly hanging up the bodies for public display. Gautam shared this thought, in passing, with Deputy Executive Director Richard Jolly, who responded with impulsive alarm.

"Kul, don't you ever mention that to Jim Grant!" Jolly admonished. "He might jump at it!"

Gautam did not mention it.

(Jolly says now that he doesn't think Grant would have "actually made such a deal" and adds that his boss was willing to work with almost anyone, "but only if he had worked out beforehand what he thought he could get them to do.")

During one visit to Haiti, when Jim and Ethel were staying at Jon Rohde's friend's beach house — they liked to snorkel there — Jim slipped in the bedroom. The floor may have been wet or he may have been in a mad rush, or both. Either way, he jammed a toe and broke it. The toe stuck out from his foot at a right angle, and the pain was searing, excruciating. Rohde tried to reset the toe, "but we could not get it fixed," he says.

Grant was scheduled to meet Duvalier the next day. Getting proper medical attention meant he would miss the meeting. So he improvised by cutting a hole in a tennis shoe and wedging his toe through it. It protruded about an inch. On his other foot he wore a dress shoe. This is how he went to see Haiti's president, jutting toe and all. "He would never give up the opportunity of meeting a head of state," says Rohde with a chuckle, "whether he had to go barefoot or what not."

Whether the vapid Duvalier took any notice of the toe or tennis shoe, he agreed to Grant's request. He would team up with UNICEF (and other partners, including WHO and USAID) to kick off a major initiative to reduce diarrheal deaths by promoting oral rehydration salts and breast-feeding. (To avoid funneling all of its resources into the coffers of a corrupt government, UNICEF would also channel financial support for the program through a network of NGOs and the local private sector.) On July 22, 1983, Duvalier and first lady Michele Bennett Duvalier hosted a grand ceremony at the white-pillared, Mediterranean-style presidential palace with troupes of children singing and dancing.

Grant's ultimate aim, says Gautam, was to bypass Duvalier and appeal directly to more enlightened government ministers and ordinary Haitians. "Duvalier was a pretty dumb fellow," says Gautam. "Jim Grant knew what we needed from Duvalier was his kind of 'yes, yes blessing.'" The head of UNICEF tried to empower others to "get Duvalier to do the right things."

In his televised address at the palace, Grant said the new initiative could save ten thousand children's lives each year if it received support from all sectors of society. "Let us not forget," he said, "that mothers are the premier and potentially most effective health workers." He reminded Duvalier, in front of the eyes of his nation, that he would ultimately determine the "difference between success and failure."

To the probable consternation of some staff, Grant made another speech during that visit at Michele Bennett Duvalier's pediatric center (the budget of which she apparently used as a personal checking account). An elegant and narcissistic woman with a penchant for lavish shopping sprees and corruption that rivaled her husband's, Mrs. Duvalier was, in the words of Steve Joseph, an "archetypal dragon lady...a horrible woman." But, according to his prepared remarks, Grant praised her profusely. "Nothing is more pleasing to an Executive Director of the United Nation's Children's Fund than to see a mother, and at that, the First Lady of the Republic, taking a keen personal interest in the well-being of children," Grant said.

"Ick" factor aside, Grant would say whatever he had to say to advance his cause. If he felt nauseated by gushing about such a notoriously awful person, he kept it to himself. (At Gautam's insistence, Grant agreed that UNICEF would not provide any financial support to Mrs. Duvalier's hospital, "because that would be abused.")

The end result of the oral rehydration campaign was striking. The use of the life-saving salts by Haitian mothers whose children had diarrhea rose from 2 percent to 34 percent within the first six months of the program and continued to increase over the next several years. Thousands of children's lives were likely saved. Which showed, Gautam says, "that even in Haiti, you could get things done."

The tussle with WHO came to a head one night in October 1983. Grant had invited a small, distinguished group of about ten guests to dinner. Among them: Jonas Salk, Philippe Stoeckel, the Rockefeller Foundation's Ken Warren, revered Australian immunologist Gustav Nossal, and Halfdan Mahler. They gathered at Grant's sprawling new house perched atop a Manhattan high-rise on Thirty-eighth Street, a few blocks south of the United Nations. It cost about five hundred thousand dollars to build and was a financial strain, putting Jim and Ethel heavily in debt to family members. The "roof house" — Grant studiously avoided calling it a penthouse — featured floor-to-ceiling windows, sun-soaked rooms, rambling decks, and panoramic views. On a clear day you could even see the twin towers in Lower Manhattan. From a distance, the large, modern, blocky house looked like an elaborate Lego structure.

The guests gathered around a long table, Grant at one end and Mahler at another. Everyone else sat on the sides. Ethel served them cucumber soup, leg of lamb, bulgur, and salad. For dessert they had chocolate mousse. Many UNICEF staff have extolled Ethel's cooking, but Philippe Stoeckel doesn't remember the food that night. The conversation grew so tense so quickly that the meal became an afterthought.

Sharp-faced, somewhat gaunt, with high cheek bones marked by deep-grooved parentheses, Mahler radiated an imposing magnetism. Early on, the conversation veered into immunization and quickly escalated into a one-way shouting match. It began, according to Stoeckel, when Mahler dismissed immunization as a practical way forward. The discussion went something like this:

"I don't believe in these vaccines," Mahler said. "I have seen the BCG vaccine [for tuberculosis]." It was problematic, he explained.

Attention snapped onto the WHO director general.

"I would rather have barefoot doctors doing primary health care with affordable means at the community level," he said. The reference to "barefoot doctors" may have been a subtle dig, an allusion to Jim's father.

Grant replied, likely flashing a wide, thin-lipped grin: "Yes, why not? . . . But why don't you add a few tools? Like oral rehydration, education, and immunization. Immunization has had fantastic results in our country. Why not use it elsewhere? Why deprive children in developing countries of immunization?"

"No," Mahler said, his voice growing taut. "This is just a way to keep these countries in our control, in the control of the developed world. Because they will have no money to buy your vaccine!"

At one point, Mahler exploded and began banging his fists on the table. "I am the one responsible for health!" he yelled. "And you are not! WHO is the one!"

He was venting what, until now, seems to have been an unspoken grievance: *How dare you try to take over my turf?*

Grant was "very cool." He didn't raise his voice. He just listened as his dinner guest raged at him.

Says Stoeckel now: "Never, ever would I have thought that dialogue on such a topic could become so heated."

It was clear, says Stoeckel, that Grant would not budge. Others at the table intervened, trying to deflate the tension and talk Mahler down.

Salk kept quiet. Part of his reticence, says Stoeckel, stemmed from a horrific fiasco in the 1950s that left him rattled decades later. Soon after the launch of his polio vaccine, one of the manufacturers, Cutter Laboratories, had released several contaminated lots. The virus had not been fully inactivated. The tragedy resulted in thousands of polio cases, up to two hundred instances of child paralysis, and ten deaths. It was a devastating scandal and stirred allegations that the Salk vaccine had been hastily rushed onto the market. His image as a national hero took a big dent. Ever since, he avoided the limelight. (Vaccine manufacturing has traveled light-years since then. Today, polio and other vaccines are highly regulated and safe.)

"[Salk] didn't want to find himself on the frontline," Stoeckel explains. "Even though he had been instrumental in setting up this dinner and this momentum for immunization with McNamara...he was happy to have Gus Nossal and Ken Warren [intervene] between Grant and Mahler."

The next morning, to wrap up matters, the group reconvened at the Harvard Club in Manhattan. The meeting in the dark, mahogany-paneled sanctum of power and privilege was subdued and focused on bookkeeping matters. Everyone, including Mahler, apparently concurred on the next step: a major conference in Bellagio, Italy, to discuss plans for a global immunization drive. They agreed to form a "child survival task force" to coordinate the work of different agencies. This was done perhaps to appease Mahler, show him some deference, but it was clear he really had no choice. (Mahler did not return a request for comment.)

The argument at Grant's house was, of course, not a fair fight. It was essentially five against one, though the irascible Dane does not seem to have been intimidated. In any event, the consensus on GOBI was mounting — if Mahler resisted, he would be cast as a colossal spoilsport. So he offered his imprimatur, however begrudgingly. He would become one of Grant's most crucial allies.

The two men eventually formed a collegial bond, says Steve Joseph, who acted as their go-between. They had a lot in common, not least that they were both at odds with their own agencies (Mahler was also viewed as wildly quixotic by many of his staff). Each was unshakably confident and stubbornly riveted to his convictions, but they were able to influence one another. Getting their agencies to work together required delicate synchronization, says Joseph, "like porcupines making love — very carefully."

Chapter 5
THE FAMINE AND THE CRUSADE

The blunt question startled him: "So how are you doing with
your immunizations?"

Though Alan Court had seen Jim Grant from afar, speaking at a staff meeting, he had not met him until now. The tall,
candid, velvet-voiced Briton had started with UNICEF in Bangladesh in 1975 and was now working in Ethiopia as a program
officer. He had come to New York for meetings.

It was late 1984, at the height of a grisly famine that would
kill as many as one million people in Ethiopia. In just one refugee camp, Korem, a hundred people were dying every day.
Each morning, bodies were wrapped in burlap sacks — many
of them babies and little kids — and taken to the camp's perim-
eter, where parents and relatives wailed in piercing grief. A harrowing BBC news report, aired on October 23, 1984, offered
an intimate window on the unfathomable suffering. The cor-
respondent, Michael Buerk, told viewers of a "biblical famine,
now, in the twentieth century." The video triggered a widespread

international reaction that culminated in singer Bob Geldof's Live Aid concerts. But the famine had been quietly spreading long before BBC cameras were turned on.

Like so many famines in the 1970s and 1980s, this "biblical" crisis had many authors other than drought and the shortage of food. Ethiopia's Stalinist government was fighting a ferocious civil war with rebels in the north. According to numerous accounts, the Soviet-backed regime had stoked the flames of famine by collectivizing agriculture, launching ruthless counterinsurgency offensives, diverting crucial relief to its militias, and forcibly relocating hundreds of thousands of people from the north to austere, and sometimes disease-ridden, camps in the south. Human rights abuses were rampant. The government's Relief and Rehabilitation Commission had made some efforts to provide relief, says Court, and had alerted aid agencies to the severity of the crisis before the BBC report.

As in Cambodia, UNICEF found itself in a political minefield. It faced the ugly prospect of partnering with a murderous and vengeful regime. The head of state — a cold, mustachioed former army major named Mengistu Haile Mariam — had presided over a reign of intimidation and political executions in the 1970s called the Red Terror. He was manipulative and merciless; working with him could legitimize his repressive and, some said, genocidal policies.

The aid group Doctors Without Borders had, in fact, been ejected from Ethiopia after openly criticizing Mengistu's resettlement program. The NGO also slammed UNICEF and other agencies for failing to speak up against Mengistu and for, in effect, abetting his crimes.

But what was UNICEF supposed to do? The most righteous position was not always the most effective. What if UNICEF had heeded the call to condemn Mengistu? It might have suffered a loss of access, and its programs — including immunization and other GOBI initiatives — could have been curtailed or shut down. The consequences could have been catastrophic.

When working with autocratic governments, Grant had reminded staff that UNICEF "is not Amnesty International." You are, he told them, in the business of "making a difference, not making a point." Staff were encouraged to work with human rights groups like Amnesty and to discreetly provide them with information, but to leave the boat rocking to others. That was generally not UNICEF's job.

Ultimately, Mengistu was yet another devil Grant had to deal with. According to Paul Ignatieff, who served as UNICEF Ethiopia's representative several years after the 1984 famine, Grant would "romance" the autocratic ruler. The two men "got along like a house on fire," he says. As a result, claims Ignatieff, Mengistu eventually gave UNICEF critical access to rebel areas to deliver badly needed relief.

During the height of the 1984 emergency, UNICEF staff, including Alan Court, were racing the clock to save as many lives as possible and working with NGOs to distribute high-protein food biscuits, medicines, and oral rehydration salts. At any given time in the Korem camp, you would see children hours away from death. "You felt like if you turned your back, the child was going to die," says Padmini, who was the UNICEF Ethiopia representative during the famine. Cholera would soon erupt in some camps — though the government forbade the use of the word "cholera," for fear it would hurt foreign trade. The combination of starvation and dehydration became so rapidly lethal that people died while standing in line, waiting to receive ORS, according to Padmini.

In New York, Court was chatting with a colleague, Manou Assadi, when Grant popped into Assadi's office. Assadi introduced them.

Grant extended his hand and said hello. He asked how Padmini was. Then he asked the question that stunned Court: "So how are you doing with your immunizations?"

Court had expected the executive director to ask about the famine, how the staff was faring in an impossibly daunting situation. But *immunization*? Now?

So he replied with jarring honesty: "Well, if we focused on immunization, the people we're immunizing would be dead, because they don't have food."

Grant was unmoved. "That's not our job," he said. "That's the World Food Program's job."

Court shot back: "I know, but they're not doing their job...so we have to step in."

This snagged Grant's attention.

"Tell me about it," he said. "Come and see me after you finish here."

Later, after evening had drained light from the windows, Court went to Grant's corner office overlooking the East River and the southern tip of Roosevelt Island. The large room was basically neat. Photos of Ethel and his three sons stood on his desk. Gifts and awards Grant had received from all over the world were set out around the room; these would eventually include a collection of papier-mâché dolls from Japan. A series of clocks were arranged on top of a bookshelf. A dark Turkish Kilim rug lay on the floor. On the wall hung a stark photo of a girl standing alone on a street in Beirut, Lebanon. Reports and files were usually scattered across his desk.

Court sat down and described the situation in Ethiopia in detail. People were migrating into the camps in phenomenal numbers, from everywhere, abandoning their homes in a last-minute attempt to find food. In some cases, a lack of food was not the problem — they simply did not have the money to pay for it. So, Court explained, UNICEF had started a cash-for-work program, giving people cash stipends in exchange for one or two days of work per week on community projects. (This was not news to Grant — the cash payments had actually been his idea, according to Padmini.) But he listened as Court described the program and how it had helped staunch the migration.

Finally, Grant said, "Let me talk to the head of the World Food Program about this."

Court was relieved, but then Grant returned to his original question.

"I'll take care of this." he said. "But I want *you* to take care of immunization."

Then he gave Court a new assignment: "Go to Colombia and see what they're doing there."

Court agreed he would. When he returned to Ethiopia, he learned some surprising news: the World Food Program representative was being transferred to Zambia, and the secretary general had appointed a new UN emergency coordinator to handle the famine. He was a Finnish man named Kurt Jansson, an able UN field veteran who had worked for UNICEF in Cambodia. Grant had recommended him.

According to Court, Jansson helped turn the tide in Ethiopia. "He was transformational," he says. "It was the result of Jim Grant taking ownership."

Jansson was indeed lauded for pulling off a startlingly difficult and thankless task, but he was also later criticized by Africa Watch for allegedly condoning government abuses and lies; some, if not all, of this may have been beyond his control. Either way, a troublesome burden had been shunted away from UNICEF.

The next time Grant was in Ethiopia, he approached Court after a staff meeting. He again asked how immunization was coming along. Court agreed that they would aggressively pursue immunization — as long as the hunger problem had been addressed. (UNICEF would continue to provide a variety of aid for famine victims in Ethiopia.)

"That's been taken care of," Grant said.

Then he asked, "Have you been to Colombia yet?"

"No," Court said. "Not yet."

"Go."

Grant went to Ethiopia several times, starting in August 1983. During a visit to the Korem camp, one detail stood out for him: the coughing. It was a harsh, hacking bark, a sickening ambient sound, in many cases a wasted body's final protest against the ravages visited upon it. He later remarked to UNICEF's eastern Africa regional director Mary Racelis: "You know, from all these tents and bushes, all you can hear is coughing…What are we going to do about it?" He decided that the answer was blankets. Already sick and weak, many people had nothing to guard against the fatal creep of the night cold. On his next trip to Japan (one of UNICEF's most consistently generous donors), Grant asked the government for a donation of blankets for Ethiopia. The answer was no, recalls Racelis, but a government minister suggested he approach the Japanese Red Cross. He did, and they agreed — they would raise money to provide the blankets. When the blankets arrived, many of them were used for the grim purpose of wrapping dead children for burial.

Even before the BBC report, Grant had been urging the world to pay more attention to Ethiopia. He had begun to significantly increase UNICEF's resources and staff presence throughout Africa; in August 1984 he launched a $67 million fund-raising appeal for Ethiopia and twelve other countries. Grant likely miffed many at the UN when he told reporters that

Western donor governments and relief agencies — including UNICEF — had been woefully slow to respond.

"The international community, preoccupied with other things, did not respond," he told PBS news host Robert Mac-Neil in November 1984. "Sometimes it takes things to get darker before the world community will respond. We remember in Kampuchea that it really had to get very bad, and then the world community responded, and we saved a people from disaster."

Kampuchea, or Cambodia, was still raw in Grant's mind. Though he pushed for a bigger, bolder emergency response in Ethiopia, he certainly did not want UNICEF to lead it — not this time. After the draining vortex of Cambodia, he could feel "the alligators snapping at my heels." Those alligators could drag him into a swamp and mire GOBI in the muck. He lobbied for the creation of a special UN body exclusively tasked with handling emergencies in Africa.

The "opening shot" of the child survival revolution was fired at about eight a.m. on June 23, 1984, at the presidential palace in Bogotá, Colombia. It did not come from a gun, but rather a small dropper bottle containing oral polio vaccine. The country's avuncular president, Belisario Betancur, aimed two drops from the bottle into the mouth of a baby, the first to be inoculated. The launch of Colombia's immunization crusade was an unparalleled national event involving 120,000 volunteers — teachers, priests, Boy Scouts, nurses, health workers, Red Cross members, police officers, and soldiers — working at ten thousand immunization posts around the country. By seven that evening, as many as 800,000 Colombian children would be inoculated against polio, measles, diphtheria, tetanus, and whooping cough. The crusade would continue on July 28 and August 25, as the children received the second and third doses.

In a photo from the first or second vaccination day, Colombia's first lady, Rosa Helena Betancur, is positioning a polio dropper carefully over a baby girl named Lina Margarita, whose cheeks were likely squeezed together to keep her lips open. The first lady is leaning forward and gently holding the baby's arm, as her husband stands nearby, grinning approvingly. Peering over a scrum of people gathered around the baby was Jim Grant, his face glowing with luminous delight.

The result of the Colombia campaign was important in and of itself, of course: these children were now protected from deadly and debilitating illnesses. But the symbolic victory was just as critical. What had happened in Colombia showed that what Grant envisioned — reaching the majority of a nation's children with basic health care — could be accomplished.

Colombia was an ideal test case, because it was a middle-income country with a fairly robust health infrastructure and immunization rates that were already comparably quite strong. In 1983, coverage for the measles, polio, and the DPT (diphtheria, pertussis, and tetanus) vaccines were all between 42 and 43 percent, while tuberculosis vaccine coverage hovered at an impressive 79 percent (for this reason, the campaign did not include the tuberculosis vaccine). The country was also already embarking on ambitious health and immunization programs, and it had a competent leader who seemed capable of delivering on his promises.

A lawyer and former dean of the law school at the National University of Bogotá, Betancur was a popular conservative who had earned widespread praise for reconciling with guerrilla groups in Colombia. One of his first actions as president was to offer amnesty to guerrillas and welcome them back into the Colombian "family." But the peacemaker could wield a sharp tongue. At a December 1982 luncheon for President Reagan, who was visiting Colombia, Betancur delivered a surprise toast in which he criticized America's efforts to "isolate" and "exclude" some Latin American nations (presumably Cuba and Nicaragua) from peace efforts, according to a *New York Times* account. "Why shouldn't we do away with the exclusions in the inter-American system?" Mr. Betancur asked.

At their first meeting in November 1982, Grant and Betancur talked over cups of *tinto*, a black Colombian coffee drink, in Betancur's office. They sat on couches, in a circle, the first lady and the minister of health flanking Betancur. In settings such as this, Grant usually leaned forward, hands folded together, getting as close as he could to his host. With each leader he met, he slightly honed his pitch. Would he appeal to a head of state's self-interest (saving children can win you votes)? Would he try to stoke a sense of rivalry with a neighboring country? Or would he make a moral argument?

Betancur was genial, almost benign-looking, with glasses and a double chin. He seemed like an empathetic man, and Grant chose the latter tack.

He made a stark, pointed, emotional appeal, and Betancur listened attentively, according to UNICEF's former Colombia representative, Jorge Jara.

"Forty thousand children die every day," Grant said, his eyes probably boring into Betancur's. "That is the equivalent of one hundred twenty jumbo jets crashing...ev-a-ree day!"

Betancur stared at his guest wordlessly.

Grant likely warned of a "silent emergency." At some point, he declared: "It is unethical not to do anything. We need to break the inertia."

Then finally: "This is *obscene*. We cannot do business as usual."

Jara recalls an astonished expression claiming Betancur's face. "When Jim said, 'This is obscene,' that hit Betancur," he says.

The grim information must not have been a complete surprise to Betancur. He had grown up in a large, poor family, the second of twenty-two children. All but five of his siblings had died young.

After a pause, the president nodded his head. "Yes, yes," he said. "Definitely, it is obscene. We cannot do business as usual. We need to break these tendencies."

Then he said what Grant wanted to hear: "We need to provide the political support for these ideas."

Still reeling from Grant's plea, the president went on to say how incredible it is that so many children are dying "when we already have the vaccines to prevent these deaths."

Betancur's minister of health, Jaime Arias, who was in that meeting, had already been planning an offensive on child mortality and ill health. He was developing three interlinked campaigns: immunization, an antidiarrhea initiative, and a program to tackle respiratory diseases. But he was having trouble getting the immunization campaign to move. He needed more propulsion, and he knew who could supply it.

"I needed the support of Mr. Grant to convince the Colombian government to do this," Arias says. "We had to mobilize all the main forces of the country."

Betancur's decision was not a facile one. There was a "big risk of failing," says Arias. If the goals were not reached, the president would suffer significant political embarrassment and would have a hard time building a consensus for other health initiatives.

Arias characterized Grant as a "very alive person... [who] transmitted a lot of energy." The UNICEF leader's enthusiasm was contagious, he says. "He transmitted that feeling to everybody. That was very important."

The entire country pulsed with that energy. Colombia was where Grant was able to try out his strategy of "social mobilization" — engage every sector of society by showing them that they all have a common interest: protecting children. The desire to immunize all the kids in Colombia was pushed by citizens, "not by epidemiologists or doctors," says Jara. It was, in that way, a "bottom-up" initiative — the exact opposite of what many of Grant's critics had alleged GOBI would become.

The Catholic Church asked all its priests to support the campaign. On the Sunday before each immunization day, the sermons in all 2,280 parishes were devoted to the importance of vaccination. Some pastors reportedly went as far as telling parishioners that if they wanted their babies to be baptized, they had to promise to get them immunized. A major bank did its part, printing thousands of free calendars, reminding its customers to get their kids inoculated. The country's two main media outlets, the daily newspaper, *El Tiempo*, and the national radio network, Caracol, agreed to promote the immunization crusade for free. With results from each province broadcast every hour by Caracol, the campaign took on the feel of an election day. Rather than wondering who would win, everybody wanted to know: *Would we make it? Would Colombia, as a nation, succeed?*

A local advertising agency created a cartoon mascot for the campaign: a doughy, smiling, obviously healthy little boy named Pitín (pronounced "Pee-TEEN"). His jovial image, with big, horseshoe-shaped eyes and a lick of hair sticking up, ran in *El Tiempo* and other newspapers throughout the country and was usually accompanied by basic health advice.

Pitín was part of a strategy to convince the most crucial stakeholders of all: the parents. Some were wary of immunization, especially since the injections could cause fevers. It was also a huge hassle, particularly in remote rural areas, to lug kids several miles to an immunization post. They had to be persuaded it was worth it.

Organizers tried to make the experience easy and even enjoyable. In urban areas, a carnival-like atmosphere pervaded the streets on each of the three days: musical troupes, theatrical performances, fireworks, and puppeteers entertained the kids and parents waiting in line.

The immunizers were government employees or volunteers, deployed by the Ministry of Health. The vaccines, syringes, cold chain equipment, and promotional materials were supplied by UNICEF and other UN agencies, including the WHO's regional arm, the Pan-American Health Organization (PAHO). PAHO was pivotal and became one of UNICEF's most dynamic partners in the years ahead, in large part due to its dogged immunization chief, Ciro de Quadros; the Brazilian epidemiologist would play a seminal role in the eventual eradication of polio from the Americas.

In the lead-up to the crusade, resistance percolated from medical and technical staff at health centers. Some resented being told to alter their procedures and panned the idea as unrealistic. Many cited weak cold chains as a reason the campaign world never work, says Jara. UNICEF had to prove them wrong and show that a cold chain would hold, even across formidable geographical terrain.

The vaccine's journey started at the site of the manufacturer and had to snake its way across the globe to the airport in Bogotá and then to a government storage facility and then to the regional health center and then to the local health outpost and then into a syringe (unless already in a dropper) and then into an often wailing child — and all the while, it had to be kept cold. But not too cold — between 36 and 46 degrees Fahrenheit, to be exact. If the temperature strayed too much above or below this range, the batch of vaccine could be ruined. The doses were stored in refrigerators (many powered by kerosene, in case of electrical outages) and transported in insulated Styrofoam "cold boxes" lined with ice or ice packs.

The country's civilian air patrol was a crucial link in the Colombian cold chain, lending its planes and helicopters to transport the doses to the hardest-to-reach places in the Andean mountains. Once they reached the airfields, the cold boxes were immediately unloaded and strapped to mules. They then began the next leg of the journey farther into the mountains. When the vaccines finally made it to their designated villages, health workers immediately had to test the temperature to make sure they had not spoiled. In some of the country's Amazonian areas, cold boxes were transported on boats.

On the second day, when officials in a town in northeastern Colombia heard via radio that a plane carrying forty thousand doses of vaccine was on the way, they realized they had a problem: the plane would be arriving after dark, and the small runway had no landing lights. The town was flanked by mountains. So they sent a radio message to local residents: please bring your cars and trucks to the runway right away. More than one hundred drivers responded, parking their vehicles in even rows on each side of the runway. They turned on their headlights. The last-minute, make-shift landing lights allowed the plane to land safely. The vaccines were unloaded and the plane immediately climbed back into the murky sky.

At the end of one of the vaccination days, the UNICEF team gathered in the Caracol radio studio to listen to the results. Microphones protruded from desks, and a red "on air" light glowed above them. The number of children originally targeted was 917,000; they had hoped to reach at least 80 percent. On this evening, the tally came in around 10:30 p.m.: the goal had been met. When everyone learned they had actually succeeded, "it was an explosion," says Jara. People howled and hugged each other and wiped away tears. UNICEF staffer Juan Aguilar recalls that Grant was so happy, he jumped into the air. The UNICEF chief then took a moment to thank everyone and proclaimed giddily, "We did it!"

In numerous speeches, he would equate the triumph in Colombia to "putting a man on the moon."

Now he had to repeat the performance.

The brief note was typed on a small scrap of paper with a simple *M* anchored at the bottom. It was handed to UNICEF's Washington, DC, lobbying chief, Kimberly Gamble, over lunch. It instructed her to work toward two goals: increasing the US contribution to UNICEF and establishing a "US Children's Survival Fund" of between $100 million and $200 million. The letter dictated that the new fund would "support global type initiatives...not less than 50 percent of which shall be contributed to multilateral activities and the remainder to be administered by USAID." The note's brevity was inversely proportional to the challenge it posed—especially during a time of across-the-board budget cuts in Washington. It was as though Gamble had been handed a ten-dollar bill and had been nonchalantly asked to pick up some Chinese takeout—for the entire population of Washington, DC.

The author of the note was Michael Shower, Jim Grant's speechwriter and close aide. Trim, balding, and often grumpily serious, Shower was known for passing out notes like these, quick missives all signed with a typed *M*. Whenever you got one, you knew it had come from the musings of Jim Grant.

Gamble did not hide her reservations. "I'm not going to live long enough to see this happen," she told Shower.

Recruited by Grant from USAID, Gamble (who now goes by Gamble-Payne) had developed a finely honed political pragmatism. She knew the Reagan administration well. She knew how little regard it had for the UN. She knew factions within USAID would resist this goal for fear it would siphon away their already threatened resources. She also knew that everything was being slashed everywhere, and that any new proposal would mean the money would have to come from some existing budget line.

She asked Shower how serious Grant was about the idea. Shower answered by raising his eyebrows and nodding his head.

"Oh God," Gamble said.

As with many of Grant's plans, one of the first steps was to get the Catholic Church on board. Gamble won the cooperation of Representative David Obey, a Democrat from Wisconsin — a well-known Catholic — and eventually wrangled the support of the US Conference of Catholic Bishops.

UNICEF's coziness with the church made many people uneasy. "The women's groups were saying UNICEF is in bed with the Catholic Church," recalls Gamble-Payne. "A lot of women inside UNICEF did not like it."

But Grant was willing to sacrifice the "gender issue" — at least temporarily — in order to get Catholics in his corner. A lot of women and men in UNICEF would increasingly pressure him to take women's rights and family planning more seriously; this did not include support for abortion (an issue UNICEF has diligently avoided), but rather "birth spacing." Ethel, who was a staunch feminist, nonetheless reminded several staff members that her husband was "a man of his generation." Grant would eventually acquiesce and take up family planning, in part as a result of pressure from the UNICEF board. The Vatican would protest and would later (after Grant's death) cancel a paltry two-thousand-dollar annual contribution to the children's agency over unfair allegations involving UNICEF and birth control.

For now, Gamble knew what her marching orders were, and she followed them. She and her team then began cobbling together votes, gathering experts for testimony, and assembling a bipartisan consensus behind the scenes — at a time, she notes, when genuine bipartisanship was still possible on the Hill.

Then, at Grant's request, she got him an official, twenty-minute meeting with the Speaker of the House, Thomas P. "Tip" O'Neill Jr. A liberal New Deal Democrat from Boston, O'Neill was big and boisterous, a consummate, old-fashioned Washington insider — and a counterweight to Reagan's swelling pro-business conservatism.

Getting on O'Neill's calendar wasn't just about meeting the powerful political Mandarin — it was about showing everyone you meant business. "If you are on Tip O'Neill's calendar, everybody in Washington knows it," says Gamble-Payne. "That means that everybody knows you have access."

Grant knew O'Neill — he seemed to know everyone in Washington — and the affable Speaker even affectionately called him "Jimbo."

It was Gamble's first time in the Speaker's office. "I felt like Alice in Wonderland," she says now. "The room seemed so big."

The two men wasted no time. "What can I do for you, Jimbo?" O'Neill bellowed.

Grant pulled out his props, likely including an ORS packet. He probably told O'Neill that forty thousand children were dying needlessly every day. He may have even used his closing line: "This is *obscene.*"

As he was speaking, O'Neill nodded and said, "Yeah, yeah, yeah."

Grant told him he wanted $100 million for a Child Survival Fund, which would be run by USAID and would provide money for simple things that could save kids' lives. It would be good for foreign aid, good for the United States, and a strategic choice that made economic sense.

When Grant became stubbornly determined about something, says Gamble-Payne, his eyes appeared almost to change color. "They were normally blue," she says, "but they would turn a certain shade of gray."

Sitting in the Speaker's office, his eyes seemed to go steely. Finally, O'Neill stopped him.

"Jimbo, Jimbo, Jimbo," he said. "No, no, no. Times are a little tough right now. Tell you what we'll do. Let's just start with twenty-five. And you'll get there, Jimbo, you'll get there. It's a good program, it's a good idea. Let's start with twenty-five and see how it goes."

O'Neill's aide then stood up, and, at the same time, the door opened. The meeting was over.

It wasn't the answer Grant wanted, but it was a start.

The Child Survival Fund was established in 1984 with an amendment to the Foreign Assistance Act of 1961. The initial allocation was $25 million — funds to be used mostly by USAID to combat child mortality (as much as $7 million was designated for UNICEF).

Some UNICEF staffers groused that all the money should have gone directly to UNICEF. UNICEF badly needed it. Why was Grant raising money for his old employer, USAID?

"Jim never wanted the money in UNICEF," says Gamble-Payne. "It wasn't about the money."

It was about placing the cause of child survival at the center of US foreign aid policy. It was about getting the United States government to join Jim Grant's fight. By insisting the money go to USAID, "he created a vested interest in USAID," says Kul Gautam. "Child survival became a big thing."

As a result, the Child Survival Fund increased year by year, becoming a recurring expenditure (despite Reagan's attempts to cut it). It eventually resulted in hundreds of millions of dollars in annual funding for child survival and maternal health programs; the money was in addition to the US government's regular contribution to UNICEF.

What had long seemed out of the question in many countries began to butt up against the edges of possibility. Immunization drives were launched in Senegal, Burkina Faso, and Nigeria, and Grant began planning a big campaign in Turkey — a country with daunting logistical and political challenges. In 1984, UNICEF increased its shipment of vaccines by 50 percent over the previous year, delivering doses to eighty countries. It also provided 65 million packets of oral rehydration salts and helped twenty countries produce the salts locally. By the end of 1985 — as a result of expanded immunization and ORS programs — as many as one million children who would have otherwise died were now alive, according to UNICEF estimates.

There were wrinkles, some of them mountain-size. On October 31, 1984, Indian prime minister Indira Gandhi was assassinated by two of her Sikh bodyguards in the garden of her residence, cut down in a spray of bullets. The attack was in retaliation for a bloody military assault she had ordered on Sikh separatists holed up in a temple a few months earlier. Before her death, Grant had met with "Mother India" several times; he and South Asia regional director Dave Haxton had secured her commitment for a full-scale immunization campaign. Now, Haxton and Grant had to make sure the immunization campaign didn't die with India's leader. Haxton's first order of business was to protect his eight Sikh employees from vicious anti-Sikh riots that were roiling the country (he insisted they camp out in the UNICEF office with their families). Then he and Grant eventually approached the country's new leader, Indira Gandhi's forty-year-old son Rajiv. They proposed that the neophyte prime minister make the immunization campaign a "living memorial" to his mother. Gandhi agreed.

Grant accelerated his pace everywhere, visiting thirty-three countries in 1984, some multiple times. In the space of one month, he flew to Nigeria, then India for a week, then to Kenya, then Burma, then Thailand, and finally Algeria. After Algeria, he went to Italy for a week before returning to the States. Almost every trip to the airport was last-minute and involved a harried rush out the door, often with Ethel handing Jim his packed suitcase. He flew Pan Am and always took the same seat, 3A. He skipped in-flight movies — he either worked or slept. Once he lost one of his little brown notebooks, only to find it more than a year later under that same seat, 3A, according to his executive assistant Mary Cahill.

During one of his many trips to Italy in 1984, at a special board session in Rome, Grant welcomed one of his most important funders and fund-raisers, Prince Talal bin Abdulaziz Al Saud of Saudi Arabia. The half brother of King Fahd, Prince Talal had first been approached in 1979 by UNICEF's liaison in Riyadh, Sabah Al Alawi, according to Maggie Black's *The Children and the Nations: The Story of Unicef*. Grant had actively courted him and persuaded the UN secretary general to appoint him as a special envoy in 1981. More important than his much-publicized concern for children were the prince's bottomless, oil-slicked pockets. UNICEF's director of personnel Manou Assadi once flew on Talal's private Boeing 727 on a trip to Kuwait and remembers ashtrays made out of gold.

Before one of Grant's early meetings with the prince, Assadi, who is from Iran, gave his boss some pointers on interacting with Arab leaders. He told him, for instance, that in Arab countries, it is customary to offer senior leaders the seat farthest from the door. "Jim Grant was very informal," says Assadi. "Things like that, he had no clue."

Grant once made a faux pas when meeting with a Muslim official in Indonesia, according to Assadi, who had heard about the encounter from a UNICEF regional director. Whipping out his packet of ORS, Grant reportedly told the government minister that not only was the solution effective for saving kids' lives, it was also a great cure for a hangover. It apparently had not occurred to Grant that his devout Muslim host did not drink.

Prince Talal became a vocal UNICEF booster and persuaded several other Arab countries to start a fund-raising consortium called the Arab Gulf Fund, or Agfund, that would support various UN causes. According to a 1981 *Newsweek* profile, Saddam Hussein, then president of Iraq, handed Talal a blank check in response to his fund-raising drive.

As the churn of fund-raising and travel and meetings suctioned away more and more time from Grant's already taxed and battered schedule, his personal life was diced into smaller and smaller pieces. He protected morsels of time with Ethel, and he corresponded with his sons and stepmother. On June 8, 1984, he welcomed his first grandchild, a girl named Joy, the daughter of his middle son, Jamie.

At some point later that year or in early 1985, Peter Adamson and Ethel persuaded Jim to go to a movie — to take him away from his work just for a few hours. They went to see *A Passage to India*, David Lean's film based on E. M. Forster's 1924 novel about British colonial India (a time and place Grant had, of course, experienced firsthand). Grant sat with his wife and his friend, but he did not seem the least bit interested in the movie. "He didn't really understand the film at all," recalls Adamson. "He wasn't really there."

Many people who encountered Grant, says Adamson, were "taken aback by the strength of his commitment and dedication...at the expense of all other aspects of life."

Chapter 6
SILENCING THE GUNS

It sounded like the beginning of a bad joke: "I met the president of El Salvador at a cocktail party last night."

Agop Kayayan was sitting at his cluttered desk in Guatemala City at around nine in the morning when the phone rang. It was Mary Cahill, Jim Grant's executive assistant, who quickly put her boss on the phone. Grant's voice was unusually charged, and he sounded very excited about something. Kayayan grew instantly nervous. The executive director of UNICEF doesn't just call you out of the blue to say he met a head of state at a cocktail party in New York.

So Kayayan, a jovial, chain-smoking Armenian-Lebanese man who was UNICEF's representative for Central America, replied simply, "Yes, Mr. Grant."

The conversation that followed, according to Kayayan, would change his life and set in motion an extraordinary series of events.

Grant continued his story about the president of El Salvador: "I asked him if we would have 80 percent immunization in El Salvador. He said, 'Mr. Grant, don't you understand, I have a war in my country?'"

Kayayan grew more anxious as he listened to the story and tried to anticipate where Grant was going with this — and what part in it Kayayan was supposed to play.

Grant went on: "I told him, 'Why don't we try to stop the war?'"

Then Kayayan knew what was coming, and the panic in him welled up.

"Then, the president says, 'It's not so easy — the Catholic Church has been trying many times.' Then I said, 'Can we try?' The president said, 'You are welcome.'"

Finally, Grant wound up his story. "Agoop," he said, adding an extra *o* to Kayayan's first name. "I want you to see how we can arrange a truce in El Salvador."

As his mind whirred, Kayayan joked: "Mr. Grant, you are saying this to the next representative...you'll have to find a new representative to do this."

"I know you're joking," Grant said. "And I know you're going to do it."

Kayayan was apprehensive, but he was also excited. "I like things that are out of the common. I like challenges," he says now.

He accepted Grant's challenge. He immediately called El Salvador's minister of health. Kayayan relayed what Grant had told him, but the minister did not seem at all surprised. He had received a similar call from the president. The men agreed they had to do something. The question that then clawed its way into their conversation was a gargantuan one: How?

El Salvador's vicious civil war, which began in 1980, would eventually claim more than 75,000 lives and unleash some of the most hideous violence in recent Latin American history — much of it perpetrated by US-backed, right-wing paramilitary death squads. The assassination of Archbishop Oscar Arnulfo Romeo by a sniper as he said Mass in San Salvador on March 24, 1980, was the opening chapter in thirteen years of terror. Romero was a forceful champion of the poor, who spoke out against the abuses committed by both the left and the right — but it was the right who felt most threatened by him. The horror quickly escalated. Romero's funeral was bombed, and attendees were sprayed with machine gun fire; as many as forty mourners were killed in the ensuing panic. Later that year, four American churchwomen were raped and murdered by members of the El Salvador National Guard; their bodies were interred in shallow graves along the side of a road. More bodies would appear, dumped above ground, in plain view, with arms missing or eyes gouged out — each one a warning from the death squads to keep quiet, each one a reminder of the vise of fear that clamped down on the country.

The most shocking atrocity occurred in December 1980, when members of the US-trained Atlacatl Rapid Deployment Infantry Battalion massacred as many as one thousand civilians — including many children — near the remote village of El Mozote. The violence was stupefying. According to Mark Danner's blow-by-blow account, published in the *New Yorker* thirteen years later, the soldiers started with the men, gunning them down and then beheading them with machetes. Next, they set about raping, torturing, and killing the women and girls, some as young as twelve. They saved the little children for last, hacking them with machetes or crushing their skulls with rifle butts.

When reports of the massacre were first published in the *New York Times* and the *Washington Post*, the governments of both El Salvador and the United States staunchly denied them. The Reagan administration considered El Salvador a critical front in the Cold War and funneled billions of dollars in aid to the government. Even the merciless mass killing of children by government military units was apparently not going to stand in the way of that. The impunity of the death squads therefore seemed impenetrable.

The president of El Salvador at the time, José Napoleón Duarte, had dismissed accounts of the El Mozote slaughter as a "guerrilla trick." A civil engineer and former mayor of San Salvador, who was once beaten and forced into exile after opposing the right-wing theft of an election, Duarte was actually considered a moderate. He was first appointed to the presidency in 1980 after joining a civilian-military junta that had pledged reforms after five decades of military dictatorship. He served until 1982 and reclaimed the office in 1984 by winning a national election. Duarte, the country's first freely elected president in fifty years, vowed to crack down on the death squads (though it became clear some were beyond his control). The man Duarte had defeated, Roberto D'Aubuisson, was a graduate of the US

Army's infamous School of the Americas and the founder of El Salvador's ultraconservative Arena party. D'Aubuisson also happened to be deranged and murderous, but this did not prevent Senator Jesse Helms and other US Republicans from staunchly supporting him. The UN Truth Commission for El Salvador later deemed D'Aubuisson guilty of ordering Archbishop Romero's murder. Next to him, almost anyone seemed palatable. Duarte was a cofounder of the country's Christian Democratic Party and a political survivor who hewed close to the political center. The stocky and beleaguered man, who sometimes wore bulbous glasses and reportedly nursed a messiah complex, had himself received death threats from both sides.

Jim Grant would, no doubt, have approached whoever was in power. El Salvador presented an unrivaled PR opportunity — if the child survival revolution could take root in a place racked by war and death and constant terror, then it could take root anywhere. He could hold the example up to any country that resisted a large immunization campaign. "If it was a success, you could tell the rest of the world, 'Look, don't give me silly arguments about why you can't do something when a country completely destroyed by war is doing it right now,'" says Kayayan. "That was Grant's major interest, and he mentioned it very, very often — too often for my taste."

But it was not his only interest. Grant would include the following stark fact in nearly every speech and press conference on El Salvador: the number of children in the country dying from vaccine-preventable diseases (an estimated twenty thousand a year) far exceeded those killed by bullets. He would call on all

Salvadorans to fight the "common enemies" of measles, polio, tetanus, diphtheria, and whooping cough. But in a country so riven by carnage, would anyone buy it?

The first person that had to be convinced, of course, was Duarte. But before approaching the president, Grant had consulted the US ambassador to El Salvador, Tom Pickering. A tested diplomat who had served in Nigeria and Jordan, Pickering had come to his post in El Salvador in 1983. Grant knew him from his days in Washington. A strong supporter of Duarte, Pickering had himself drawn the ire of the death squads — a right-wing plot to assassinate him was reported in the *New York Times* in June 1984. He lived in San Salvador's wealthy San Benito neighborhood, in a house guarded by Marines and surrounded by "a very high tennis court fence for rocket protection." On his backyard patio, next to a swimming pool, the tall, bald, businesslike ambassador would host guests for breakfast.

In the fall of 1984, according to correspondence, one of those guests was Jim Grant. He and Pickering spoke several times. During one of those conversations, Grant asked his old Washington friend what he thought about UNICEF spearheading a mass immunization campaign in El Salvador.

"He was discussing the importance of getting these kids vaccinations and inoculations," Pickering recalls.

The ambassador listened to Grant and then tossed out an idea: "Why don't we try for a ceasefire?"

Grant immediately glommed on to the concept. During moments like this — when a new, transformative idea bobbed up — Grant's eyes would often sparkle with childlike mirth.

"Do you think that would work?" Grant asked.

Pickering said he thought it would, because the guerrillas had already agreed to limited ceasefires on other occasions (though nothing as grand and complicated as this would entail). Duarte had also initiated talks with the guerrillas about a peace process.

The two men then discussed logistics. Pickering asked how long it would take. Grant guessed a week. Was he ready to mobilize? Could he get all the training and resources in order? Without hesitating, Grant said yes, he could take care of it.

"It was the usual Jim thing," Pickering says. "He was never in any doubt."

Brokering a ceasefire in the midst of national civil war for the purpose of immunizing kids would be a first — at least on this scale. Nils Thedin, a Swedish elder statesman on the UNICEF board, had articulated a vision several years earlier of children as "a zone of peace." In the late 1960s, before Jim Grant's time, UNICEF and the Red Cross had delivered aid to both sides during the Nigerian civil war. During the Vietnam War, UNICEF provided relief to children in both North and South Vietnam. But a national military truce to aid children? That was novel. It struck some as truly zany. Would either side really go for that? Wouldn't it be seen as sign of weakness? The paranoia in El Salvador had become calcified — not even Jim Grant could chisel through it.

Adamson recalls one meeting at UNICEF headquarters when Grant mentioned the ceasefire idea. The suggestion was met with a pause and "an almost audible gasp."

The plan invited a label of extreme naïveté. Military conflicts can't just be stopped — it almost sounded like the fanciful musing of a tie-dyed couch surfer whose only experience with armed combat was watching *Apocalypse Now*. But Jim Grant knew war intimately. As a lieutenant in the US Army during World War II, he had helped hold off the Japanese siege of the Burmese town of Myitkyina and would later win a Bronze Star.

Once while flying in a two-seat plane to interrogate some Japanese prisoners, Grant and his pilot had taken a detour to throw grenades at Japanese positions. The plane was hit with a bullet from below, and they were forced to land on a sandbar on the banks of the Irrawaddy River. They scrambled to fix the plane and, as they were doing so, a Japanese boat began speeding toward them. The boat had a gun, and it started firing. The plane was hit two or three times as the pilot furiously tinkered with the engine. Finally he got the plane working again, and he and Grant took off just in time, skimming over the water and narrowly escaping capture by the Japanese.

Toward the end of the war, Grant had worked under the command of General Joseph Stilwell and had later been tasked with helping General George Marshall negotiate an ultimately failed truce during China's civil war. He had remained in China after World War II to work for the United Nations Relief and Rehabilitation Administration (UNRRA), helping deliver aid to the Communists (the jeep he drove had sixteen bullet holes in it from various excursions).

Grant knew what he was proposing in El Salvador would not be easy. But Pickering did not see it as quixotic. "To me, it was a 'crazy like a fox idea,'" he says. "I said, 'Geez, let's try this... we could get people to start thinking about ceasefires and ending this conflict.' From my point of view, it had a lot of political possibilities." He adds, "I had to really depend on Jim to sell it, but he was willing to sell it."

"Willing" is a gross understatement. Grant was positively giddy about it.

As an American and a former US government official, Grant had to distance himself from his country, admits Pickering. "I think he wanted to do it without the US around, given the fact that we were a real partisan and a major player on the government side," he says.

Before Grant made any moves, Kayayan had to lay the groundwork. He and the government's minister of health agreed that in order to negotiate a workable truce, the minister would naturally handle the government side and UNICEF would handle the guerrillas. But Kayayan could not simply make an appointment to meet with the rebels. So he did the next best thing — he went to see the archbishop of San Salvador. Arturo Rivera Damas had stepped into Oscar Romero's shoes after his assassination, inheriting one of the country's most dangerous jobs. Despite the obvious risks, Damas had continued Romero's practice of denouncing the violence committed by both sides during Sunday sermons. Though not as aggressive as Romero, he became one of the few voices of dissent in a country largely silenced by systematic murder.

"[UNICEF's] relationship with the Catholic Church in El Salvador was crucial," Kayayan says. "Without the Catholic Church, we could not have done what we did."

Kayayan made an appointment with Damas and his assistant bishop Gregorio Rosa Chávez. Damas was heavyset, jowly, calm, and wore thick glasses. He "always looked indifferent, like he was thinking of something else," says Kayayan — not the sort of bearing you might expect from a truly courageous defender of human rights. In contrast, Chávez was young, slim, and brimming with energy. With arched eyebrows, boyish looks, and a humble aura of determination, he was the more dynamic of the two. They both were absolutely essential to UNICEF's audacious plan — the Catholic Church held unparalleled sway with the rebels and with almost all Salvadorans. If Damas and Chávez didn't sign on, it was dead in the water.

Grant had already urged Kayayan to forge a close bond with the church. The warm, wisecracking, nonreligious man would eventually become known by some as "Monsignor Kayayan," because of a joke he would tell to a gathering of Central American bishops several years later. In addressing the group, Kayayan asked in advance for forgiveness if he made any mistakes in speaking about the church. He then quipped, "I'm only a simple bishop from the Armenian Orthodox Church," and grabbed the thick red suspenders he always wore and held them out, as if to suggest that this was the typical attire of an Armenian bishop. The bishops laughed, but one did not get the joke. During a coffee break, an elderly Honduran bishop approached Kayayan and said, in complete seriousness: "Monsignor, I was very happy to hear about the Armenian Church. How is it?"

During that first meeting in Damas's office, Kayayan did not joke around. He feared he would not get very far. The ebullient, forty-one-year-old UNICEF representative began speaking in general terms about immunization and the need to save children from preventable diseases. Damas, at first, appeared unmoved. "It looked like it would take him a long time to understand what we were proposing... physically. That he wouldn't get excited," Kayayan says.

At first, Chávez sat in silence, keeping mum in deference to his superior. Kayayan kept speaking but began to feel daunted by the lack of reaction. "I had the feeling, I'm going to have a hard time," he says now.

Damas and Chávez eventually asked a few questions about money and what would be expected of the church, and Kayayan said UNICEF would shoulder much of the cost. Then Damas finally replied, his tone sagging with negativity.

"But we have tried this so many times," the bishop said. "The Catholic Church tries, at every festivity, to bring about a truce so the families can visit each other and circulate."

Kayayan thought that was it, the bishop was getting ready to tell him no. Then, after a pause, Damas brightened.

"For children," he said, "we will try as many times as needed."

According to an account later written by Chávez, "the arguments made by Kayayan were irrefutable." Among them: "Children have nothing to do with the war; they are beings above suspicion."

Grant later met with Damas in November to lock in his commitment and then sent him a follow-up letter reminding the archbishop of the promise he had made. The letter mentioned that Grant had met with Pope John Paul II on numerous occasions to plot the church's overall involvement in the child survival revolution. He quoted a pledge the pontiff had made to UNICEF: "The Holy See has said that 'the entire Catholic aid network organized in the various countries of the world and especially in the developing nations...will lend its maximum support to these important simple proposals.'" In other words, you don't want to disappoint the big boss, do you?

President Duarte also needed further convincing, despite his initial agreement at the cocktail party in New York. When the idea became more than a lofty topic breezily bandied about over drinks, he apparently grew wary about the political and logistical ramifications. Part of his reluctance may have stemmed from a fear that Grant's ceasefire could complicate his own nascent (and eventually failed) peace talks. As specific dates and other details were batted around, he replied that he would have to consult his "advisers," which, notes Kayayan, was a euphemism for "the generals."

"The initial moments of negotiation for truce were very shaky," Kayayan says. "The archbishop had his doubts, and neither side was enthusiastic."

In his written account, Chávez recalls that he and Damas met with both members of the army and the guerrillas. The army's reaction was "surprise and bewilderment" and was colored by a fear that the rebels "will take advantage of the truce to occupy positions, re-supply, heal their wounded, etc." Chávez writes that the army at first refused, saying it "could not suspend military operations that were already scheduled." Apparently, Duarte would have to force them to do so — if he could.

The guerrillas took a slightly softer line. Their reservations "were practically the same," according to Chávez's account, but they were "not entirely opposed to the idea."

Nonetheless, the Farabundo Martí National Liberation Front (FMLN), which comprised five different opposition groups, had good reason to be skeptical of any official proposal. Given the government's record of denying atrocities, why believe anything it had to say? Winning the rebels' cooperation was a formidable challenge, even for the only Salvadoran institution they trusted — the Catholic Church.

To anchor the buy-in of a head of state, Grant's tactic was basic, says Kayayan: "Give politicians a success story while they still are in government." This is what he sold to Duarte — the president had an opportunity that might never come again, a chance to do something of great importance for all Salvadorans (and, of course, for his own political career). Duarte clearly saw the potential for his own benefit: he specifically requested that the immunization campaign take place before municipal elections in March that could help him consolidate his power among lawmakers.

Once the government's pledge of cooperation was assured — but before they had heard anything from the guerrillas — Kayayan got a little ahead of himself. At the suggestion of a staff member's wife, he called a few journalists to share the big news. In a conference room at San Salvador's Camino Real Hotel — where most foreign journalists stayed — he sat down with two reporters and began to describe the immunization campaign. He withheld mention of the ceasefire plan. As he spoke, he quickly realized the reporters were bored. Finally, one of them said, "Mr. Kayayan, don't you know the country is at war?"

Thinking to himself, *What a question*, he replied: "Of course I know it's at war."

"So how," the reporter pressed, "are you going to organize a vaccination campaign?"

Kayayan answered calmly. "We are arranging a truce."

The boredom evaporated instantly. One reporter quickly ran up to Kayayan and asked if he could call his colleagues, other reporters, and pass on the tip. "You can," Kayayan said. After he realized the mistake he had made, Kayayan was surrounded by reporters.

It had hit him while he waited for the other correspondents to arrive. "We didn't yet have an answer from the guerrillas...maybe I was making a stupid move."

He quickly explained the situation to the hungry scrum of journalists, and they all agreed to hold the story until the guerrillas had replied.

Waiting for word from both sides was one of many worries that tormented Kayayan (and that may have contributed to his three different stomach ulcers). Another was the logistical challenge of mounting a nationwide immunization campaign in a country without the basic infrastructure to support it. El

Salvador was broke, relying on the United States to pay many of its bills. The health care system was simply nonexistent in many places. Roads were disastrous, especially in the mountains, and in some cases were strewn with land mines. Many bridges were destroyed. The country didn't have a refrigerated storage facility for vaccines, relying instead on a local beer company to store them and keep them cool. A cold chain network would have to essentially be assembled from scratch.

Making Kayayan's job all the more tenuous was the lack of a UNICEF office in El Salvador (Grant would soon open one). In the meantime, UNICEF staff from other countries met in the lobby of the hotel where they all stayed (not the luxurious Camino Real, but a cheaper alternative). The front desk served as their receptionist, Kayayan says.

During one of Grant's visits, as they sat in the airport lounge, the executive director asked Kayayan who would be running the day-to-day operations. "This man right here," Kayayan replied, turning to a compact, green-eyed Colombian named Hernan Jaramillo, who had accompanied them. Grant looked at Jaramillo, whose commitment and workaholic drive would prove pivotal.

"Mr. Grant, if he succeeds, I want you to remember that he is the one," Kayayan continued. "If he fails, we will hang him by his foot."

Grant's eyes, wide and incredulous, shifted to Kayayan. Like the old Honduran bishop, he had not gotten the Armenian's jest.

"Agoop," Grant began, "why do you want to hang him by his foot?"

Kayayan smiled. "So he dies very slowly."

Finally, his eyes registered the humor, and he laughed. It would not be the first or last time Grant was slow to get a joke, according to several staff members. Sometimes, he would laugh a minute or two after the punch line had been delivered, long after everyone else had moved on to a new topic. This humor lag seems to have been inherited from his father, Dr. John Black Grant, who admitted in his 1961 oral history that, as a student, he "had an absolute inability to understand a joke...Still have, says my wife."

Once the church finally came back with the guerrillas' response — they would honor an undeclared truce — the immunization campaign gained shape and speed. The initiative was dubbed the Days of Tranquillity, and a frenzied period of organization and communication ensued.

More than three thousand government health workers fanned out across the country, making house-to-house visits to explain the importance of vaccines to parents and to count the number of children under age five in need of inoculation — a tricky task in some areas, where itinerant communities moved frequently to avoid detection by the army. The wariness met by the health agents was not purely political: some parents had never been vaccinated themselves, and some had never once seen a doctor.

The launch was originally scheduled for Christmas 1984 — a "gift" to the children of El Salvador — but the protracted negotiations scratched that plan. The amended dates were bumped into 1985 and set for February 3, March 3, and April 21 — all Sundays to allow families to come without parents missing work. The three days would enable each child to get initial immunizations and two follow-up boosters. The timetable's other unspoken purpose: enable President Duarte to capitalize on the glow of goodwill in advance of the elections in late March.

The numbers were quickly tabulated and a target fixed: four hundred thousand children.

To reach them all with the full, three-course series of polio, measles, and DPT vaccines, the campaign needed a total of 4.5 million doses, 2.8 million syringes, 3,000 cold boxes, 700 vehicles, and 21,000 gallons of fuel.

Grant had already assembled an alliance of partners and funders to help support the $1.5 million campaign: the Pan American Health Organization, the International Committee of the Red Cross (ICRC), the United Nations Development Program, USAID, and a fleet of local Salvadoran organizations, including radio and TV stations, the Boy Scouts, and Rotary and Lions clubs. The government paid for the bulk of the program and fielded eight thousand health workers and twelve thousand volunteer immunizers. UNICEF would chip in $500,000, including the vaccines and cold chain equipment.

As in many of UNICEF's endeavors, the ICRC was vital. They went where no one else could go. In this case, in guerrilla-held towns near the Honduran border where government health workers feared to set foot, the Red Cross agreed to do the vaccinating. Since they would have a hard time finishing the job during the three designated days, they decided to take the risk of sending their immunizers out on non-ceasefire days as well.

Grant flew down to San Salvador the Saturday night before the first Day of Tranquillity. Kayayan and other UNICEF staff were on edge — what happened tomorrow would either be an epic victory or a disaster. And a lot of it was beyond their control. If either side chose not to keep their word, the whole affair would collapse into a welter of death and recrimination. The fractured nature of the conflict fed the maelstrom of doubt. "It's not like you had a unilateral border line," notes Kayayan. "It's not two armies sitting in front of each other. You are talking about small groups with very bad communications and hard feelings on both sides."

The campaign was inaugurated the next morning with the wailing of a baby girl at the presidential palace. Duarte held the infant in his lap as flashes popped and TV cameras recorded the event. After a needle was plunged into her behind, she screamed in protest, and Duarte picked her up and patted her back. Nearby stood Jim Grant, beaming.

At a press conference, seated side by side in ornate high-back chairs behind tall glasses of iced tea, Grant and Duarte looked oddly mismatched. Wearing big glasses, his face drooping, somber, dour even — Duarte was inscrutable. Grant folded his hands in front of him, telegraphing a quiet excitement. His eyes glinted and his shirt pocket bulged — probably with a few packets of ORS.

"Señor Presidente," Grant began a halting, heartfelt, pause-riddled address. "This is a great day in El Salvador — not only for the children of El Salvador...but for children throughout the world...

"Last year in El Salvador, more children died...from not being immunized...than died because of fighting in the country. To my knowledge, this is the first time...in the history of the world...when all parties...in a country like El Salvador today...agreed to fight a common enemy first."

As his words staggered out, his hands swept in small circles, as though he were urging someone to hurry up and finish a thought.

He then thanked and congratulated the president, pronouncing his name "Dor-tee."

Despite the mispronunciation, President Duarte liked Grant and even began emulating him. On a later occasion, before a televised press conference, Duarte stopped Kayayan in the hall and asked if he happened to have a packet of ORS, oral rehydration salts. "I don't," Kayayan told the president, "but Mr. Grant surely does." Kayayan found Grant.

The executive director of UNICEF was tired and puzzled.

"Why does he want ORS?" he said. "Does he have diarrhea?"

"No," Kayayan replied, perhaps stifling a chuckle. "He wants to do the same thing you do."

Grant nodded, fished a packet out of his pocket, and handed it to Kayayan.

When Duarte addressed the television cameras, he declared that El Salvador would not only vaccinate children, it would save them from the biggest killer, diarrhea, by using oral rehydration salts.

Then he brandished the packet of ORS and held it aloft for all to see.

"He had learned this from Mr. Grant," says Kayayan. "I looked at Mr. Grant, and his mouth is open, he can't believe it... [The president] was imitating exactly what he used to do."

On Sunday, February 3, 1985, at more than three thousand sites in nearly every corner of El Salvador — at health centers, schools, churches, and town squares, in the dense barrios of San Salvador and in remote villages of adobe brick homes — parents lined up to get their kids immunized. Many had come because their priests had encouraged them. Some had heard about the campaign on commercial radio stations or on the FMLN's clandestine Venceremos radio channel. Others had read about it in one of the million leaflets air-dropped across the Massachusetts-sized country or even glimpsed the slogan *prevenir es... vacunar* on a lottery ticket.

Grant's "social mobilization" strategy had once again paid off. Spreading word of the immunization drive in every conceivable venue was intended not just to let parents know about the free service, but to instill in them a demand for better health care for their children. In some places, the immunization teams — dubbed "life squads" by Bishop Chávez — were the very first contact local residents had with any kind of health care, ever.

On that first day, Grant went to the small hamlet of Corral Viejo, where a local volunteer told the Associated Press that residents had to walk ten miles to the nearest health clinic and that, as a result, most children there had never seen a doctor. She said that each year about half of the village's small children died of preventable diseases.

Indeed, it was a big event for the village. Children had donned their "Sunday best" to get their shots. In Corral Viejo and many other places, the vaccination booths were adorned with balloons and streamers. Once children had submitted to the needle, they were given a bat and encouraged to break open piñatas filled with candy.

In guerrilla-held towns, rebel soldiers did some of the vaccinating along with Red Cross staff. A UNICEF photo taken the day of the campaign shows a female guerrilla, an automatic rifle slung over her shoulder, bending over to vaccinate a young child. In some places, government doctors allowed themselves to be "abducted," so that they could be taken to rebel areas to administer vaccines; they were later released. Chávez recalls, in his essay, that guns were used on that day — but only to open bottles of soda.

At the end of the day, Duarte told reporters that his minister of defense informed him the truce had held. "For that I am glad," he said, "because we have a day of peace, a day of life, a day of hope."

The commander of the FMLN, Joaquin Villalobos, issued a similar statement: "We cannot in any way be in disagreement. The vaccination campaign is of great importance for our people."

Kayayan was at the airport at the end of the day and called into the office for news. "No fighting anywhere!" was the exuberant reply shouted through the phone. Sitting next to an airport pay phone, the receiver clutched to his ear, Kayayan stomped his foot down triumphantly and yelled "Banzai!" This was, in part, for the benefit for a young female Japanese UNICEF staffer who stood nearby. And it worked — hearing the victory cry, she promptly jumped into Kayayan's lap and hugged him.

When the results were tabulated, they must have produced a mix of elation, relief, and slight disappointment. The teams had immunized 217,000 children on the first day, far shy of the goal of 400,000. But the fact that the truce was kept — that they were able to essentially stop a war to save children's lives — was a surreal triumph.

They got ready to do it again.

It wouldn't have worked if they hadn't broken the rules.

Kayayan used to give his staff members brown paper bags filled with cash, in case they encountered problems in the field. If, say, during an immunization campaign, a truck carrying vaccines got lodged in viscous mud — what were your options? You did not have much time to think about it. You needed a tractor. You asked a local farmer to borrow one. But he, of course, wanted to be paid.

"What do you do?" says Kayayan. "Give a check or credit card? For people to laugh at you?"

No, you give him cash. You keep the truck moving, so the vaccines don't spoil in the heat.

This likely ran afoul of UN financial rules. But if UNICEF had followed those rules — if every expenditure had been formally approved and vetted — Days of Tranquillity may not have been possible, says Kayayan. "When you are doing something like this in El Salvador in the 1980s, there are some bureaucratic rules you cannot follow."

Grant understood this, says Kayayan. "He cut the red tape for me...he was our friend in New York." The head of UNICEF did not mind, he says, if you broke the rules "for a good reason."

Grant himself flouted numerous procedures and protocols, including during the second or third Day of Tranquillity in El Salvador. He let the staff know he would be arriving in San Salvador late and needed someone to take him directly from the airport to the site of an immunization post in a guerrilla-held area at the other end of the country. It would be impossible to make it via car or truck.

UNICEF's Guatemala coordinator Thierry del Rue, a plucky Belgian economist, had a plane and a license to fly it. He offered to take Grant himself, though he had serious reservations.

"It would have been very easy if someone wanted to shoot us," he says. If the plane had gone down with the executive director of UNICEF on board, he adds, "it would have been a catastrophe."

Del Rue met Grant on the tarmac, and they got ready to board his 1948, single-engine, four-seater Navion plane.

Someone standing nearby mentioned that such a flight was prohibited for security reasons.

"I don't care," Grant said. "We're going."

During the nearly two-hour flight, the roar of the engine was too deafening to allow conversation. Del Rue had to guide the plane very slowly between two mountains — this is where he felt most vulnerable. They were a tempting target up here, plodding along, pinned by the mountains.

He finally set the plane down on a short gravel airstrip at a dilapidated airport that looked abandoned. A caravan of UNICEF cars was waiting. After a short drive, the group was warmly greeted by the guerrillas. A government minister had also come, arriving in a car with darkened windows. The rebels welcomed everyone, says del Rue, offering coffee and cookies.

There were numerous last-minute hitches — and with them, bent or snapped rules. On a Friday afternoon before a later Day of Tranquillity, an urgent message came crackling through a walkie-talkie: "No ice!"

Ice was required, of course, to keep the vaccines cool. Without it, notes Kayayan, vaccines become "water with salt." They become useless. Apparently, the ice supply had run out two days before the next truce. Hernan Jaramillo, the diligent Colombian who managed the logistics, picked up the walkie-talkie. He barked an order to staff: "Buy ice everywhere!... Go to stores, go to homes, buy all the ice you can." He told them to first come to the office to get some cash.

Jaramillo was "the action guy," says Kayayan.

He extracted UNICEF from a number of tight fixes. One evening, before the second or third ceasefire, Kayayan organized a press conference to announce the next impending truce. Earlier that day, he had reserved a reception room at the Camino Real Hotel and invited thirty reporters. "We were given assurance from the church it was going to be yes," Kayayan recalls.

But as night crept across San Salvador, the "yes" had not come. Grant had flown down and was at the hotel. The thirty journalists soon started filtering in, and Kayayan found himself in a familiar position: surrounded by reporters with nothing to tell them.

"Just a minute," Kayayan told the group. "Just a minute."

Finally, he admitted he didn't have confirmation from the guerrillas. "It was like a funeral," he says.

Grant was calm and did not betray any anxiety or displeasure. As he chatted with reporters, Jaramillo sidled up to Kayayan.

"Don't worry," he whispered. "I'm going to the archbishop's place."

"Hernan," Kayayan protested, "it's nine o'clock at night. You don't bother an archbishop at night."

"I'm going," he said, and left.

Kayayan then ordered in some food and drinks. Everyone politely sipped beers and sodas and waited in a stifling haze of unease. Del Rue, who was in the room, recalls a "moment of very high tension."

In about forty-five minutes, Jaramillo bolted back into the room, an expansive smile splitting his face. He hurried over to

Kayayan and whispered that Deputy Bishop Chávez had confirmed that the guerrillas had once again accepted the truce. Kayayan quickly told Grant, who promptly asked for everyone's attention.

"The truce is on for the weekend!" he announced.

Suddenly, the "mourning session turned into a wedding ceremony...the journalists had a party."

On another evening, recalls del Rue, UNICEF staff were eating dinner in the hotel restaurant as the hotel band struck up a familiar tune: "We Are the World." Featuring forty-five famous performers, the song was written by Michael Jackson and Lionel Ritchie to raise money for famine relief in Africa. Grant quickly shot out of his chair, bounded onto the stage, and started belting out the words (no doubt completely off key): "We are the World...we are the children...we are the ones who make a brighter day...So let's start giving!"

He beckoned others to join him, and they did, scrambling onto the stage.

"It was very funny," says del Rue, "all the staff of UNICEF singing in this hotel."

The last two Days of Tranquillity were even more successful than the first one: 262,000 children were reached on March 3 and 241,000 on April 21. The truces again held, with one exception. On March 3, five immunization sites were closed because of government bombing, according to Grant's handwritten notes. The notes were based on reports from the guerrilla radio channel.

The three almost entirely violence-free days were indeed remarkable and fleeting anomalies. In the weeks preceding and following each day, the killing raged, unabated. In his sermon on March 3, Archbishop Damas again appealed for peace from the pulpit, asking both sides to honor UNICEF's ceasefire. According to a United Press International report, he also decried what he called a "cloud" of deaths that was darkening El Salvador, noting that eighty-six people had died in the last week alone.

Throughout the rest of El Salvador's civil war, which ended in 1992, the Days of Tranquillity would be reprised year after year. No matter how bad — how sinister and cruel and blood-soaked all the other days of the year were — these days were sacred. Thousands upon thousands of children lived as a result.

Chapter 7
BUY ITALIAN

"Holy Shit."

The words came through the phone in a barely uttered whisper, after a pause — a pause long enough to make Marco Vianello-Chiodo think, at first, that he had lost his connection with Jim Grant.

But Grant was there, and he was listening.

In his hotel room in Boston, the head of UNICEF was absorbing what Vianello-Chiodo — sitting thousands of miles away in Rome — had just told him. Those two words were his response.

Vianello-Chiodo was in his native Italy in May 1985 to ask for money. That was his job as the director of UNICEF's Program Funding Office. He had been visiting Francesco Forte, a Socialist government minister in charge of Italy's foreign aid budget. The imposing Vianello-Chiodo, who stood six feet seven and wore a lush beard, had suggested that the government of Italy support UNICEF's push for childhood immunization. Italy could make an unparalleled impact, he had said. Forte had told him to write a letter making a specific request, and Vianello-Chiodo had decided to waste no time — he would write the letter right then and there. He asked to borrow a typewriter. It happened to be the typewriter used to write speeches for government officials, with giant characters between a quarter and a half inch tall. He threaded the paper in and hastily drummed out an official note in extra-large type, asking the government of Italy to give UNICEF $100 million.

And the government of Italy said yes.

After Colombia's immunization crusade — as big campaigns were mounted in country after country — Grant's propulsion was rapidly outpacing UNICEF's resources. He needed a cash injection. Now he had one.

But like most big sums of money, it came with some irksome demands. In exchange for the contribution, the Italian government wanted UNICEF to "buy Italian" and hire Italian staff, among other things.

When he had confirmed the donation, Vianello-Chiodo called Grant at his hotel room in Boston. His boss didn't answer, so he left a message. Grant called back at midnight Rome time and apologized for waking Vianello-Chiodo (he apologized for this a lot).

The fund-raising chief then told him about the pledge from the Italians and the "strings" that dangled from it.

No reply.

"Are you listening?" Vianello-Chiodo asked.

"Yes," Grant finally said.

"So?"

Nothing. Not a word from Grant.

"You are not going to refuse a hundred million dollars?" Vianello-Chiodo asked. He made the point that the money would allow Grant to expand his revolution and would help put the world behind UNICEF.

Then, finally, came the faint *"Holy shit."*

Why had he taken so long to answer? It may have been simple shock. His mind may have been clambering to keep up with the cavalcade of possibilities let loose by this amount of money.

Either way, Vianello-Chiodo was relieved. "I knew you were going to accept it," he told his boss.

The donation was transformative, and it would be followed by other infusions of money. But many people were not happy about the quid pro quo. At a regional staff meeting in Abidjan, Ivory Coast, according to Vianello-Chiodo, several staff members voiced qualms about the Italian donation. "They were furious because they had to buy Italian cars," he recalls. "And the only car that could go anywhere was a tiny Panda four-by-four, which is a rickety little affair, and so they were furious about that."

The Italians pressed Grant hard. UNICEF's Fouad Kronfol, then Africa section chief, recalls a tangibly uncomfortable meeting between Grant and Italian officials, including one who was pelting demands at the UNICEF chief in a "rather condescending" way, says Kronfol.

"They were being a little bit too obnoxious," he recalls, "but Grant swallowed it all . . . he had a very thick skin."

As he sat there watching the Italians talk down to his boss, Kronfol remembers thinking that if he had been in Grant's seat, "I would have stormed out of the meeting."

Instead, Grant listened patiently and, as each demand was hurled at him, he calmly replied that he would see what he could do.

The ebullient "master fund-raiser" wrangled money from lots of other places, too. As he relentlessly browbeat heads of developing countries to up their immunization rates, he hassled richer countries to boost their financial support for UNICEF. He would remind them that UNICEF's revenue was all voluntarily contributed. Unlike "specialized" UN agencies such as the World Health Organization — which got regular allocations from UN dues — UNICEF was a "fund" and, as such, had to raise almost every penny it spent. Grant made it a very popular investment. During his tenure, the United States' total annual contribution to UNICEF went from around $44 million to more than $130 million. Funds also flowed in from the private sector — Grant would take money from pretty much anyone, including oil titans Exxon and Texaco. About a quarter of UNICEF's income came from "national committees," nongovernmental organizations that were set up in wealthier countries to raise money and awareness for UNICEF.

Despite rising antipathy toward the United Nations and a suffocating recession, Grant ultimately presided over more than a tripling of UNICEF's financial resources during his tenure. As its coffers grew, so did its clout. In a 1988 editorial, the *New York Times* noted that UNICEF's positive reputation was an anomaly among

UN agencies. Applauding the US Congress for increasing its sup-port for the Child Survival Fund and UNICEF programs, the *Times* noted that Congress had not treated the rest of the UN very well: "Congress continues to starve the U.N., the Organization of Ameri-can States and a host of development agencies." The UN children's agency, "the little engine that could," as Grant liked to call it, was blazing brighter than any other star in the UN firmament.

It was only fitting that Grant would use the occasion of the UN's fortieth anniversary on October 24, 1985, to garner more attention for his cause. At Grant's urging, UN secretary general Javier Pérez de Cuéllar invited world leaders to a conference the day following the anniversary to recommit to the once elusive goal set by the World Health Assembly in 1977: universal child-hood immunization by 1990.

Speaking to UNICEF staff a few months earlier, Grant had said that the aspiration of reaching all children with immuni-zations by 1990 "might really take hold and become a serious goal...and not just one of these cartoonist's goals with which we are so accustomed."

Two reasons the goal was now a serious one: Colombia and El Salvador. Grant had shown it could work in both places. It was now a lot harder to ignore or forget the 1977 commitment. Another potent prod was the Pan American Health Organization's announcement in May of a coordinated plan to wipe out polio in the Americas (major strides against polio had recently been made in Brazil). UNICEF had also secured the buy-in of the world's two most populous countries — India and China. Without either of them, universal childhood immunization was a sheer impossibility.

As many as one thousand people attended a ceremony at the United Nations, and fifty-seven world leaders signed a pledge reaffirming their governments' commitment to meet the ambitious target. One of the nongovernmental signatories was Rotary International, which used the occasion to announce that it would raise a game-changing $120 million to help eradicate polio; over the next three years, it would astonish everyone by pulling in more than twice as much (by 2015, it would contribute more than $1.3 billion). The service organization had been involved in the polio battle since 1979 and had recently teamed up with Albert Sabin, the inventor of the oral polio vaccine (and Jonas Salk's bitter rival). Grant enthusiastically welcomed Rotary to his revolution and would later remark: "Thank God Rotary was born."

The ceremony was standing room only, guests packed shoulder to shoulder. Some diplomats complained that the meeting had violated protocol, recalls former UNICEF staffer Allegra Morelli, who organized the gathering. One guest remarked aloud: "Who is the crazy person who organized this mess?" Standing nearby, Morelli answered that she was.

Looking out over the teeming room, Grant began his speech with a quote from Shakespeare:

> *There is a tide in the affairs of men*
> *Which, taken at the flood, leads on to fortune;*
> . . .
> *On such a full sea are we now afloat,*
> *And we must take the current when it serves,*
> *Or lose our ventures.*

He did not mention, according to his prepared remarks, that the source of the quote was Brutus, one of the murderers of Caesar in Shakespeare's *Julius Caesar*.

But the metaphor served his purpose. He used it as a somewhat clumsy goad. "Let us indeed suppose that those of us who bet on life can succeed," Grant said. "Let us prove to the world in these next five years that on such a full sea are we now afloat, and we shall take the current!"

In its coverage of the event, the Associated Press noted that, just the day before, UN member states could not even come to a consensus on the wording of a declaration marking the world body's anniversary. The immunization pledge, however, "was a chorus of unanimity."

Now, Grant had to figure out how to actually do what he said could be done. And fast. Five years was not a long time.

Some of Peter Adamson's most enjoyable moments at the UN were "watching Jim deal with experts."

One of those moments came in a meeting between Grant and several WHO officials. After Halfdan Mahler's promise of support, the health agency had emerged, however begrudgingly, as a full-fledged partner in the push for universal childhood immunization (the WHO's immunization chief, Ralph Henderson, had been a diligent proponent of vaccination—even if Mahler and others had been unenthusiastic). Its technical expertise and monitoring capacity were indeed essential. But hints of elitism and inflexibility still flickered.

Adamson watched as WHO officials told Grant that immunization rates couldn't simply be doubled and redoubled — the infrastructure wasn't there, the cold chains were inadequate, the electricity coverage was insufficient.

"They were making this point to Jim as though they had to teach him a few elementary things about immunization," Adamson recalls. Grant had heard much of it before, of course.

To anchor their point, the WHO experts mentioned Pakistan as an example. Which was a mistake.

Grant immediately began reeling off immunization statistics from Pakistan — they were among the dense and growing compilation of numbers that swarmed in his head. And he could snatch any one of them when it suited.

"Well, if you look at the figure for Pakistan for DPT1," Grant began, "you see it's around 70 percent." DPT1 refers to the first of three rounds of the diphtheria, pertussis, and tetanus vaccine.

He went on: "DPT2 is about 40 percent, and DPT3 is around 20 percent."

Then the knockout line: "If you can reach 70 percent on DPT1, then there is no reason, infrastructurally, why you can't reach it with DPT3. This is not an infrastructure or supply problem. It's a demand and communications problem."

The WHO officials were flustered. They did not expect the head of UNICEF to know more about immunization than they did.

Says Adamson: "Two minutes after they were patronizing him, they were left wondering what to say."

Chapter 8
THE SALESMAN

"He's a military dictator," Steve Woodhouse began. "He's not interested in kids."

The jovial British head of UNICEF's Syria office — who helped pull Grant out of a soak pit in Pakistan a few years earlier — had met his boss at the airport in Damascus. They sat in the gilded, wood-paneled VIP lounge, probably sipping coffee, as Woodhouse briefed Grant on his upcoming meeting with Syrian president Hafez al-Assad. With scant time between meetings and flights, the head of UNICEF did a lot of work in airport lounges.

Genial and reassuring, Woodhouse had the bearing of an affable high school guidance counselor. He tried to impress upon Grant that he didn't think he would get very far with Syria's repressive leader, known for his cruel tendencies.

The father of the cold-blooded Bashar al-Assad, who has terrorized Syria in recent years, Hafez al-Assad was also widely feared and perhaps even more ruthless. In 1982, he brutally put down a Muslim Brotherhood uprising by razing much of the city of Hama. Estimates of casualties ranged up into the tens of thousands.

Woodhouse summed up his reservations for Grant: "Look, I'm not very optimistic."

Grant looked at Woodhouse. He had listened intently, nodding and taking in everything he said.

But he did not agree. The two proceeded to the presidential palace.

Dressed in military fatigues, al-Assad greeted Jim Grant with a reserved handshake. They sat side by side in slightly angled chairs. Woodhouse and al-Assad's aide sat behind them. Interpreters lingered nearby. Coffee was served in small cups.

With a big forehead, sharp chin, thin mustache, and a stern bearing, al-Assad did not give away much. He wore a placid "poker face," Woodhouse recalls.

As he looked at his dour host, Grant's face began to glow with sudden intensity. He was "almost like a madman," says Woodhouse, with the "eyes of a Rasputin."

Then, without any warning, he let loose a whopper.

"Mr. President," he said, "how would you like to beat the Turks?"

There was a tinge of mischievous excitement in Grant's voice, as though he were asking the president of Syria to help him pull off a really great prank.

Al-Assad's poker face thawed instantly. His gaze snapped sharply onto Grant.

Woodhouse was shocked and appalled by what his boss said. But he also understood that objective number one had been achieved: Grant had commandeered the president's attention. Now he had to keep it.

Al-Assad finally replied: "I thought you were the UNICEF executive director."

In other words, *Isn't that a wildly inappropriate thing for you to say?*

Sounding perturbed, he added, "What do you mean, 'Do I want to beat the Turks?'"

Grant first answered, "Yes, I am." Then without missing a beat, he told al-Assad that "your former colonial master during the Ottoman Empire days" had recently immunized the majority of its children against several killer diseases.

He likely smiled — his quick, gotcha grin — then continued. Beginning his sentence, "I'm sure, Mr. President," he egged al-Assad on and said he knew he could do even better than Turkey.

Reminding Syria's dictator of the country's former overlords was risky at best. Such a tart comment could have gotten Grant and Woodhouse thrown out of the country. What of the immunization campaign then?

But al-Assad did not throw them out or react at all adversely. Instead he listened. Grant began to describe what Turkey had achieved, how such a big country had mobilized its entire population against considerable obstacles.

At the time, according to WHO estimates, immunization coverage for one-year-olds in Syria was between 27 and 29 percent for polio, measles, and the third dose of DPT; for the tuberculosis vaccine, it was higher, at 53 percent. As many as tens of thousands of young lives were lost every year, simply because most Syrian kids were not immunized.

Earlier, Woodhouse had asked Grant why he was focusing so many of UNICEF's resources on immunization. Grant cited a lesson he had learned while working for President John F. Kennedy as deputy assistant secretary of state in the early 1960s. What Kennedy had taught him, he said, was not to hit complex problems head-on. Instead, envision the problem as a wall of bricks. "Try to identify a few bricks — if you take them out, the wall will collapse by itself," Grant had said. "I see immunization as one of those bricks." Immunize a country's kids, and the wall of ill health, early death, misery, and lack of services will start to crumble.

As al-Assad soaked up Grant's story, the UNICEF leader laid on a little flattery and began to drop a few more crumbs to entice him farther down the path. "I know you can beat the Turks," he said. "I know you're a strong president. Once you decide to do something, it will get done. You are in charge of your government in a big way, and I'm convinced you could mobilize the country."

Woodhouse realized that al-Assad was beginning to grasp how all of this could advance his own position. The president "could immediately see there would be some political benefit for Hafez al-Assad," recalls Woodhouse, "if he could show the Syrian people he had the power to do good for the majority, and at the same time, beat the old colonial powers, the Ottoman Empire."

The president was sold. "Tell me more, Mr. Grant. What do I need to do?"

Grant ticked off what would be required: making sure the entire population knew about the immunization schedule, mobilizing health staff throughout the country, setting up the cold chain, positioning vaccines, syringes, and equipment.

Speaking to his aide, al-Assad then commanded: "Call the minister of health immediately. Call the minister of information immediately. Call the minister of defense immediately."

The ministers appeared within minutes. Grant repeated, with more detail, what needed to happen. Then gesturing toward Woodhouse, he said, "This young guy, Woodhouse, will be happy to work with any committee of people you put together to make sure that all the planning is done properly."

Within the next three months, Syria launched an immunization campaign. UNICEF provided vaccines, equipment, coordination, training, and other assistance. And after all the results were tallied, Syria's immunization coverage had doubled and, in some cases, nearly tripled in the space of one year. Polio coverage for one-year-olds jumped from 29 percent to 86 percent, DPT3 shot from 29 percent to 86 percent, measles rose from 27 percent to 64 percent, and the tuberculosis vaccine went from 53 percent to 98 percent. In every category except measles, according to 1986 estimates, it had done just what Grant suggested: it had beaten Turkey. For measles coverage, the countries were exactly tied at 64 percent.

Woodhouse was "blown away" by Grant's ability to persuade a military dictator to do something good for children. His boss's strategy, Woodhouse learned, was not to appeal to global leaders' compassion or empathy, but rather to identify their concerns and then piggyback UNICEF's agenda on those concerns. This tactic was employed all over the globe, with miserable despots and enlightened statesmen, government generals and rebel commanders, democratically elected presidents and calcified monarchs — with whoever held the levers of power. He came to these meetings armed with plenty of props — growth charts, polio droppers, oral rehydration packets — but also often with more knowledge about the country's children than the leaders themselves possessed.

Folded up in his pocket, Grant sometimes carried the table of contents of a book entitled *Getting to Yes: Negotiating Agreement without Giving In*, coauthored by his longtime friend Roger Fisher, and William Ury. Among the entries: "Don't Bargain Over Positions," "Separate the PEOPLE from the Problem," "Focus on INTERESTS, Not Positions," "Invent OPTIONS for Mutual Gain," "Insist on Using Objective CRITERIA." Grant did all of these things, but his method of persuasion was often even simpler: find that one weak point, that one critical brick that could be plucked from the wall.

In Morocco, after the UNICEF representative could not gain any traction with the administration of the autocratic King Hassan II, Grant made a visit to the North African country. According to former UNICEF program director Dr. Nyi Nyi, who heard accounts of the meeting from Grant and a Moroccan government official, the encounter began as a one-way lecture by the king. Grant politely listened as the king, known for his

eloquence and political dexterity, spoke at length of the great-
ness of his country. Morocco, he told Grant, bore many similari-
ties to its former colonial ruler, France. It was, in fact, "France
south of the Mediterranean," he said.

When the king paused to take a sip of water, Grant inter-
jected: "Your Majesty, what you say is true, except for one thing."

The king's curiosity was piqued. "And what could that be?"
he asked.

"Your children die at a rate ten times that of France."

The king looked at Grant. He turned to his health minister,
who sat nearby. "Is that true?"

The health minister confirmed that, unfortunately, what the
head of UNICEF said was indeed correct. Apparently this information had never been shared with the king until now.

"We can't accept that," the king proclaimed. "Do whatever
Mr. Grant wants us to do."

The staff from the Moroccan Ministry of Health visited
UNICEF headquarters in New York, where Nyi Nyi welcomed
them. An immunization campaign was launched. The country's
coverage rates for polio, DPT3, and tuberculosis would eventually climb from none at all in 1980 to more than 80 percent by
1990, according to WHO estimates. Coverage for measles would
reach 79 percent.

"He knew what would strike a chord," says Nyi Nyi. "He
would play one country against another."

He was also utterly shameless, never missing an opportunity
to make his pitch, no matter how tacky or inappropriate. In the
Dominican Republic, after an official field visit in 1985, President

Salvador Jorge Blanco hosted an august state dinner in Grant's honor. He was asked to make a speech. On the stage with Grant stood the president, wearing an expensive-looking suit, and three or four men in full military regalia — possibly generals or bodyguards. Grant began to tell the crowd of several hundred people what the Dominican Republic could do to save more children. About halfway through his speech, he stopped. According to Peter Adamson, who had accompanied him, he then reached into his pocket and pulled out a ribbon of red and blue stickers. Printed on each were the words CHILD SURVIVAL REVOLUTION. He walked over to President Blanco and the men surrounding him, peeled off some stickers, and began applying them liberally on the president's suit and the men's uniforms. "I am making you five-star generals of the child survival revolution!" Grant announced cheerfully.

President Blanco smiled, perhaps stunned.

Back at the hotel, Ethel chided, "Jim, you are such a ham."

Adamson says it is hard to imagine any other international leader getting away with a stunt that might well have been perceived as "tactless at best" and possibly even offensive. "Yet, because of who he was," Adamson says, "it was fine."

Grant's motives were so obvious, he adds, that even his greatest critics could not dispute his genuineness. Because everyone knew that all his enthusiasm, all his marketing ploys, all his badgering and berating — that it was never about him. It was always about saving kids. There was no ulterior motive, no hidden agenda.

In India, during the mid-to-late 1980s, the government was ambivalent toward outsiders promising external aid or bilateral support, according to former Indian government official Gouri-sankar Ghosh. He is aware of one notable exception. "The only person who was not only well received, but also warmly received — starting from the prime minister down to state governments — was Jim Grant," says Ghosh, who would go on to work for UNICEF. "Even if India had a visit by the UN secretary general, it would not create as much headline news as a visit by Jim Grant."

Samora Machel, the revered African freedom fighter who had liberated Mozambique from Portuguese rule in 1975, trusted Grant so much that he once agreed to a sudden and, some might say, wildly unreasonable request. On the way into the heavily guarded presidential palace in Maputo, the country's capital, to see Machel, Grant clutched a briefcase under his arm. UNICEF's Mozambique representative Marta Mauras advised Grant to leave the briefcase behind — security was too tight.

"Jim, you cannot take that," said Mauras, an assertive Chilean sociologist. "It's going to be taken away."

Grant ignored her. He didn't answer, didn't even look at her. Then, suddenly, like a fugitive trying to ditch his parole officer, he bolted. Briefcase under arm, he darted into the palace. He rushed past the guards, as Mauras and UNICEF staffer Carl Tinstman ran behind him. Somehow, he made it inside.

Something in that briefcase was very important, and Mauras and Tinstman would soon find out what it was.

President Machel was waiting for them on a long, red velvet couch with four cushions, surrounded by several aides, an interpreter, and a government minister. Bearded and in military garb, the stout, former rebel leader commanded a striking presence. Machel was a Marxist and his philosophy, in one significant way, mirrored Grant's: both men believed that the benefits of society should be made available to all. A vociferous critic of the evils of colonialism and apartheid, Machel once famously remarked, according to the *New York Times*: "The rich man's dog gets more in the way of vaccination, medicine and medical care than do the workers upon whom the rich man's wealth is built."

Grant likely would have agreed.

Mozambique was then throttled by a nasty civil conflict that pitted the ruthless Renamo rebels (backed by the apartheid government in South Africa and formerly by white-ruled Rhodesia) against Machel's government. Horrific human rights abuses abounded, most of them committed by the Renamo rebels. But Machel's sense of justice was marred by his own despotic tendencies. According to Human Rights Watch, the military leader's postcolonial regime subjected dissidents to re-education camps and set up a secret police force that tortured prisoners and carried out extrajudicial executions.

Machel stood up to greet Grant. The head of UNICEF was then signaled by an aide to sit in a nearby chair, also upholstered in red velvet. Grant proceeded to give his child survival spiel and brandished a packet of oral rehydration salts as an interpreter translated his words into Portuguese (though Machel was rumored to understand and speak English). Then Grant said, "Mr. President, I have a favor to ask you."

"Yes?" said Machel.

He opened his briefcase. As if triggered by the snapping motion, Machel's aides stood up. No one had mentioned what was in that briefcase, and they now appeared concerned.

Grant pulled out a folder. Inside it was a document, two or three pages long.

As Tinstman recalls, Grant then said, "I have taken the liberty of developing this formal agreement for us to sign. If it's all right with you, perhaps we can both sign it right now."

According to Mauras, Grant then explained that it was a "commitment for all children."

This was news to Mauras. Grant hadn't said a word to her about the agreement before this meeting. Ostensibly, he had kept it secret to avoid sounding off alarm bells at the presidential palace. He wanted to walk out with a signature. He didn't want to wait for vetting and bureaucratic approval.

The president's aides, in the words of Carl Tinstman, "went ape shit."

Frowns formed on their faces, and their heads shook vigorously. An aide bent down and whispered in Machel's ear. "We could tell by the body language ... that Samora Machel was being told not to sign it," says Tinstman.

Which was not at all bad advice. For one thing, the document was in English, not Portuguese. And, as the minister pointed out, "We haven't seen it. We need to read it first."

Not an unreasonable demand.

At this point, Grant stood up and, "against all protocol," says Mauras, he asked Machel to make room for him on the couch. The president and father of independent Mozambique obliged and scooted over. Grant sat down next to Machel, as though he were a family friend, and handed him the document.

Tinstman remembers that Machel raised his eyebrows, as an aide whispered insistently in his ear. The president then held up the document and glanced at it but did not take time to read it. Mauras notes that Machel needed glasses to read anyway, and he wasn't wearing any.

Then Machel looked at Grant. "This is a good thing for me and my country and the country's children?" he asked.

"Absolutely, Mr. President, of course," Grant said.

That was all it took. "I will sign," said Machel. And against the advice of all his aides, he did just that.

Grant peered down to inspect the signature and noticed that Machel had only signed his first name, "Samora," in big, sweeping script.

"Mr. President," Grant said, "you have to sign the full signature."

This last request Machel refused. He told Grant: "There is only one Samora in the whole world."

Another gamble had paid off. But the weight of that signature would not last long. About a year later, Machel would die in a mysterious plane crash. Many suspected that the apartheid government of South Africa was responsible, though the case has never been officially resolved.

As Jim Grant canvassed the globe, UNICEF country staff quickly learned what a "Jim Grant field visit" meant — a breathless, 24/7 whir of activity from the minute he touched down to the instant he departed. Everyone was exhausted and frayed and perhaps secretly relieved by the time he left. A typical day began at or before sunrise with back-to-back meetings with a roster of government officials and local NGOs, then lunch (which was often just another meeting with food), then perhaps a visit to a village or health center or refugee camp, then dinner, then more meetings at the office. Grant always took more time than the schedule allotted and was nearly always late, as his staff scrambled to maintain appointments. Sometimes it was because he became ensconced in conversation with a government leader; other times it was because he took part in activities he had come to observe. Grant would administer vaccines (usually just oral polio drops), crank a hand pump to bring up water, hold a weighing scale steady so a child could be lowered into it, and, of course, mix doses of oral rehydration salts. He also sat down to chat with village elders and mothers, whether it was on chairs, stools, or the ground. And sometimes he would stay for a while. When a chorus of children would gather to sing for him, dance, or play drums, he would stand up and clap vigorously. Or he would join them, bobbing awkwardly into their midst with a beaming grin on his face. During a performance in China, when a half dozen child dancers began a formal show on a stage, Grant jumped up, grabbed Ethel's hand, and pulled her onto the stage to dance with them (Ethel accompanied him on many trips). This was not the way most UN officials or Western leaders behaved, and it took many by surprise.

The last day of a Grant field visit usually ended with a marathon session of thank-you note writing. Jon Rohde had moved to India in 1986 and worked as a consultant for a global health nonprofit and also for UNICEF. Rolf Carriere remembers staying up until dawn on several occasions with Grant and others at Rohde's house in New Delhi, drinking wine and writing thank-you letters to members of Prime Minister Rajiv Gandhi's government. "[Grant] would have to be at the airport at six a.m. to fly on to the next place," says Carriere, who then ran UNICEF's health and nutrition programs in India. "He would work throughout the night, and we would all be there with him."

This letter-writing all-nighter became standard practice. The letters had to be written before Grant left, so he could sign them. They were not brief notes. Each one summarized what had been discussed and reminded a minister or bureaucrat or even a head of state what he or she had agreed to and what, in Jim Grant's opinion, would be needed to make it happen. Written in the most deferential diplomatic tone, they were nonetheless pointed reminders: *you promised to do this for your country's children, and I'm going to hold you to it.* For those staying up until an ungodly hour to help compose the notes, it was hard to complain when your boss was staying up, too.

After an eighteen-hour day of meetings in Ankara, Turkey, Grant and several staffers, including Steve Woodhouse, returned to their guesthouse late in the evening. Most were exhausted and probably ready to collapse. But, as Woodhouse recalled, the day was not over yet. "C'mon," said Grant effervescently. "We'll have a meeting in my room to discuss next steps." He then bounded up a long flight of about forty stairs, the first one to reach the top. Everybody else was younger than Grant but struggled to scramble up after him. On another occasion, when one staffer complained that Grant was driving people too hard and asked how they were all supposed to cope, Grant's reply was "I think you all need to sleep faster!"

One high-level staff meeting in a Bangkok hotel conference room dragged on into the early morning, as Grant grilled country representatives one by one about their immunization programs, like an instructor administering a withering oral exam. *Why is your coverage so low? What are your biggest obstacles? Who do you need to speak with to get things moving? What can you as the representative do?* If you hadn't done your homework, or didn't have adequate answers, you were exposed and embarrassed in front of all your colleagues.

Finally, at one a.m., India representative Eimi Watanabe raised her hand, like a tentative kid at the back of the classroom.

Grant pointed to her.

"Can we continue this in the morning?" she asked.

Grant looked at her. "No," he said.

The meeting went on.

He would refuse many such pleas — whether it was to end a meeting or reconsider an eleventh-hour staff posting. Several UNICEF veterans have stories of getting a call from Grant, often in the wee hours, when he would share the surprise of a new job halfway around the world — in some cases with only a few days' notice. According to his executive assistant Mary Cahill, one woman protested Grant's decision to send her to Saudi Arabia — a country known for its harsh and brazenly unequal treatment of women.

"What if men ask me to have sex with them?" she asked.

"Simple," he replied. "You tell them no."

In another instance, immediately after Steve Woodhouse had moved his family to New York at Grant's request, Grant called and said he now wanted Woodhouse to go to Senegal. It would be a short-term assignment to help with the immunization campaign. Woodhouse pointed out that he had just relocated his whole family to a new city. Then he tried another argument.

"I can't speak French!" he pleaded.

Grant was unmoved. "Neither can I," he said. "That doesn't matter."

Woodhouse went to Senegal.

It was not just the late nights or last-minute global reassignments that grated on people. Grant was completely altering the way UNICEF worked in the field. Before him, many country representatives did not meet with heads of state and did not personally lobby them. They were supposed to get along with those in power, not challenge them. And immunization was the government's job — how can a UNICEF field operative be held responsible for something the government is supposed to do? Grant's response, according to former assistant Carl Tinstman: "Yes, it's the government's job, but not all governments are doing it as well as they should, so it's *your* job as the UNICEF representative to make sure the government does it."

Some representatives protested that they feared trying to force their governments to do things would get them thrown out of the country. Plus, it was not always easy to get a meeting with a minister, much less a president. Tinstman remembers one senior representative raising his hand during a meeting and making a plaintive plea: "Mr. Grant, you want me to meet with the president? I've never done that. I've never met with any president."

"Well, you will now," Grant said. "If you're having difficulty, I'm going to visit your country, and you and I are going to see the head of state together."

This modus operandi pried open unparalleled channels of influence with world leaders. "The access really increased — it was absolutely extraordinary," says longtime staffer Fouad Kronfol. More than anyone else ever had, he asserts, Grant managed to "prick the imagination of all the heads of state and convince them to do more for their children."

Tinstman, a versatile American who rapidly adapted to new situations, traveled with Grant on numerous occasions. His job was to help his boss prepare for meetings and get him from here to there. It was also, as he puts it, to be "a donkey." "You have to carry a computer, you have to carry papers. You have to carry all kinds of stuff."

And you had to keep up with Jim Grant. Making this even more difficult was Grant's penchant for traveling with only one carry-on. Which meant that "you're bloody well only [bringing] a carry-on suitcase also," Tinstman says.

Grant had no time for laundry or dry cleaners either. He packed everything in his carry-on, washed his clothes in the hotel bathroom sink, and hung them around the room to dry. He wore a special, wash-and-wear, wrinkle-free Brooks Brothers suit that he would clean himself. To get the wrinkles out of it, apparently all he had to do was hang the suit in the bathroom, run the shower hot, and fill the room with steam.

Fancy accommodations were not required. The most important consideration was staying wherever the government had recommended. In one case, in Uganda, this was a dilapidated old hotel, in a room with no toilet seat and a door that didn't fully shut. Grant didn't complain.

He sometimes traveled solo. Many people who met Grant at the airport were surprised that he did not have a big entourage, and, in this respect, the contrast with other UN leaders was striking. "I would sometimes be at the airport when other UN agency heads would come in," says Richard Reid, the American logistical dynamo who had overseen the Turkish immunization campaign. "And one of them had three different people carrying his bags. He was like a British viceroy arriving in Afghanistan with two hundred and sixty-two camels. Just astonishing how simple Jim was and, at the same time, so able to make the waves part." Nonetheless, all of this irritated Ethel, who believed that Jim did not take proper care of himself. It also spawned a trend in UNICEF: the "cult of no-suitcase."

Joe Judd, who worked in a number of UNICEF country offices, recalls one of his supervisors fretting about whether to check a suitcase while on a trip with Grant. "My boss said, 'I can't take a big suitcase. Jim Grant will think I'm not with it,'" says Judd. "It became absolutely ridiculous…I think the sales of wash-and-wear shirts went up in the world."

The spartan carry-on tradition was born out of sheer, unvarnished practicality — make every minute count. With so many connections packed into such short periods of time, the potential for losing a checked bag rose exponentially. There was also a tint of bravado. "When you got off that plane, you were right in the thick of things," says Judd. "There was going to be no pause, no slowdown, no surrender to waiting for a suitcase."

The refusal to pause or rest caught up with Grant sometimes. At an airport in Swaziland, he was racing down the plane's stairway during a rainstorm. An airport shuttle was parked about three feet away. To avoid the rain — and presumably to save a few seconds — Grant leaped from the stairs to the shuttle. Badly misjudging the distance, he collided with the top of the shuttle door and crumpled to the ground. Tinstman, on his first trip with Grant, was mortified. "I thought, 'Oh my God...now we've lost him.'" He and several other passengers helped Grant up. Tinstman could see a lump growing on his boss's forehead. Dazed, Grant sank into a seat and rested his head on the seat in front of him. "Are you all right?" Tinstman asked. "Do you need a doctor?"

"No," Grant mumbled. "I'm all right. I'm just a little stunned."

While meeting with the prime minister of Japan, after a full day without sleep, he dozed off as his host was speaking. As he later recounted to several staff members, the prime minister tapped him on the shoulder.

"Mr. Grant?" the prime minister said. "Perhaps you would like to use my bathroom to freshen up?"

He fought his fatigue fiercely. "His tiredness was defiance," says Adamson. "I could see him wanting to sleep...Whereas other people would give in to it, you would see him bringing himself around."

To chip away at his burgeoning sleep deficit, Grant would take catnaps — twenty- or thirty-minute snatches of slumber. In the car, plane, train — he could conk out anywhere. Former UNICEF Rwanda and Somalia staffer Ian MacLeod remembers traveling with Grant in a mammoth Hercules military plane as it flew into or out of Somalia. There were little metal benches in the back of the plane. Grant took off his suit jacket, curled up on a bench and was out instantly. MacLeod was amazed. "There's infernal noise in the back of a Hercules," he says. A half hour later, Grant popped back up, slipped on his coat, and adjusted his tie. "He woke up and looked like he'd slept for twelve hours," marvels MacLeod.

When Grant started suffering bouts of stabbing back pain from a slipped disc, he did not slow down or adjust his schedule. If his back gave him trouble, no matter where he was, he would lie on the floor for some temporary relief. Reportedly, this sometimes meant lying in the aisle of a plane, midflight. He would conduct meetings flat on his back in the middle of the floor, as everyone gathered around and peered down at their executive director.

During a trip to New Delhi, Alan Court (who had helped lead UNICEF's response to the 1984 Ethiopian famine) heard a knock at the door of his hotel room. It was 11:30 p.m. He opened the door to see Richard Jolly, who said Grant wanted to see Court. "But try to make it quick," Jolly cautioned. "Jim's not well." Court put on some pants and a shirt and walked down to Jim's room. Ethel answered the door and invited him to sit down in the common area. "You know Jim has a back problem," she said before going into the bedroom to fetch her husband. Jim hobbled out, in obvious pain, and gingerly lowered himself onto the floor beneath Court. He lay flat and looked up at his guest.

"What would you say if I were to offer you the position of representative in Chad?" Grant said.

Court was stunned. Here was his boss lying on his back on the floor, offering him a job. Court sat on the edge of his chair hovering over Grant. He said yes.

Court was with Jim and Ethel on another trip when they experienced a brief moment of respite. In Kathmandu, Nepal, in November 1986, while meeting with the king, Jim had over-run the clock by forty-five minutes. He and Ethel missed their flight. Court, then a program officer in Nepal, booked a later one. Suddenly, they had some time to kill. They decided to visit the nearby Boudhanath Tibetan Buddhist temple. Ethel put her arm in Jim's, and they walked along the paths below the ancient stupa that loomed in the night. They strolled in the glow of oil lamps as the chanting of monks drifted on a gentle breeze. The rest of the group hung back — a moment like this was rare.

By the end of 1986, the chorus of naysayers and critics dwindled as Grant's child survival revolution gained momentum in every corner of the developing world. Nearly one hundred countries and more than four hundred nongovernmental organizations had joined the campaign for universal child immunization. Donors and millions of volunteers from all sectors of society across the globe — priests, imams, monks, rabbis, teachers, students, police officers, soldiers, artists, nurses, doctors, athletes, mothers and fathers — had united to create what Grant would call "a grand alliance for children."

UNICEF spent $57 million on immunization activities in 1986, providing 500 million doses of vaccine — a 24 percent increase over the previous year. Global immunization coverage had more than doubled since 1980, now reaching over 40 percent in all categories. The supply of oral rehydration salts — the other "twin engine" of child survival, as Grant dubbed it — had grown by six times over the past four years, in large part due to UNICEF's advocacy. These two interventions were now saving an estimated 1.5 million lives every year, according to UNICEF.

The man who had sparked it all liked to keep the spotlight off himself or, at the very least, pull others into its gleam with him. Grant liberally doled out credit for these achievements, making a particular effort to lather praise on his erstwhile adversary, WHO. "Make sure WHO looks good," he frequently instructed. This was not about being nice. Grant knew he could not prevail without WHO or without the International Committee for the Red Cross or without USAID, among many others. He continued to recruit allies and funders for his "grand alliance" — the more diverse his coalition and the broader the base of support, the more quickly obstacles would fall. Though he tried to remain in the background, though he was exceedingly modest, Grant's quiet fervor was sustained by a "great sense of self," says Cahill. "He had a great belief in himself and a great belief in the cause."

Packed between his constant trips abroad were dense batches of meetings in New York, Washington, and Atlanta — with donors, staff, the UNICEF board, the Child Survival Taskforce, congressional committees, various UN committees and bodies. And many mornings at the Grants' "roof house" were working breakfasts, catered by Ethel (as one staffer recalls: "there was poor Ethel, making bacon and eggs, while Jim carried on"). He rarely watched TV or movies and never took in any sports; he once remarked to one of his sons: "I can't believe how much time I save by not watching sports!" Often the only time UNICEF's head of personnel, Manou Assadi, could find with Grant was in the limo on the way to JFK Airport; after Grant got out, Assadi would ride back to UNICEF headquarters by himself.

An agitator, a pest, an irritant extraordinaire, Grant took every opportunity — clambered upon any podium, pedestal, or bully pulpit available — to plead the case of the world's poor and dying children. On television news shows and on college campuses, in the halls of the UN and the corridors of power in Washington, he continued to decry the "obscenity" of the preventable deaths of millions of children. On the eve of UNICEF's fortieth anniversary on December 11, 1986, when the annual *State of the World's Children* report was released, he told the *New York Times* that "the most shameful fact of the late 20th century is that every week, over a quarter of a million of the world's children are being killed, largely needlessly." He frequently used a quote he attributed to writer and Holocaust survivor Primo Levi: "When we know how to relieve torment and do not, then we join the tormentors."

Because he knew statistics failed to convey the true horror of mass child deaths — and because those deaths were mostly ignored by the mainstream media — Grant deployed simple, blunt metaphors. The number of children dying each day, he said, "is the equivalent of having two hundred jumbo jets packed with children crash every day with half killed and half crippled for life." Or he invoked an event that had been covered in the news: the number of Indian children dying each day from vaccine-preventable diseases was higher than the total death toll of the Union Carbide disaster in Bhopal. His analogies didn't always fly. Speaking of the shift in global attitudes toward children, he once described UNICEF as "the yeast of this historic change." However apt the analogy, it's hard to get inspired by yeast.

As his movement grew, emergencies both "loud" and "silent" flared up in dozens of countries. UNICEF constantly struggled to respond. The agency's regular programs — those not included in Grant's revolution — also had to keep operating. Many staff members felt that Grant gave short shrift to a host of other issues: water and sanitation, child protection, women's empowerment, the fight against HIV — anything not blinking brightly on his radar screen.

UNICEF's resources were growing markedly at the time, but the pie was still only so big; under Grant, child survival would always get the biggest slice. Without survival, of course, not much else matters. A blunt sentiment expressed by several staffers: *You can't educate a child if he's dead.* (Though education was an issue Grant had long valued and was, of course, tightly intertwined with survival. Before GOBI, he had, in fact, initially considered making primary education the focus of his "quantum leap.")

Ultimately, the child survival revolution and Grant's single-mindedness were as strategic as they were moral. His first priority was to figure out how to help as many children as possible: What could be done to save the most young lives? The next step was finding a "doable" solution. Part of it was the science: vaccines and ORS were both cheap and effective and ready to be put to widespread use. But it was also about marketability—could he sell it to donors? If something was abstract, or required a long time to explain, its "doability" would diminish. GOBI lent itself to a quick elevator pitch. And what many of his critics failed to realize was that child survival was only phase one, or as Rohde put it, "a foot in the door." If GOBI did succeed, Grant planned to use it as a launch pad for progress in other areas (water, education, primary health care, etc.). But first he needed that walloping, seismic success.

This is not to say that he should come out completely unscathed for skirting difficult topics, such as the fight against HIV and AIDS. The burgeoning epidemic in the mid-to-late 1980s seemed messy and uncomfortable (Grant was squeamish on issues related to sex), and delving into it risked drawing the ire of the Catholic Church—plus, there was no magic bullet, no vaccine, no ORS packet. He would eventually give HIV more than token treatment, but many felt it was too little and too late.

His attention was also divvied up among regions of the world, and one onto which he heaped copious amounts was Africa. Fouad Kronfol, then UNICEF's Africa section chief, had encouraged Grant to place more emphasis on Africa, and several board members had asked him why UNICEF's presence was so paltry in some African countries. Grant set out to remedy that, expanding and upgrading dozens of offices across the continent and launching a major fund-raising appeal for Africa in 1986. Noting that the "tidal wave of human suffering" that racked parts of Africa in 1984 and 1985 had receded, Grant reminded donors that progress was "deceptive" and that millions of lives were still at risk. Between 1980 and 1994, UNICEF's spending in Africa more than quintupled, going from $54.5 million per year to $303.5 million.

"Mr. Grant was one of the key UN leaders that made the UN relevant to Africa," says Abdul Mohammed, a former UNICEF staffer and currently the chief of staff of the African Union High-Level Implementation Panel for Sudan and South Sudan. "He was very committed to Africa. He felt the UN and agencies like UNICEF could make a difference. He also felt that some of the international humanitarian roles crafted in the aftermath of the Second World War must be adjusted to take Africa's reality into account."

To help keep the world's eyes on Africa, Grant teamed up with former Boomtown Rats singer Bob Geldof to launch Sport Aid, a follow-up to Geldof's Live Aid concert. Though Ethel found Geldof's manners horrid — during a visit to the Grant's roof house for breakfast, he reportedly swore up a storm and put his feet on the furniture — Grant knew the scruffy rock star had a knack for generating publicity. They hoped Sport Aid would equal or beat Live Aid, which had raised more than $100 million. Though it drew some twenty million runners from around the world for a "Race Against Time," it fell well short. According to UNICEF, the event brought in more than $30 million to be split between the children's agency and Geldof's charity. One reason for the fund-raising deficit: Sport Aid clashed with Hands-Across-America, an American fund-raiser which focused on helping the poor in the United States. Many US news outlets, it seemed, virtually ignored Sport Aid in favor of the American event. Responding to reports of aid fatigue surrounding both events, Grant wrote a letter to the *New York Times*, hailing the achievements of each and noting "the people of the world are not 'aided' out... They wait for their governments to catch up with them."

By now, Grant's relationship with the UNICEF board and with UN bureaucrats was smoother. As his successes mounted, they questioned him less. But some sizable bumps in the road still cropped up, some arguably a result of the head-spinning, ends-justify-means sense of exigency he had unleashed.

The UN's Board of Auditors dinged him and UNICEF in an August 1986 report that noted numerous financial errors and irregularities. Among the findings: UNICEF had purchased two office buildings at a cost of $424,367, "although no appropriations had been provided in either the original or revised budget estimates"; payments had been made to UNICEF staff for relocation expenses "in the absence of an appropriate evidence of relocation"; and UNICEF had failed to submit revised budget estimates for the purchase of additional computers, instead transferring money from one budget line to another to cover the expense.

Though he may not have been aware of these particulars, Grant had given some field operatives carte blanche to move money around — or spend funds before they had them in hand—in order to meet urgent needs that couldn't wait for bureaucratic approval. These were generally not grave violations, but in the ossified bureaucracy of the UN, such activity hoisted red flags. Some field staff may have gone too far. But Grant did not want to know about any financial fallout. He preferred to skip UN committee meetings where budgetary matters were discussed, according to former comptroller, and later deputy executive director, Karin Sham Poo.

A year earlier, a few months after starting at UNICEF herself, Sham Poo had discovered a serious cash flow problem—a result, in part, of Grant's rapid acceleration of activities. He had been unaware of it, because, says Sham Poo, "nobody had the guts to tell him that UNICEF was spending more than they had."

Sham Poo had steeled herself, made an appointment to see him, and disclosed the bad news. "He did not look happy," she says. She remembers that his face was still, stern, unmoving, but out of it gleamed his penetrating, metallic blue eyes. "His eyes were *so* blue," she says. Those eyes could stop you, freeze you where you stood. Grant asked her what this all meant. She explained that UNICEF would have to rein in expenses, halt the paying of some bills, and lay off temporary staff. He relaxed, his face loosened. He got up, walked around, and sat down again. Then he said, "Do what you think is necessary. I'll support it."

When the alarming report on the audit came out in 1986, Sham Poo was on a UNICEF visit to Mali. Her boss, Deputy Executive Director Karl Eric Knutsson, sent her an urgent Telex: *Cancel your trip. Come back immediately. The Board of Auditors is not qualifying UNICEF's audit.*

"Jim Grant was extremely upset," she recalls, "because to get a nonqualified audit report could be a big hamper on fundraising." He did not yell or scream or curse, at least when Sham Poo spoke to him. He was simply stone-faced, much as he had been when she told him of the cash flow problem. This is when you knew he was upset.

Sham Poo felt the findings were unfair — "a lot of garbage," in her words. There were some errors and technicalities, but it wasn't purposeful mismanagement. No one had pocketed any money. Though he did not want to, Grant attended a meeting at the UN and issued a statement. It was eventually resolved, but the stain it created lingered for years.

Grant shook off distractions as he drove UNICEF more and more relentlessly. But one crisis became very hard for him to ignore. It was one of the darkest moments of his tenure and could have happened regardless of who sat in his chair.

In March 1987, police in Belgium busted a huge international child pornography ring that included a volunteer on UNICEF's Belgian national committee. The volunteer, Michel Felu, had allegedly been using the basement of the UNICEF Belgium office to sexually abuse children and produce and store more than a thousand child porn images.

The revelation was sickening and shattering. The pedophile porn ring also included a former minister of the Belgian government, as well as parents who were charged with renting their children out to be abused. Felu and thirteen others were eventually convicted by a Belgian court, according to the Associated Press. The conviction of the former head of UNICEF Belgium,

Jozef Verbeeck—who was accused of knowing about the activities and doing nothing to stop them—was later overturned on appeal. He was acquitted.

When the news first hit, UNICEF was at the center of a maelstrom. "UNICEF has always stood for the love of children — an image now grotesquely defiled," wrote *Newsweek*. In one respect, this statement was true, but it was also unfair. No one at UNICEF headquarters, including Jim Grant, apparently knew anything about this until the ring was discovered by police. They were as horrified as everybody else. The Belgian UNICEF committee — like the dozens of other national committees around the world — operated independently of UNICEF headquarters and had its own governing board. Felu was not a UNICEF employee. Still, he was a member of the UNICEF family.

UNICEF issued a statement expressing its shock and reaffirming its commitment to protect children from acts of exploitation. The statement also alluded to what was perhaps Grant's greatest fear: a potentially grave injury to UNICEF's reputation and fund-raising ability. "The first to suffer from the discredit which would unjustly fall on this organization as a result of this affair would evidently be the children of the third world," the statement warned in part.

The chairman of the Belgian national committee board, Gilbert Jaeger, who was not implicated in the case, wrote to Grant in August informing him that he would be stepping down. In response, Grant wrote on September 4: "I share your hope that the judicial proceedings will clear away the dark clouds which have hung over the entire organization since the unsavoury events of the recent past occurred and the trial will exonerate UNICEF and the Committee which serves it." He added that the public's trust in UNICEF "is our most valuable asset and we should protect and nurture it as well as we can." He then pledged to "prepare guidelines" to "reduce, if not eliminate, the likelihood of potential 'black sheep' entering the fold again."

The trial eventually yielded Grant's wish: it became clear that UNICEF was not in any way complicit, and that Felu was indeed a "black sheep" who had exploited his position with the Belgian committee.

Throughout the entire affair, Grant did not want to talk about the case, according to several staff members. Certainly his concern about fund-raising was a valid one — the children UNICEF served could have been affected by a drop in donations. In that sense, speaking publicly about Belgium was a risk.

There may have also been a strategic consideration. The issue of child abuse fell outside the periphery of child survival. If he had made a big proclamation, it could have drawn attention away from GOBI.

But what about the children who were actually abused in Belgium? Didn't he also have an obligation to them and to other victims of abuse? Grant had become the most visible and powerful children's advocate the world had ever seen.

This case gave him, as the head of UNICEF, a special opportunity to shine a sorely lacking light on an extremely pervasive and shadowy problem that existed in every country. He could have taken the occasion to issue a clarion call to stamp out the detestable sexual exploitation of helpless boys and girls. There was some pressure from within UNICEF for him to do just that — put out a press release, confront the issue head-on, and do right by the children in Belgium and elsewhere who were appallingly exploited by malicious adults.

But he didn't. He kept quiet.

UNICEF supported many programs geared toward protecting children from abuse and neglect, but they were not a top priority for Jim Grant, not yet anyway. Not even a scandal of this revolting magnitude could change that.

It may well have tortured him, but he would not let it slow him down. He would stay fixedly, relentlessly, ruthlessly on message.

Chapter 9
ONE LIFE THAT COULD NOT BE SAVED

It began in the water. As the day sloughed off its heat and the fervent sun melted into a soft, gauzy haze, Ethel Grant went for a swim. Gliding across the hotel's wide outdoor pool, she felt something in her chest — a twinge, a sudden stab of pressure. She swam to the side, pulled herself out, and sat there on the edge of the pool, keeping still, breathing. Her eldest son, John, saw her and came over to ask if she was all right.

Ethel waved it off, because that's the kind of person she was. She kept her hair short, wore simple clothes, and assiduously deflected attention. And like her husband, she could be stubbornly sanguine — not one to let physical discomfort get in her way. Thin and fit, she jogged regularly, played tennis, pedaled an exercise bike, and eschewed anything with butter in it. At sixty-three she did not tire easily and was always up for the next activity. Even so, it must have flickered in her mind then, as her feet dangled in the water, that heart problems had plagued her family. Her father had died of heart failure, and her sister struggled with a heart condition.

But tonight, they had plans. They were going to see the Taj Mahal by moonlight. Everyone in the group — Ethel and Jim, their son John, her sister Catherine and brother-in-law Ted, and Jon Rohde and his wife, Candy — had agreed to meet in the lobby at six o'clock sharp. Ethel lifted her feet out of the water, stood up, and went back to the room to change. That pang in her chest could wait.

It was April 1, 1988, Good Friday. After an official state visit to New Delhi, India, Jim had taken a few days off to meet family in Agra. Ethel was with him; before India, they were in Bhutan for UNICEF business — reportedly one of the most enjoyable trips they had taken together. Jim came to India often — without India, of course, he knew he could not reach the global goal of universal childhood immunization. Since his life-changing visit to Calcutta in 1944, the vast country had exerted a strong and perennial pull on him. In the early 1950s, when he had served as a legal adviser to the US aid mission, the Grants had lived in New Delhi, and their youngest son, Bill, had been born in India's capital city. Their grandson would be born there, too; their eldest son, John, now worked for USAID in India, and his wife was several months pregnant. An Indian government official would later marvel at what he called Jim Grant's "bond of cosmic human activity" with the nation. Today, that bond would be tested.

The last year or so had ushered in more milestones, as the child survival revolution — officially known as the child survival *and* development revolution — hopscotched from one country to another. In October 1987, to accommodate the organization's rapid growth, UNICEF moved its headquarters into a more spacious building on Forty-fourth Street in Manhattan, called UNICEF House. Grant collected more allies, and immunization rates continued to climb. Screen legend Audrey Hepburn infused new dynamism when she was appointed as a UNICEF goodwill ambassador in March 1988.

Grant had initially been opposed to appointing Hepburn. The idea was first broached by Victor Soler-Sala, a cultured, carefully spoken Spaniard who had worked for UNICEF since 1957 and was then in charge of celebrity relations. The UNICEF chief quickly shot down the suggestion, quipping, "Isn't she a has-been?" When Soler-Sala left Grant's office, Grant told Cahill, "You've got to screen a little better and save me from these crazy ideas."

Cahill and Soler-Sala conspired to change his mind, and eventually they succeeded. Audrey Hepburn would become UNICEF's most famous and effective celebrity ambassador, generating a level of attention and interest in the fight for child survival that, in some ways, surpassed even what Grant could muster. She had a special affinity for UNICEF; as a teenager in Holland at the end of World War II, she had been one of the millions to receive aid from UNICEF's predecessor and Grant's former employer, the United Nations Relief and Rehabilitation Administration. After meeting Hepburn, Grant quickly realized his mistake and—like many men at UNICEF—developed a crush on the thoroughly unpretentious and magnetic Hollywood darling.

"She just adored Jim," says John Isaac, a UN photographer who became Hepburn's friend. "She told me how much she admired him."

With a note to Grant in November 1989, Hepburn included a photo of herself surrounded by giggling children in Bangladesh. "Dearest Jim," she wrote. "Just to say THANK YOU for your warm, so encouraging cable, and thank you for sending me to Bangladesh...I wanted dearly to go...Now I know why. See you in New York on the 20th of November." It was signed "Love Audrey," with a little heart drawn above her name.

He had wrestled with other decisions in the past year (though the Hepburn one should have been a no-brainer) and had further bolstered UNICEF's stature as an advocate and thought leader. After much internal debate and last-minute tinkering, he helped conceive and launch the controversial Bamako Initiative — an attempt to revitalize health care in African countries and to make it more locally driven by providing quality medicines at a low cost and by requiring patients to pay fees for those medicines and other services (the fees were intended to promote sustainability but drew heavy criticism; some people simply could not afford them). In 1987 he released two provocative reports, the first of which accused the apartheid government of South Africa of causing mass child deaths by fomenting civil conflict and economic destabilization in nine neighboring countries, including the former Portuguese colonies Angola and Mozambique. The second report, written by Richard Jolly and others, called for measures to protect children from the deleterious and even fatal consequences of so-called structural adjustment policies — economic belt-tightening measures foisted upon developing debtor countries by the International Monetary Fund and the World Bank.

Both reports — and their concussive conclusions — garnered considerable media coverage and helped stir an outcry over injustices visited upon children because of the cruel and cold-hearted actions of adults. This was a testament to the aura of audacity fostered by Grant — people wanted to see what UNICEF was going to say, what position it was going to take. When UNICEF held a press conference, many reporters saw it as a must-attend event — what was Jim Grant up to now? (No UNICEF executive director, before or since, has drawn even a smidgen of the attention amassed by Grant.) Grant was, in fact, becoming the undisputed star of the entire UN system and sometimes even received a bigger reception than the secretary general himself.

Grant was a little worried about the political fallout from the anti-apartheid report, which was called "Children on the Frontlines." UNICEF Mozambique representative Marta Mauras, who had accompanied Grant to meet Mozambican president Samora Machel, had first proposed the concept at a meeting of UNICEF's Africa representatives. "I said, 'We have to do some kind of a study that will prove apartheid is killing more children than we imagined, not just in South Africa, but also in southern Africa,'" Mauras recalls.

Richard Jolly immediately took up the idea. He recruited his friend, American economist Reginald Green, to write the report and then persuaded Grant to back it. When it was ready, UNICEF called a press conference in London. Mauras met

Grant at Heathrow Airport, and they got into a taxi. As the car sped into the city, Grant read the final draft. He looked up and bluntly asked Mauras: "Are you completely sure about what we're doing here, Marta?"

"Yes," she replied. "We have to go ahead with it."

His reservations were not unfounded. The political ramifications were huge, says Mauras. But so was the potential reward. South Africa's barbaric system of racial segregation and discrimination was already under siege, and this report could help deliver a jarring blow.

At the press conference, Grant didn't hold back. He told the reporters that, as a result of conflict and other factors, Angola and Mozambique now had the highest child mortality rates in the world. A Mozambican or Angolan child, in fact, died every four minutes, Grant said, according to an account by United Press International. "The situation is sufficiently dark in these countries," he went on, "that if it continues, of the one million children born in these two countries in 1986, by 1990, their fifth birthday, one out of every two will either be dead or crippled for life."

The report set off tremors throughout the international community and may have contributed to the fall of the apartheid regime, according to Mauras.

"The South Africans felt the sting," she says.

The India trip was a chance for some precious downtime. It also gave Grant a chance to catch up with Jon Rohde, with whom he usually stayed when he visited New Delhi. Rohde worked for a global health nonprofit. But ever since the beginning of the child survival revolution, he had also been Grant's de facto consigliere, his closest and most trusted adviser on health matters. Rohde didn't want a UNICEF staff job — he found UN bureaucracy and internal politics too off-putting. (He would officially come on board in 1993, when Grant finally convinced him to serve as the organization's India representative.)

But even then, his loyalty was not to UNICEF. "I never worked for UNICEF," he says. "I worked for Jim."

Like other Grant acolytes, Rohde viewed the UNICEF chief as not only a mentor. Grant was a moral beacon, a visionary guru who inspired almost religious devotion. But the connection between Grant and Rohde was even stronger, almost familial.

In a letter to Grant several years later, Rohde proclaimed: "I always leave you, buoyed up and ready to take on the dragons of poverty! Indeed, the only reward I need for whatever little I do is to spend a few days with you every now and then."

It was almost dark on that Friday night when Rohde and his wife stood in the hotel's grand lobby, underneath the chandelier, waiting for Jim, Ethel, and the rest of the group. Then Rohde spotted Jim crossing the lobby, Ethel on his arm. Jim walked his wife over to Rohde. He looked uncharacteristically serious.

"Now," Jim said, turning to Ethel, "tell your favorite doctor what you told me." Worry tinged his normally buoyant voice.

Ethel looked at Rohde, probably somewhat self-consciously. "Well, I was swimming," she said. "And I felt really refreshed. Then I had this pain in my chest, and I — "

And right then, midsentence, under the chandelier in the middle of the hotel lobby, she collapsed. Rohde caught her before she fell to the floor, and they laid her on a nearby bench.

"Shit," Rohde muttered, and quickly bent down and listened to Ethel's chest. He felt her pulse. He knew that she had just had a cardiac arrest.

John Grant rushed over. He and Jim crouched down. Jim looked at Rohde, his eyes wide and scared. Rohde told him: "This is one I'm going to win."

Then he directed Jim's son John to "breathe" his mother, while Rohde began pumping her chest, trying to jump-start her heart. John Grant quickly lowered his mouth to his mother's and began forcing air into her lungs. Like her, he was thin, vigorous, and moved with purpose — especially now.

As Rohde's arms pistoned up and down on Ethel's ribcage, he turned to his wife, Candy. "Get on the phone," he ordered. "Get me a defibrillator. And call an ambulance."

His head then swiveled to Jim. "Jim, talk to Ethel. She's probably still conscious. Talk to her."

Jim Grant leaned toward his wife of forty-five years, his life partner and best friend and closest confidante — a woman who had given up her career to support him, who had, in many ways, allowed her life to be subsumed by his — and took her hand. He was in shock, but he spoke calmly. He said her name. He told her she would be okay.

It was unclear if Ethel could hear him. Her eyes stared up blankly, but her pupils were moving. Rohde kept pumping her chest. A hotel manager hurried over, and Rohde told him he needed a defibrillator, *now*.

The manager, formally dressed in a coat and tie, nodded nervously and disappeared. He eventually came back, panic etching his face. He said he was sorry, the hotel — a major luxury resort — did not have a defibrillator. He had made phone calls but could find nothing.

The ambulance finally arrived. It was, in the words of Jon Rohde, a "shitty van." They carried Ethel out of the lobby and carefully placed her on a stretcher in the back. There was not much in the way of equipment, medicine, or anything else. There were built-in benches along the walls, and everyone perched on them and held on.

Candy had made a flurry of calls and had found a cardiology practice that claimed to have a defibrillator. Rohde told the driver to take them there.

The driver lurched off, barreling away from the hotel. After a few minutes, the van slowed, then stopped, stymied by a vast, dense, unmoving sea of cars, motorbikes, bicycles, and rickshaws that lay sprawled ahead of them into the night. The driver turned on a siren, but it made no difference.

Jon Rohde was still pumping, and John Grant was still performing mouth-to-mouth. Jim Grant held his wife's hand and watched helplessly from the bench where he sat. He told her that her favorite doctor was taking care of her.

"We've got everything under control," Jim said to his wife. "We're moving through the town, and everything's fine."

The van crawled its way through the cacophonous congestion of Agra's evening rush hour, horns blaring and tires screeching and people hollering—and all the while, Rohde kept pumping.

Only a few hours earlier, Rohde had posed for a photo with Jim and Ethel inside the ancient red-stone city of Fatehpur Sikri. In the picture, the three are grinning widely in the blazing sun as the magnificent, intricate Mogul buildings rise up behind them. After everybody had toured the site and returned to their van to rest, John Grant had said he wanted to explore some more. Jim, Rohde, and everybody else had replied that they were too tired, and that it was too hot—everybody, that is, except Ethel. She had eagerly bounded off with her son for another hike around the ruins.

The hardy mountain girl from Skyforest, California, had never shied away from physical challenges. In November 1946, after surprising Jim by arriving unannounced in Beijing (traveling by plane and freighter), she had joined him in working for UNRRA. She even volunteered for a trip down China's Grand Canal via barge to oversee a big delivery of milk powder and other aid. The shipment was going to Communist areas in Shandong province, south of Beijing. Ethel was with her boss, a woman named Gladys, and their plan—once the delivery was complete—was to return to Beijing in a jeep that had been loaded onto one of the barges. But when they arrived, they discovered that someone had forgotten to put antifreeze in the jeep. It was late November or early December at this point, and the engine block had frozen solid. When Christmas came and went with no sign of Ethel, Jim began to worry. He went looking for her, visiting an UNRRA office in Tianjin. While he was there, Ethel miraculously stumbled in, depleted and, in Jim's words, "bedraggled." She had just walked 150 miles. She happened to be pregnant at the time and suffering from morning sickness. She would eventually lose the baby.

Later, after Ethel had returned to the States, she would lose yet another baby, this one stillborn. At the time, Grant, who was still in China, "never felt...so helpless," according to his oral history. These intense personal tragedies would later fuel his determination to combat infant mortality many years later.

Now, as night encased the ambulance carrying his dying wife in Agra, India, Grant faced another rare moment of total helplessness. He sat there and watched as Ethel lay disconcertingly still and as their eldest son, John, desperately tried to keep her alive.

Finally, they made it through the throng and arrived at the cardiology office in the warren of a packed, teeming bazaar. It was dark, but they could make out a small shack with a sign posted out front announcing that medical services were available. They hoisted Ethel's stretcher out of the van and wheeled her in.

The place was low, narrow, and practically bare — save for a few paper scraps scattered on the grimy floor. A lone lightbulb hung forlornly from the ceiling. They lifted Ethel onto a table.

The taciturn cardiologist emerged, carrying what he said was a defibrillator. In an instant of sudden horror, Rohde realized that the device was, in reality, "a fake old radio set with tubes in it that lit up."

He looked at the contraption, baffled. Then he got mad. This quack had wasted precious time. Had he actually used this on patients in cardiac arrest? Was he even a real doctor? Rohde didn't have time to contemplate the implications. "This will not do!" he said, as he continued to pump Ethel's chest and as rivulets of sweat trickled down his face. John Grant was still giving his mother mouth-to-mouth. Her pupils were still responsive. They could still save her, but they had to move. They had to try someplace else. Ethel's chances ebbed with every minute that passed. There must be a working defibrillator somewhere, anywhere. "Get us out of here!" Rohde yelled.

They wheeled her back to the van.

"Take me to the university hospital!" Rohde commanded. Sweat soaked his shirt. His muscles burned, but his hands never stopped moving. If they did, Ethel would die.

After more interminable traffic, they pulled into the university medical school and stopped in front of the main door, but were told they had to try another entrance. They drove around the campus in the dark, looking frantically, slowing, speeding up, until finally they found the right building. They brought Ethel in and were directed to the emergency room. Rohde and John Grant had alternated pumping and breathing, and they were each still working feverishly. The second they stepped into the room, Rohde knew they would have to go elsewhere.

"It was a filthy, blood-spattered, equipmentless hole in the wall," he says.

Exasperated, he pleaded with a nurse.

"We've got to get a defibrillator!" Rohde told her. "There must be one in this hospital somewhere."

The nurse replied that there was one in the internal medicine ward upstairs. Again they were on the move, working on Ethel as they rolled her through the crowded corridor, praying that they would at last find a working defibrillator. They lifted the stretcher with her on it and carried it up a flight of stairs; all the while, Rohde kept pumping.

They barged into the internal medicine ward and found a large room with about thirty beds, almost all of them occupied. As they lifted Ethel onto an empty bed, a terrified nurse jogged in, carrying a defibrillator. A bolt of optimism shot through Rohde. Finally, they had found it. Maybe they could still bring her back. But when he picked it up, one of its wires dangled uselessly, disconnected from the paddle, almost as if someone had committed a calculated act of sabotage. Their hope crumbled. Rohde could not believe it. He had spent most of his career in the developing world, working in extremely daunting, austere, pathetic conditions. He was used to improvising, even when there was not much to improvise with, but there were certain things you could just not do without. And when someone had a cardiac arrest, a defibrillator was one of them.

Rohde knew that it was probably over, but he could see that Jim would not accept that. The head of UNICEF stood nearby, his face ashen, his eyes pleading. He kept saying, over and over, "Don't give up, don't give up...please, Jon, don't give up."

Rohde looked at his boss. "There just isn't a chance anymore, Jim," he said.

"Just keep trying," Jim replied quickly. "Please don't stop."

Rohde picked up the defibrillator. He could see that on both ends of the separated cord, a few loose threads of wire protruded. Pinching them between his fingers, he twisted the ends of the wire together until the cord was attached. He knew it probably wouldn't work, but he was doing this as much for Jim now as he was for Ethel. He placed the pads on Ethel's chest and gave her three jolts. The jury-rigged defibrillator worked, but barely. Ethel didn't respond. She lay motionless on the bed.

There was one other thing he could try. He asked for an intracardiac needle — the kind of long needle used to shoot adrenaline straight into the heart. They didn't have one. They did have adrenaline, which they gave him along with another type of needle — a needle that didn't look long enough to reach Ethel's heart. Rohde used it anyway, raising it up and plunging it into her chest. It was the absolute last hope of saving her. It might work, a small voice inside him said, it could.

It had been an hour and a half since Ethel's cardiac arrest. Jon Rohde and John Grant were drained, debilitated, drenched, but they still kept trying to revive her. Finally, Rohde stopped. Ethel was gone.

Today, Rohde is tortured by the most wrenching kind of second-guessing. He thinks they might have been able to save

Ethel had they gone to the local army barracks and announced that the wife of an under secretary general of the United Nations was dying. The army would have had a defibrillator. "It never dawned on me that we could go to the army," he says now. "If we had, things would have been different, because she was doing well for quite a while."

Had Ethel's cardiac arrest occurred in New York or in another, richer country, there is a very good chance she would have made it. She died for the same reason millions of people in developing countries die: the tools or medicines or vaccines that could have saved them were simply not on hand. As Grant had himself pointed out hundreds of times, it was a deadly gap between what was needed and what was available. It is a cruel irony that a man who had strived to bring lifesaving interventions to the poorest corners of the world could do nothing to save his own wife from what was most likely a survivable cardiac arrest. Grant and Rohde had both visited many bleak rooms in overrun clinics, not unlike the room they stood in now. And there, on the margins of the most marginalized places, they had met dull-eyed boys and girls lying in old, ratty beds, quietly dying from things no one — especially children — should die of. They had met parents who had faced the ultimate grief of surviving their own children. And for millions of these ostensibly doomed families, these two men had set about building an immense levy against loss and suffering and death — a medical bulwark to hold back the silent carnage of measles and tuberculosis and diarrhea and malnutrition.

None of this, of course, could help Ethel Grant.

They didn't stay in Agra that night. Instead, they wrapped up Ethel's body in a sheet, put her in a UNICEF van — not the "ambulance" in which they had spent the last harrowing hour and a half — and a UNICEF staffer drove them to New Delhi. During the trip, Jim talked as he wiped away tears, recounting his life with Ethel, giving voice to all the moments that now played vividly in his mind. He may have told of how they met at a fraternity party at Berkeley. Their wedding in December 1943, weeks before he was shipped off to the war. How she journeyed to China after the war to join him. How she made famous waffle brunches on Sunday mornings for visiting dignitaries. How they raised their family all over the world — in India, Sri Lanka, Turkey, and Washington. As the darkest night he ever knew scrolled by his window, it was almost as though Jim were trying to keep a part of Ethel alive.

When they arrived in New Delhi, they drove to the UNICEF office, where an official took Ethel's body. Jim stayed at Jon Rohde's house that night, and the next morning Ethel was cremated according to Hindu custom. Rohde held a reception at his house, which was flooded with diplomats and officials coming to pay their respects to Ethel — and not just because she was Jim Grant's wife. Many of them had been to dinners she had hosted and some had been welcomed into the fold of the Grant family by its magnanimous maternal emissary. If Jim radiated extreme energy, she matched him in warmth. She had, no doubt, helped him win over many an ally.

The following day, Jim Grant flew back to New York, carrying his wife's ashes in a small box. His executive assistant Mary

Cahill and a few other UNICEF staff members met him at the airport. "Ethel is no more," he said in a low voice. His eyes had dimmed, and his skin had turned a pale gray — he was not the Jim Grant they knew. But in one respect, he was unchangeable.

Within a few days, he went back to work.

Chapter 10
THE ALIVE GIRL

Big, sweet, and somehow knowing, her smile is bracketed by deep dimples. Her head is cocked slightly to one side and wrapped in a bright, colorful, poufy turban. Confident and unafraid and just the slightest bit playful, her expression radiates vivacity and possibility. Buttoned straps hang over her small shoulders. She seems to be wordlessly daring anyone whose gaze fixes on her to be as expectant and hopeful and cheerfully defiant as she is.

Selamawit Gebreyes was four or five years old when a photographer took her picture, and she unexpectedly became the face of the child survival revolution. Her blithe, pixieish image would be featured on brochures, stamps, and big posters seen by millions of people around the world. She would help UNICEF raise untold sums of money.

She was unaware of her fame at first. Indeed, people who saw her beaming face would not likely have imagined the arduous, austere struggle she faced every day. It was a typical existence for a family in a cramped, confining slum in Addis Ababa, Ethiopia. She lived with her mother, three brothers, and grandmother in a garage — a dilapidated, windowless, one-room extension from the back of a bigger house. They had no electricity or running water. There was no toilet. There were no beds or furniture. The walls of their home were crumbling, and the tin roof leaked. It was almost always dark inside the cramped, tiny room, even during the day.

Selamawit's mother supported them all by selling onions, peppers, and traditional Ethiopian injera flatbread in a nearby village market. Her father, a soldier in the Ethiopian army, had died before Selamawit had ever met him, according to an account of her life compiled by the UNICEF Ethiopia office.

His absence was painful. The quiet, watchful little girl saw the fathers of other children in her neighborhood. She watched them giving their daughters and sons bread, sodas, and candy. She did not have these things. She did not have a father.

The crying of young children all around was incessant. Many were sick with diarrhea and other illnesses. In urban neighborhoods like this throughout the developing world — where there was no trash collection, where sewage and garbage often mingled in the street or in tepid canals — deadly diseases raged. When small children died, Selamawit could hear their mothers wailing. She herself "felt an apprehension of death," according to the UNICEF account.

To make extra money, two of her brothers shined shoes after school and guarded parked cars to make sure no one stole them. One of the boys' customers was a staff member from the British

Save the Children organization. The woman and her male partner took a liking to one of the brothers, who would visit their apartment and do various errands for them. One Saturday, he stopped by for a teatime visit, bringing along his mother and little sister.

Staying with the Save the Children staffer at the time was a professional photographer named Louise Gubb. She was working on a freelance basis for several UN agencies, including UNDP and UNICEF. When she met the Ethiopian family, Gubb was immediately struck by Selamawit. "Her face projected the innocence and joy of childhood," Gubb recalls in an email. She asked the girl's mother if it was okay to take her picture for UNICEF, and the mother said yes. They went out onto a balcony to snap the photo.

Then, according to numerous UNICEF accounts and articles, Gubb asked Selamawit what she wanted to be when she grew up. The poised girl supposedly did not hesitate, replying in her native language, Amharic: "To be alive!"

Gubb does not recall whether she actually asked the famous question; it is possible, she says, that someone at UNICEF came up with that line for marketing purposes. Either way, she says, the photo of the striking little girl spoke for itself. "She was so vibrant, so full of life and delight, despite the gnawing poverty in which she and her mother and siblings lived," says Gubb, "that she encapsulated the essence of UNICEF's message."

She sold the photo to UNICEF for thirty-five dollars. UNICEF officials immediately saw the fund-raising potential. Jim Grant had long been looking for a symbol for the child survival revolution — now he had one. A range of collateral was produced with Selamawit's face and words. On the poster, the question "What do you want to be when you grow up?" floated over her image. Printed below in big capital letters was the reply: "ALIVE!"

Selamawit did not know about any of this. The British Save the Children staffer gave her family money, and UNICEF provided clothing for her and her brothers. Despite these gestures, her hardships only grew worse.

The family had lived for fourteen years in the dark little garage attached to the bigger house. The occupant of the bigger house was a Greek man, who had taken pity on the family and had allowed them to stay there. When he died in 1988, Selamawit and her family faced eviction.

Around this time, a confluence of fortuitous events took place. UN photographer John Isaac, a gregarious Indian man who had earned a slew of prestigious awards for his arresting images, decided he would try to find out whatever happened to the UNICEF poster child. He went to Addis Ababa. On a Sunday in March 1988 he visited the family in their home. "She was in a little hut [and had] no money, nothing," Isaac recalls.

Even so, the grandmother performed the traditional Ethiopian coffee ceremony for Isaac, an elaborate affair for an honored guest that usually involves roasting coffee beans, pounding them with a mortar and pestle, and then brewing them. Isaac then learned that Selamawit's leg had been badly injured in some sort of traffic accident (it's not clear exactly what happened, but she may have been struck by a car while walking in the street). She was somehow able to get medical treatment and told Isaac that doctors, at first, feared they would have to amputate her leg. Fortunately, a woman doctor was able to save it. Ever since that day, Selamawit had decided she wanted to be something else when she grew up besides alive — she wanted to be a doctor.

The family also told Isaac that Selamawit's school fees had become too expensive, and that she might not be able to continue her studies. He gave them some of his own money. He even visited her teachers and told them the fees would be paid.

When he returned to New York, Isaac went to see Jim Grant. "Jim would like me to tell him stories," Isaac says now. He told him how UNICEF's poster child was faring, about the terrible poverty that had ensnared her family. He showed Grant pictures he had taken of Selamawit.

Isaac had decided to share this information with Grant specifically — because he knew Grant would take him seriously. Grant did.

The UNICEF leader had also heard about Selamawit's life from the photographer who had first taken her photograph, Louise Gubb. At some point, probably before Isaac came to see him, Gubb was in Grant's office to take his picture. She had been recommended by her friend Maggie Black, the author and UNICEF historian. Noticing the "Alive!" poster hanging on Grant's wall, she began to tell him Selamawit's story. "In order to relax him for the photo shoot, I chatted about Selamawit and the background to that photograph," she recalls. "He showed great interest."

Whether it was Isaac who spurred him, or Gubb — or both — Grant wanted to meet Selamawit. He wanted to see if he could help her. He would remark to several staff members that she had, after all, "done more for us than we could ever do for her."

During a trip to Ethiopia in May 1988 for an important summit, Grant asked UNICEF communications program officer Yohannes Tsadik to find Selamawit. Bring the girl and her mother to his room at the Hilton in Addis Ababa, he said, at the end of the day. Tsadik obliged.

Selamawit was now around nine. It had been at least five years since that chance encounter when Gubb took her picture. She and her mother arrived at Grant's hotel room after eight p.m. He welcomed them inside, shaking Selamawit's hand and then her mother's. "How are you?" he said. They both stood, seemingly unsure of whether they should sit.

"Please sit down," Grant said, and the mother and daughter sat next to each other on a couch. Grant and Tsadik sat across from them in chairs. The mother was reserved and did not say much. Grant told Selamawit that he was going to order her some ice cream and then asked her mother if she wanted anything; she said she would like some mineral water. When room service arrived, Grant picked up the ice cream cone and handed it to Selamawit. She took it, her eyes wide. She had likely never tasted ice cream before. "She liked it," recalls Tsadik. "She was so happy about it."

Grant told them he would consult with the UNICEF Ethiopia office and do what he could to help their family. His tone was friendly but cautious, recalls Tsadik, perhaps because he was unsure of exactly what he could promise.

The shy girl was awed by Grant. Either on this occasion or a later one, Grant told Selamawit that she would grow up to become a "great lady" and be very successful. It was crucial, he added, that she stay in school.

Though surely Grant did not intend this, she began to view him as a father figure, says Tsadik. "He treated her so nicely," he says. "Such a big man, a well-known man, famous man, bringing himself down to the level of this little girl, buying her food, giving her money, buying her ice cream — so that's how she considered him a father."

The meeting at the Hilton was a welcome bright spot for Grant, who was still recovering from the shock of Ethel's death. Worse was her obtrusive absence — she might have been with him on a trip like this. She would have loved meeting Selamawit. He must have wondered what she would have thought of her.

Once back in New York, Grant proposed something totally out of the bounds of normal practice: UNICEF would provide Selamawit's family with long-term, regular cash assistance for school, food, and rent for a better house. The problem was that UNICEF did not sponsor individual children or families. The aid it provided was mostly channeled through governments, NGOs, and local organizations. But this, Grant insisted, was a special case.

Still, he had to figure out a way to justify the highly unusual arrangement. A trust fund was briefly considered but ultimately ruled impractical. The argument that Grant and his adviser

Michael Shower eventually concocted was put to staff in a memo from Shower: Selamawit's photograph, which was widely used for fund-raising purposes, could "qualify in the category of 'personal services' and should be compensated accordingly."

The initial agreement with Selamawit's mother, drawn up at UNICEF headquarters in September 1988, stipulated that UNICEF would support Selamawit and her family for three years. Grant felt this was too short a period of time. On a draft of the document he wrote: "What happens after 3 years? Selamawit will be 13 and finished only 6 years of schooling — her brothers who are older will have had more. I propose that, after the first three years, we continue to pay Selamawit's schooling, as long as she stays in school, through high school, and as long as she stays in school, we contribute to house rent and to subsistence."

Grant prevailed, and UNICEF agreed to subsidize the family until Selamawit's graduation from high school in 1999. This included about $1,300 per year, enough to cover school fees for Selamawit and her brothers, rent, food, and money for furniture.

UNICEF also moved Selamawit and her family from the decrepit, one-room garage that had been the only home she had ever known to the main house that had always loomed over them — just feet away but nonetheless in another world. With the UNICEF stipend, they could now afford to rent it. UNICEF renovated and furnished the six-room house. The family had suddenly vaulted into an entirely new and better life. Everyone had a proper bed. They had electricity and plumbing, a bathroom and a kitchen. They even had a dining room table. Selamawit's grandmother, who had become ill and so depressed she started refusing to eat, was now "in good health and happy to be alive," according to a memo sent to Grant by UNICEF staffer Stanislaus Adotevi, who visited the family in their new home.

Local UNICEF staff arranged for Selamawit to be admitted to Nazareth School, a competitive private Catholic girls' school in Addis Ababa. She started in the third grade and did well during her first year. "She understands this is a chance of a lifetime and is determined to succeed in her studies," Adotevi wrote.

Grant would check in on her, every now and then, to make sure she was still in school and doing well. And for the next seven years, as long as he remained executive director of UNICEF, she was both. But several years after his death, her good fortune began to come apart. She was unable to finish school. UNICEF continued providing some support for her family's basic living expenses but could not go on doing so forever. In 2008, when she was around twenty-nine and had children of her own, UNICEF paid her a final "goodwill gift" of $3,500. At this point, Jim Grant had been dead for thirteen years. (Efforts to contact Selamawit were unsuccessful.)

At the twenty-fifth anniversary summit of the Organization of African Unity in Addis Ababa on May 26, 1988, Grant brought a special guest. Into the cavernous meeting hall, past a forest of tall flags, he walked with his hand on the shoulder of a small Ethiopian girl. Wearing a white robe, a neatly trimmed Afro, and a white necklace, she looked elegant, mature, and nervous. Grant led Selamawit Gebreyes up to the stage. He guided her to a spot to the right of the podium and then turned to her and smiled reassuringly.

She kept her hands crossed in front of her and looked down. Every now and then, her eyes took a quick scan of the big clamorous room, which contained thirty heads of state from throughout Africa as well as the secretary general of the United Nations. It is hard to conceive of a more intimidating atmosphere for a nine-year-old child who has never been in such a setting before.

Grant leaned toward a tangle of microphones.

"Mr. Chairman, your excellencies, Mr. Secretary General, distinguished participants, honored guests," he began, glancing over at Selamawit, as camera flashes started popping. "It is a great honor...to address this session...in the year of the...African child."

He then held up his hand briefly and made a somewhat awkward, pause-laden introduction to the girl who stood next to him. "Mr. Chairman...if I may first...take this opportunity to introduce...the African...child...Selamaweet..."

Reaching up, he gently clutched her arm and pulled her closer to him and continued: "...who has done the most of any child...to help promote...the child survival...and...development revolution."

He spoke of his desire to find a "symbol" for this revolution and said he knew he had discovered it when he saw Selamawit's photo. As he spoke, his hands, every now and again, spasmed in small frenetic loops, as though operating separately from his body—the hands of an overexcited child.

He relayed the story of how Selamawit's picture was taken and then held up a copy of the poster that had made her a celebrity. "It has been seen by hundreds of millions of people, been on the cover of magazines," Grant said. "It says on the top, 'What would you like to be when you grow up?' 'Alive'..."

He folded the poster.

"Now, five years later, it is my privilege to actually meet her in person...here in Addis Ababa."

He told the audience that she was ranked second in a third grade class of one hundred and added that she was "of course, fully immunized."

"Mr. Chairman, with your permission..."—here Grant held up his finger, like a lawyer asking to approach the bench—"may she say just a few words...to this distinguished summit?"

He adjusted the microphones and then stepped back. A man walked up and placed a stool behind the podium. Grinning widely, Grant took Selamawit's hand and helped her to climb up and stand on the stool, so she could reach the microphones.

Standing at Grant's height, she looked out at the crowd for a few seconds, her eyes big and discerning. Then suddenly, she began speaking breathlessly in Amharic, pushing the words out as quickly as she could, pausing two or three times to inhale. Her voice was high and faint.

When she finished, applause rippled across the hall.

"I am told," Grant said, "that what she has said to us in Amharic is, 'My name is Selamawit...A few years ago...someone asked me, *What do you want to be?*...I answered, *I want to be alive*. Now I am alive...I want the same for all children in Africa...so please help them. Thank you.'"

He looked at her and nodded his head very quickly, a crisp military gesture — a signal of approval, as if to say, *Ya done good, kid*. Then he lifted her off the stool and gingerly set her down.

Chapter 11
EVERYTHING IS NOT ALL RIGHT

In the middle of 1988, many people at UNICEF started to realize they might actually succeed — they just might make history. The global target for universal childhood immunization (UCI) had emerged from a fog of skepticism and, while not yet in reach, now hovered plainly in sight. They had come so far, so fast. Countries large and small — from China to Saint Lucia — had responded heartily to Grant's call to immunize their children. Coverage rates had already doubled and tripled in some places — despite a suffocating recession, despite wars, despite nonexistent roads or roads that were mined, despite the near absence of health infrastructure, despite resistance from local doctors and medical personnel. An estimated 1.9 million children's lives were being saved each year as a result. When the goal was set a few years earlier, even the most bullish believers had their doubts. Some had felt that even if they made it halfway, that would still be an extraordinary accomplishment. Many lives would still be protected. Many families would still be spared the ultimate grief. In other words, maybe reaching the goal was not the main point — if that goal had nonetheless produced a significant payoff.

Grant did not see it this way, according to several former staff members. Meeting UCI was all or nothing, a conquest to be won essentially at any cost. Grant couldn't really afford to be anything but absolutist about it — if anyone detected in him the slightest hint of hesitation or complacency or willingness to accept anything less than a total victory, the whole thing could start rattling and wobbling and falling apart.

The actual goal was not 100 percent immunization coverage. In 1977, the World Health Assembly (WHO's governing body) had proposed immunizing "every child in the world" by 1990. But Grant believed the global target should be more achievable and suggested it be fixed at 80 percent. Though not "universal," it would hopefully approach "herd immunity" — the point at which a critical mass of people is immunized, making it much harder for an outbreak to occur and offering a degree of protection even to those who haven't been covered. That was not the only factor, says Ralph Henderson, who then ran WHO's immunization programs. Grant wanted the 80 percent goal, he says, because he "could sell it credibly to national leaders." In Africa, the target was set at 75 percent — in recognition of the unrivaled challenges facing the continent.

Keeping track of all the numbers and of each country's performance was Dr. Nyi Nyi. The short, intense, no-nonsense Burmese man was then the director of UNICEF's program division. Known as Grant's "enforcer," he donned a beret and often wore a completely inscrutable expression. An unquenchable reader — described variously as a "flipping genius" and a "bull-dog" — Nyi Nyi could keep a swirling constellation of facts in his head, much like Grant himself. The former Burmese government minister was a formidable and widely feared taskmaster. If you were a UNICEF country representative, and Nyi Nyi began scrutinizing your performance, you had better be ready to defend yourself. He would probably know your country's statistics better than you did. He was withering when he needed to be. And everyone knew he acted at Grant's command.

Nyi Nyi's office at UNICEF headquarters was known as "the torture room on the thirteenth floor." Files and papers were piled so high on his desk that when you first walked into his office, you could not tell if he was sitting there or not. And when he needed to find a particular document amongst the dense towers of paper, he knew exactly where it was — he could retrieve it in seconds. He was in the office at 6:30 every morning, and he would stay until at least seven at night. He estimates now that he spent about five months of the year traveling, a month or two less than his boss.

His loyalty to Grant was total. In describing him years later, Nyi Nyi says unreservedly: "When you met him, you fell in love with him."

Nyi Nyi's ruthless devotion, if off-putting to some, was also crucial — without someone like him prodding UNICEF representatives to prod their governments, it is unlikely such considerable strides would have been made.

Some people felt the frenzied push for UCI — and in particular Dr. Nyi Nyi's relentless browbeating — was so extreme that it bordered on abuse. Many representatives were throttled by panic. Some complained to their colleagues: What was being asked of them was unreasonable; they were being judged by a brutally unfair standard; how could they work in conditions like this?

Nyi Nyi says his interrogations were simply to get information. "If I don't grill [them], I won't get the information," he says now. "If I don't have the information, I won't be able to help them... Like performing a diagnostic test on a patient — you have to find out what's wrong." His main purpose, he says, was to help the representative come up with a solution to overcome whatever was in the way.

But the unyielding pressure to meet the targets — and Nyi Nyi was not the only source — may have spawned some ugly offshoots. According to several former staff members, some countries fudged their immunization coverage numbers to make it look as if they were doing better than they actually were. Some UNICEF staff members may have even been complicit in "cooking the books" — perhaps because they were terrified of giving Grant or Nyi Nyi bad news. How much Grant knew about this is unclear. While he did not expressly ask for false figures nor tell people to manipulate information, he doesn't seem to have actively discouraged it either. Several staff members suggest that he viewed the matter as another pesky distraction he simply chose not to deal with.

Rohde got into bitter arguments with Dr. Nyi Nyi over this issue. He believed that Nyi Nyi was pressing people too hard, and as a result they were coughing up false figures. At one point, says Rohde, "Nyi Nyi said, 'I don't care how you reach 80 percent, but we've got to reach it.'" Rohde raised the issue with Grant, who replied that Nyi Nyi knew what he was doing. "I think [Grant] dodged the issue to the point that it was uncomfortable," Rohde says now.

Nyi Nyi claims he never pressured anyone to alter immunization numbers and, in fact, vigorously guarded against it. If he suspected numbers had been changed, he would order another round of evaluation to ferret out the real figures. "I would not allow fudging," he says.

One of Grant's most dynamic field operatives, an American named Richard Reid, was involved in several big immunization campaigns and says concerted efforts were made to ensure the accuracy of the data. "I think we were extremely strict and did all kinds of follow-up and house-to-house surveys," he says.

Nyi Nyi, a meticulously spoken Buddhist, notes that his religion forbids him to lie. Beyond that, he adds, duplicity is impractical. His mother once imparted advice that he says he has followed his whole life: if you make a habit of telling lies, you won't remember what lie you told to whom. Fudging immunization stats is a form of lying, he says, and he would never have tolerated this or encouraged anyone to do it. He says his famous interrogation sessions were, in part, designed to expose dishonesty. He would then insist upon using the correct figures, though he would make a point to never publicly shame anyone — "you want to preserve their enthusiasm."

But as 1990 drew closer and some UNICEF representatives grew more frantic, the reliability of immunization numbers became a vexing, stubbornly lodged thorn in UNICEF's hide — no matter how much Grant wanted to ignore it.

Bearing the brunt of Grant's mania on a daily basis — probably more than anyone else — was Mary Cahill. A sharp-witted, keenly observant Irish woman with uncommon multitasking abilities, Cahill ran Grant's office and served as his de facto chief of staff (there was no actual "chief of staff" at that point). She had to match his energy and his hours — Grant performed the jobs of three or four people, and hence so did Cahill. She often trekked into the office on Saturdays, at Grant's insistence. The work was ceaseless, demanding, and largely thankless.

"Mary worked probably eighteen hours a day, and she was always behind the scenes," says Doreen Lobo, the former assistant to Grant's speechwriter Mike Shower.

Cahill's devotion to Grant rivaled Nyi Nyi's, and Grant needed her perhaps as much. She started in June 1982, and it took her close to a year to understand and appreciate her manic boss. At first, she says, "I thought he was a lunatic."

She got used to his fanatical pace. Though perennially late and always rushing, he would still listen to whoever came to see him — even if they spoke at excruciating length about something peripheral or irrelevant (there are a lot of "talkers" at UNICEF). Grant might have stopped listening during such conversations, but he would never brush anyone off, according to Cahill. "He never made anyone feel stupid," she says. "He never said to a person, 'That's ridiculous.'"

Though he often quietly disregarded what people told him. And in some meetings, his behavior could be perplexing. He would sometimes lean back in his chair and close his eyes. And keep them closed for a half minute or longer. "You'd think, *Jeepers, he's gone to sleep*," says Cahill.

But then, after a thick, thoroughly uncomfortable span of silence, he would abruptly snap back up and say, "Three things." Then he would fire three incisive questions at his guest, who would be scrambling to keep up.

Cahill tried to relieve the surging stress for other staff members, particularly visiting regional directors, who often arrived in New York and were immediately swept up in a gale of meetings. "It was all work and no play," she says.

So she organized some fun. At her urging, Grant and his three deputies agreed to buy the visiting regional directors tickets for a Broadway show like *Les Misérables*. Mary and Mike Shower planned a special dinner: Mike made meatballs, and Mary brought salmon, salad, wine, and homemade chocolate mousse. Cahill, Grant, and his deputies would join their guests for a potluck feast in the office, and then they would all head out for a night at the theater. "It became a tradition," she says.

Cahill also made a tradition out of Grant's birthday, May 12, which usually fell right after a laborious, two-week board meeting. "I used to do silly things," she says.

She once stayed up until four in the morning making a papier-mâché replica of Jim Grant. She fashioned the figure out of newspaper, glue, and wire, and painted on a navy blue suit. She made a tiny papier-mâché packet of ORS and stuck it in the doll's hand. An avid equestrian (in her scant free time), Cahill clipped some of her horse's gray hair and glued it on the doll's head. She even made a miniature bookshelf with tiny copies of *The State of the World's Children* reports, created by reducing photocopies over and over again.

After Ethel's death, Cahill was a vital source of support. She often heard Grant mumbling to himself about things he needed to do — things Ethel might have taken care of before. "His focus on work helped him overcome the void," she says.

Cahill knew better than anyone how demanding Grant could be. She ultimately never resented it, because she knew that he worked harder than anybody. And she, of course, knew what was at stake. Many staff members recognized that the difficulty and the exasperation and the long hours came with an immeasurable reward. UNICEF was now a changed place. Grant had instilled in its people a newfound belief in themselves and their organization. They were altering history, redefining the boundaries of global health and children's advocacy. Many would later realize that working for someone like Grant, someone who gave them the chance to truly change the world, was a once-in-a-lifetime experience.

But the galvanic camaraderie also masked growing pockets of unease.

There was a small group of Grant favorites known as "Jim's boys" — usually men he considered brilliant and indispensable (and some of them truly were). An official committee at UNICEF handled all staff appointments and promotions based on a selected range of criteria. Everyone had to accept the committee's rulings — everyone, that is, except a handful of people, mostly Jim's boys, who were promoted according to Grant's whim. This understandably rankled many hardworking people, who had played by the stated rules. But from Grant's perspective, he wanted the best people possible in important positions — children's lives literally depended on it. However fair, the bureaucracy was also arthritically rigid.

After an executive staff meeting, Manou Assadi, the Iranian head of personnel, approached Grant in the hall. He wanted to warn him about the growing discontent over his ad hoc promotions and transfers.

"Jim, do you know why the shah of Iran fell?"

Grant didn't answer.

"Because people around him told him, 'Your Majesty, everything is all right.'"

He then added: "Jim, everything is not all right."

Grant listened to Assadi. But he did not say anything in response.

When a senior official suggested checking the somewhat suspect background of someone Grant wanted to hire, he summarily batted the concern away. "When I have to fix a plumbing problem," Grant remarked, "I don't want to know the background of the plumber. I want the problem fixed."

He avoided contentious personnel matters, much as he dodged unpleasant financial concerns. This tendency would earn him a reputation as a bad manager, though this was not entirely fair — in some ways, he was a singularly stellar manager. But when it came to administrative, financial, or personnel issues, he simply wasn't interested. He didn't want to deal with it. One senior staff member recalls sitting in audit meetings with Grant. "As soon as something unpleasant came up, Grant would walk out of the door, and he would all of a sudden have something very important to do," he says. "And we would be left with his deputy...and all of us would throw up our hands and say, 'Here we go again.'"

In December 1983, several years earlier, one of "Jim's boys" had been caught allegedly embezzling and defrauding the UNICEF China office of as much as $144,000. When confronted with the news, Grant balked. Jim "could never accept that [he] was a crook," says former China representative Joe Judd. "He blamed the two auditors, and he blamed me."

According to a memo from the deputy director of UNICEF's Office of Internal Audit, the man "concealed and falsified official information and documents; committed systematic acts of fraud and embezzled or facilitated defalcation of UNICEF funds and committed [a] series of administrative wrongdoings."

Judd, who otherwise greatly admired Grant, says the UNICEF chief "sometimes lost perspective" and "let himself be fooled." Grant "was of a mind, if somebody was doing something great and there was a little shady stuff going on on the side, you had to weigh the two," adds Judd. "There may be justification for unintentional mismanagement, but there is no justification for fraud and intentional mismanagement."

Amazingly, Grant did not seem to consider the matter to be a big deal. He told another staff member that the man accused of filching as much as $144,000 was "the best program officer ever" and added, "I'm sorry that because of some small administrative problems, he had to be fired." Notes the staff member: "the fellow had been steadily stealing... That was offensive."

Grant would, in fact, initially refuse to take action against several individuals accused of violations, according to several former senior staff members. Whether a sign of fierce loyalty or a troubling blind spot — or a combination of the two — the tendency would abrade many, even Grant's loyal supporters. It would also undercut the immense goodwill he had engendered. Grant wanted to believe the best of everybody and hated firing people, even when it was starkly clear they should be dismissed.

In the China fraud case, the man was let go and agreed to pay UNICEF back.

There would be other cases like this over the next few years. Says Judd: "It is demoralizing to UNICEF staff around the world when they learn about these things."

Changing Jim Grant's mind could take years. Allegra Morelli knows this as well as anyone. The sincere, dogged Italian woman, who held several positions at UNICEF and was close both to Ethel and to Grant's stepmother Denise, "had many fights" with her boss.

"I was always saying, 'You cannot save a child with immunization and then let him die of poverty,'" recalls Morelli.

Grant did not at all disagree with this. He viewed immunization as a political entry point — a host of other services could be delivered on the path blazed by vaccination teams. Morelli knew Grant was no one-trick pony — his vision of international development was vast and shifting. Still, getting him to focus on goals that fell outside his "doability" zone could be a Sisyphean endeavor.

One of those goals was the Convention on the Rights of the Child. The proposed human rights treaty, then in working draft form, would afford children around the world basic rights and protection from abuse and exploitation. Grant thought it would divert momentum away from UCI, and that it didn't stand a very good chance of being ratified anyway. Plus, he would point out, the UN already had the Declaration on the Rights of the Child, which was adopted in 1959 — in other words, we've been there, done that already (except that the declaration had no teeth, not even baby ones; it was a statement of principle, not a legally binding treaty). Many of Grant's advisers agreed. For a long while, the "convention" was a no-go.

But Morelli made it her personal quest to persuade Grant to support it. Because once Jim Grant threw his weight behind something, that something moved.

"He was very much against it," she says. "It took me five years to convince him."

Kimberly Gamble, who lobbied for the convention in Washington, DC, noted that the Reagan administration was an obstacle and that Grant didn't think it was worth the political risk. "Jim said, 'Why should we go up against Reagan on this?'"

So how did Morelli sway him?

By making the point that the convention was not an encumbrance — it was a tool. It was a giant cudgel that Grant could wield to deafening effect. It would give UCI and child survival a major boost by making the world pay more attention to the basic question of children's welfare. Children were ignored in a lot of places. The convention would give them — and Grant — visibility.

Grant would later say that it was Morelli's "eloquent, emotional, forceful plea" that compelled him to back the convention. He had also insisted that a component specifically addressing child survival be added; Article 6, guaranteeing a child's "right" to live, was included.

In the late 1980s, Grant began speaking more and more vehemently about this "Magna Carta for Children." Once on board, says Morelli, "he went full steam."

He would employ the same strategy he had used for UCI: play one country off another. He would tell UNICEF Bolivia representative Jim Mayrides that he needed Bolivia to ratify the convention in order to goad Brazil into doing the same. Mayrides recalls: "He said, 'Look, if you can get the Bolivians to ratify it, and if you can get the Bolivians to do all these things in child survival, then I can go to the Brazilians and say, 'Here are these poor indigenous people in the hills, and they're doing this, and you guys down here in Brazil can't get it done?'"

With the convention teetering atop Grant's Jenga-like to-do list, he hurtled ever faster toward 1990. No one was holding him back anymore — Ethel was not there to ask him to rest and take care of himself. All the while, a growing concern began nipping at him: How could he firm up these historic undertakings, how could he make sure they didn't slip like loose sand through his fingers?

He began talking about holding a big meeting — a meeting the like of which the world had never seen before. Every head of state on earth would be invited. It would be the first global "summit" in history, and it would be focused on children.

Surely another Grant fantasy, many assumed. But now everyone knew you could not write off Jim Grant's ideas — no matter how wild or grandiose.

He nurtured yet another aspiration, a soaring but mostly unspoken dream: winning the Nobel Prize. UNICEF had snared the lofty Norwegian honor in 1965. Recent accomplishments already far surpassed anything the agency had done almost twenty-five years earlier — but would the Nobel Committee agree? A second Nobel could give UNICEF supersonic momentum. Who could say no to Jim Grant then?

As the biggest deadline of his life speedily ate through his calendar, something else would soon vie with UCI and the convention and fund-raising pressures for his disappearing slices of time. Something big. A roaring storm, a new emergency, was about to swallow Jim Grant. This time, he couldn't pull himself out.

Chapter 12
LIFELINE

The Sudanese general was sweating. He had opened the collar of his military uniform and now sat in the crowded, low-ceilinged, un-air-conditioned room, training his eyes on the floor. A large, *Casablanca*-style ceiling fan spun overhead, stirring the languid, hundred-degree air, but not doing much to cool it. Around an oblong conference table scattered with papers huddled about twenty people, Sudanese government ministers and UN agency officials, all of whom abided the tense silence. Across the table from the general, fixing him with hard, cold eyes, was Jim Grant.

"We have been let down," Grant said, his voice devoid of its usual buoyancy. "Someone has let us down."

In late May 1989, Grant was in Khartoum, Sudan, to oversee a critical emergency operation to avert mass starvation in the country's southern regions. A vicious civil war, raging for the past six years, had obstructed relief efforts, exacerbated an already calamitous drought, and left as many as 250,000 people in dire need of food. The previous year, as had become clear in recent months, as many as 250,000 had already died. Now, in some small towns, dozens of people were dying every day, most of them very old or very young.

In March, Grant had brokered a ceasefire of sorts, convincing the government and the rebels to hold their fire in several "corridors of tranquillity." It was agreed by both sides that aid could be peaceably transported to these areas by plane, truck, barge, and train — but the train was the most important. With its forty-eight cars, it had the largest capacity. More than one hundred thousand tons of grain had to reach the south within weeks if widespread deaths were to be prevented. It now looked like the deal might be unraveling.

The whole endeavor was dicey. A truck convoy had been ambushed a month earlier, and eight rebel escorts had been killed. The antiquated rail lines were sheathed by weeds, sections of track had warped, and bandits had stolen ties. UNICEF had worked with the Sudanese government to repair the rails, but the train had then been stalled for a month by other obstacles: a rail workers' strike, mechanical problems, and government recalcitrance. Tens of thousands of lives depended on that train moving now.

That morning, it finally moved. But it didn't get very far before a band of one hundred armed thugs had hijacked it and kidnapped three relief workers (including the UN Development Program's Khartoum chief, Brian Wannop), hauled them into the woods, confiscated their belongings, and threatened to kill them.

The thugs had eventually been talked into letting their hostages go by some Sudanese rail workers, but the train—loaded with 1,500 tons of food—once again sat idle. The attack had occurred in an area controlled by a general who was also a government minister, and who happened to be sitting at the table that afternoon in Khartoum. The general had apparently earlier pledged that his clan of raiders would let the train pass.

The attack had cast a sudden pall over an already troubled operation at a critical point. Richard Reid, the brisk, lean American who had worked for the Peace Corps and Save the Children and was then UNICEF's regional director for North Africa and the Middle East, wrote an account of the Khartoum meeting in *Jim Grant: UNICEF Visionary*, the anthology about Grant published by UNICEF. He recalls the taut unease in the room. "The fact that we had already run into an impediment...made things seem both scary and imminent," he says. "We were afraid that if more attacks on the train occurred, more intimidation, that the train line might not work, and it was going to, of course, carry the largest bulk of the supplies and food."

It was the only time Reid had ever seen his boss visibly angry—so angry his cheeks had flushed red. "Jim just turned to the guy...and just leveled him with a stare," says Reid. "Jim had his eyes when he started, and then the general looked away."

Grant then scanned the room and returned his gaze to the general, a tall man who had become plump in his middle age.

Silence suffused the room for several seconds. The general kept his eyes lowered, and everyone waited for Grant to speak.

Finally, he said: "There was an attack on the train this morning by an armed militia." A few people shifted in their seats. No one spoke.

Grant described the event and then said: "I wonder how this happened?"

No reply.

"We're here to save lives," he continued. "Not endanger them. All of us." Then he raised his voice and added: "Isn't that right?"

In some towns in southern Sudan, aid workers asked families how many children they had lost, and a woman or man would point to a sad little mound next to their hut, or two mounds, or three. The fighting and famine had uprooted and scattered up to two million people, who had fled to shantytowns in Ethiopia and throughout Sudan, many staggering into small, government-held towns near the border between the southern and northern regions of the country. Makeshift refugee camps grew around these towns. There was little food; some people ate worms. On October 13, 1988, the *New York Times* reported that eight thousand people had died in the border town of Abyei since June and that almost all the children under age two in the town were dead. Some had succumbed to starvation, many others to measles (proof of Grant's exhortation that immunization was critical, even during a famine). Some people were too weak to bury the dead, and corpses lay next to their huts. Hyenas would come in the night and drag the bodies away.

The war stemmed from a decades-long conflict between the Muslim north and the Christian and animist south. Both sides had intentionally used food as a weapon of war, blocking aid agencies from reaching civilians. Starvation had been engineered. The government had closed off Abyei, a collection of mud-and-stick huts and a few tin-roofed government buildings, all rimmed by dense swampland. The residents were mostly members of the Dinka tribe, southern cattle herders who were a source of recruits for the rebel Sudan People's Liberation Army (SPLA). Militias loyal to the government savagely targeted the Dinkas, enslaving them and massacring noncombatants. Reports of regular, sickening atrocities filtered out of the south. In March 1987, in the village of al-Da'ien in Darfur province, a tribe armed by the government in Khartoum viciously murdered as many as a thousand Dinka children, women, and men, burning some of them alive.

UNICEF was among the first to deliver assistance to Abyei, flying in emergency food on its Twin Otter plane. "It was an attempt to break the ice," says Detlef Palm, a UNICEF logistics officer in Sudan at the time. "It was almost a provocation." The children he saw were stick-thin and listless, their shoulder blades protruding like grotesque wings. "Not a single child looked okay," says Palm. When he walked through the village, he met a resident priest who behaved strangely, running and hiding behind huts and then whispering and beckoning to Palm.

Palm assumed the man had been driven insane by the enormity of what he had seen.

In October 1988, the US government organized a multiday airlift of as much as ninety tons of grain for the residents of Abyei. UNICEF helped facilitate the operation and also provided medical supplies. There was a question as to how much aid was actually going to the residents and how much was being taken by government soldiers (indeed, during the previous trip to Abyei, Palm had noticed that some food had been placed "under lock and key" by nearby soldiers — even though children were dying in plain sight). Refugees kept straggling in. The aid was stopgap, patchwork — not even remotely enough. Humanitarian agencies, NGOs, and donor countries knew a major disaster was looming. Many people believed it was already too late.

A key moment came during a phone call between Grant and Palm's boss, UNICEF Sudan representative Cole Dodge. Assertive, erudite, and coolly confident, the American anthropologist was a Peace Corps veteran and a "Jim's boy." Probably one of Grant's most daring field representatives, he was a humanitarian virtuoso who had helped broker a ceasefire in Uganda and who was willing to assume a startling amount of personal risk. Dodge was in the UNICEF Twin Otter plane when missiles were fired at it on two separate occasions. On one of them, in January 1988, the warheads exploded in view of Dodge's window. "It was quite spectacularly beautiful," he says.

The experience was alarming, but Dodge had been through worse. "I don't remember it as a threatening circumstance in the same way as having a gun right to your head." Dodge had had a gun put right to his head, and a knife to his throat — both while working in Uganda.

It was in the cockpit of the Twin Otter that Dodge called Jim Grant. He used the plane's radio. Placing the call here meant a better connection than landlines would allow. Once he got Grant on the line, the boss told him that while on a flight from Paris to New York, he had opened a newspaper and had seen a grisly and shocking photo. It had shown tiny children standing next to the corpses of people who had starved to death in the town of El Meiram. "We've got to do something," Grant told Dodge. "Even if there's no way to do it officially."

Dodge agreed. He had, in fact, already been meeting with the country's prime minister, Sadiq al-Mahdi, on a regular basis to discuss what was possible in the south. UNICEF always operates at the invitation of a country's sitting government, and the government of Sudan only allowed it to work in the north. The south was off the radar and off the table.

But Dodge had managed to work out an unofficial agreement with the prime minister and the rebels to allow aid flights to some towns in the south (not including Abyei), starting as early as 1987. It was based on "implied consent" and was a "tumultuous arrangement and affair because both sides were suspicious," according to Dodge. If Khartoum thought Dodge was getting too cozy with the SPLA, he could be declared persona non grata (or PNG'd) and kicked out of the country (this had recently happened to another UN official). The flights also earned the ire of four foreign ambassadors, who complained to the UN secretary general that UNICEF was acting unilaterally.

This didn't faze Grant. "Jim was on the side of risk-taking and of things on the edge," says Dodge. "The mission was more important than niceties and regulations." Grant's main concern about the flights was insurance. "The normal insurance was carried out of New York, and they wouldn't touch it at all," Dodge notes. Grant told him to approach Lloyd's of London. Dodge did, and the company gave him some quotes for covering the dicey endeavor. When Dodge sent the quotes to senior officials at UNICEF headquarters in New York, he was told not to proceed. "New York said, 'No way, José,'" he recalls. "But it was Jim who said, 'Yes, we're going to do it.'"

But Grant still wanted a formal, on-the-books agreement with all sides. He asked Dodge to get official letters from the rebels, the government, and the ICRC (with whom UNICEF would be cooperating and which had also been trying to gain permission to deliver aid to the north and south). The letters from the rebels and the Red Cross came fairly easily; the government was a different story. After the complaints made against Dodge by members of the diplomatic community, rumors lurched around Khartoum that he and UNICEF were playing too fast and loose. "It was very edgy," says Dodge.

When he met with al-Mahdi, the prime minister (with whom Dodge had a personal relationship) refused his extended hand. He accused Dodge of aiding his enemies and prolonging the war. Something had soured him. How could Dodge possibly get him to sign a letter of consent now?

He went back to al-Mahdi's office four or five times but could not get past his secretary. Then an idea elbowed its way into his head: his friend from the World Bank played tennis with the prime minister — maybe he could snag al-Mahdi's signature. Miraculously, he did just that, and handed the signed letter back to Dodge. He called Grant immediately and blurted out, "I have it!"

The signed letter, along with an agreement finally obtained by the ICRC from the government, helped set the stage for what would become a colossal, precedent-breaking humanitarian endeavor known as Operation Lifeline Sudan. It would last sixteen years and involve several UN agencies and more than thirty-five nongovernmental organizations. Dodge left the country before it began. Grant posted him to Bangladesh, where he would help engineer a "near miracle" in immunization coverage over the next several years.

Palm was soon summoned to New York. A mid-level UNICEF employee, the unassuming German was nervous about meeting UNICEF's executive director. He bought a tie for the occasion but did not know how to knot it; he had never worn one before. A New York shopkeeper knotted it for him. In front of Grant and several senior staff members, Palm gave his logistical assessment of what was possible in the south of Sudan and how many locations UNICEF could reach. Grant eased his nerves and then said, "We're going official with this."

Palm flew back to Nairobi, Kenya, where he was based. Within a week, he learned that Grant had put $1 million at his disposal. He immediately began procuring vaccines, food, and other supplies for the starving children of Sudan.

Grant wanted to see Abyei for himself. It was a big security risk — airplanes flying in the area sometimes returned with bullet holes in their tails. In 1986 and 1987, according to the Associated Press, rebel fighters shot down two relief planes, killing seventy people. Dodge had been fired on twice while in the air. But Grant insisted on going.

Once on the ground, "he was very shaken by what he saw," says Abdul Mohammed, an emergency coordinator for the Sudan Council of Churches who accompanied Grant and would later join the staff of UNICEF.

Walking into the village, Grant took in the scene and muttered, "Oh my God." The situation was probably grimmer than anything he had ever witnessed, save maybe the Great Bengal Famine in 1944.

The famine's toll in southern Sudan was "worse than the famous Korem camp (in Ethiopia) in '84," says Alex de Waal, an Africa researcher and executive director of the World Peace Foundation at Tufts University. "It was worse than anything" that had been recorded before, he adds, noting that the death rates in Abyei and El Meiram in 1988 were four to five times higher than those in the Korem camp.

Grant quickly overcame his shock, removed his jacket, and rolled up his shirtsleeves. He rubbed his hands together vigorously — as if to say, *Okay, let's fix this*. He fished out a camera and started snapping photos of the sunken-eyed, wasted children. He sat down with mothers and asked them when their children were last fed. "He transformed himself from being shocked to being affectionate," says Mohammed.

One woman pleaded with him in whispers, grabbing his hand and pulling him into a hut with a plastic tarp roof. Inside lay a tiny baby girl, maybe eighteen months old. Her belly distended, her eyes empty, her arms the width of Magic Markers, the child was on the cusp of death. She cried weakly. When greeting people in their homes, Grant would often cheerfully ask, "How are we today?" Inside the hut he knelt down. He took the child's limp hand and spoke softly to her. He may have said he was sorry. Then he stood and either took the mother's hand or placed his hand on her shoulder; she was despondent, her eyes vacant — "eyes that have seen a lot," says Mohammed. There were a few other children inside. Grant told a UNICEF staffer to hurry and get a doctor, though he knew it was likely too late. This baby needed more than ORS. He waited for the doctor to arrive and examine the child. Mohammed does not know what happened to her.

UN secretary general Javier Pérez de Cuéllar needed someone to helm the entire UN emergency response in Sudan, a startlingly complicated and increasingly urgent task that required wooing donors and the media and commanding the respect of the government and the rebels. An earlier UN effort to deliver aid to the south of the country, called Operation Rainbow, had been shut down shortly after it began in 1986; the government had discovered the man coordinating it had been speaking to the rebels and expelled him from the country. As a result, many were pessimistic about future initiatives. "That basically intimidated the UN," says de Waal. What was needed, he adds, was "someone who was not going to be intimidated."

Within the UN system at the time, the choice was obvious — especially since Grant and Dodge had begun to lay some of the groundwork. After Grant had accepted, he ran into a colleague on a plane and asked him whether he thought he could succeed. The man told him he stood a good chance. "People are saying I have a 25 percent chance," Grant replied. "I think I will."

Grant knew the only way he could prevail was to persuade the entrenched, warring parties in Sudan to lay down their arms. He needed to reprise the Days of Tranquillity from El Salvador. This time, it would be even more difficult. Donor government representatives and diplomatic leaders had already tried and failed to prod the government into action. One question scampering skittishly around the nooks and alleys of the aid and diplomatic community in Sudan: *What makes Jim Grant think he can do it?*

The chances were improved by a changed political climate in Sudan in early 1989, according to de Waal. Sadiq al-Mahdi had long stubbornly resisted the prospect of a peace process, but his stance had recently been softened by new pressure from political parties in Sudan and from the United States government. This, says de Waal, "made it possible for all sorts of things to happen on the humanitarian front." As for Operation Lifeline, he says, "it took someone like Jim Grant to make the international [community] take seriously the need and the possibility to do it, but it was these two other political developments that opened the door."

In early March, Grant met with the swaggering al-Mahdi. Standing six feet one and taking four-foot strides, al-Mahdi was an affable and imperious man who wore flowing white robes and a white burnoose on his head. A former president of the Oxford Union, he liked intellectual discussions.

After a tense exchange, during which al-Mahdi initially swatted away Grant's concerns, he eventually gave in to the UNICEF chief's request. In his written account, Reid recalled that one turning point in the discussion came when al-Mahdi said that Grant's gruesome projections of starvation in South Sudan sounded "worse than Ethiopia" and added "that can't be true."

Grant had replied, "It is worse than Ethiopia."

That rattled the prime minister.

Once Grant had al-Mahdi's agreement, he went to see the stocky, imposing president of the Sudan People's Liberation Army. John Garang was a member of the Dinka tribe but had attended Grinnell College in Iowa and reportedly had traces of a Midwestern accent. He wore green fatigues and a green cap.

They met under a mango tree in the desert, sitting on folding chairs in a circle of about twenty people. According to Reid, when Grant asked Garang how many children he had, the question drew laughter from the rebel leader's brusque bodyguards. But Grant cheerfully persisted: "You have four million!" He told Garang he was the "father of all the children here."

Within a few days, Garang provided his answer: yes.

Reid was in the meetings with al-Mahdi and Garang and watched his boss win them both over. "It was amazing," he says, "how Jim had caused two mighty oaks to fall in just a few strokes."

Operation Lifeline Sudan was officially launched on April 1, 1989, a $132 million endeavor to transport more than one hundred thousand tons of food to millions of people in the south. The food had to be delivered before the imminent start of the rainy season, which would hamper travel and make some areas impassable. At a press conference, Grant said that the effort was a "race against time...a mission impossible that could be possible with the cooperation of everybody."

A month later, after the rainy season had begun and progress had been slower than Grant had hoped, he sat in a hot Khartoum conference room glaring at the general whose armed gangs, he believed, had attacked his train.

After admonishing the general — not by name, but by implication — he let the silence spread through the room; he let everyone bake in it, squirm in it.

Then he announced that the train would resume its run.

"If you know anyone else that wants to try to stop this train," he declared forcefully, "tell them, 'Hands off! Hands off!' Or we'll shine the headlights of the world on them."

The general was "completely terrified," says Farid Rahman, a Pakistani who had recently replaced Dodge as UNICEF's Sudan representative. "He was an aggressive man," Rahman notes, "and he had a tribal mentality, and I think he was feeling affronted, here was a train that was going to go through his territory all the way to the south."

Rahman recalls the general brazenly speaking up at some earlier point. "He said, 'We can't guarantee the safety of this train'...which was, in a way, saying the whole train project is going to fail."

But after Grant's indignant speech, "he absolutely shut up."

In two days, the train was moving again, and the food reached those starving in the south.

Setbacks continued, including attacks on convoys by raiding militias accountable to neither side. Grant visited a Red Cross tent hospital where seven or eight UNICEF volunteer drivers from Kenya lay on gurneys recovering from burns and AK47 bullet wounds. Their convoy had been hit, and they had all miraculously survived. But their injuries were severe, and several groaned in pain.

Grant walked slowly into the wide, white tent and bent down to speak to each of them. He thanked them for risking their lives to save children. Tears stood in his eyes as he made his way among the gurneys — an uncommon display of emotion. Most of the men were too weak to speak, but a few recognized Grant, and their eyes widened. One man reached out and touched his arm.

"He was very much like a priest," says Reid, who accompanied him. "He was very much in communion with them."

Lifeline gained momentum and supporters, and aid began to flow along the eight corridors of tranquillity. Prime Minister al-Mahdi became increasingly enthusiastic about the effort, spending more and more time on it. One June 29, he met with Grant and Reid for eighty minutes.

The next day, everything changed. On the morning of June 30, Reid heard a knock on his door at the Khartoum Hilton. He opened it and saw two stern armed guards. Perplexed, Reid protested, "I was hoping to go out and have some breakfast."

The guards told him he was not to leave his room and that they would bring him food. Reid called Grant, who was also staying at the Hilton.

"Have you looked outside?" Jim asked. "It looks like we've had a coup."

"Oh, God," was Reid's reply.

Grant sounded calm, not at all panicked. At some point that morning, Rahman had told him about the coup — that Sadiq al-Mahdi had been arrested and a general, Omar Hassan Ahmad al-Bashir, had taken power. It was bloodless; no one had been killed. Rahman had also said that the new leaders had specifically requested Grant's presence at a meeting later that day, at which a member of the new government would address the diplomatic corps. And then Rahman had strongly advised his boss not to go.

"As the special representative of the secretary general...you would be giving them a tacit recognition of their illegal act," said Rahman, who was efficient, by-the-book, and more cautious than his predecessor, Cole Dodge. "I will go."

Grant agreed. Rahman left; he was allowed to move about. Grant, Reid, and two other staff staying at the Hilton were apparently under "semi house arrest," says Rahman.

They stayed in their rooms. Outside, it was eerily quiet. Reid got the impression that Grant was "beavering away" on something, so he didn't bother him. The question that now hung ominously before them — the question that must have pried its way to the top of Jim's teeming list of priorities — was this: With Sadiq al-Mahdi no longer in power, what happens to Operation Lifeline Sudan?

They would soon find out.

Rahman went to the diplomatic meeting; it was uneventful. The new leader, al-Bashir, did not make an appearance. Afterward, an official of the new government called Rahman. He had a message for Jim Grant — would Mr. Grant like to meet al-Bashir? Without consulting Grant, Rahman immediately said no. The head of UNICEF was "not very keen" on meeting with al-Bashir, he told the man. Then Rahman turned the question around: if the president would like to see Mr. Grant, Mr. Grant might consider that request.

Soon Rahman got another message: yes, President al-Bashir would like to meet Mr. Grant.

Rahman, Reid, Grant, and a few other staff members got ready to meet Sudan's new president — the very first delegation to do so. Reid recalls being led out of his room by armed guards. They weren't rough, but they weren't friendly either. When they got to the street, he spotted Grant sitting in a military jeep. A flag jutted from the fender. Reid got in. He doesn't remember exactly what Grant said next, but he thinks it may have been a half joke: "This should be an interesting ride, Richard."

A convoy, including several jeeps and UNICEF's official vehicle — a Toyota Crown Royal Saloon — ferried the group through a hushed Khartoum. During the bumpy, ten-minute ride, Grant said little if anything. He seemed preoccupied, watching the buildings and streets trundle by.

The jeep stopped in front of a run-down, inconspicuous government building. The guards helped them out, led them up the steps, and opened the doors. They were ushered into a "small, dingy room," recalls Rahman. Then they were led into another spare room. There was a table with papers strewn across it.

Behind the table stood a small, tense, sallow man in a rumpled military uniform that appeared to have been worn for several days. Stubble coated his face. Grant smiled broadly as he introduced his group. The man finally sat down, Reid recalls, and then they sat down. He greeted them in a friendly but official manner. Three other men stood nearby. "Shaggy-looking fellows," says Rahman. "Highly unimpressive."

This was Omar Hassan Ahmad al-Bashir, the country's new leader. A decade and a half later, his name would be synonymous with the appallingly bloody violence and crimes against humanity in the Darfur region of Sudan; in 2008, he would become the first sitting head of state to receive an arrest warrant from the International Criminal Court in The Hague. As they stood before him on that quiet night in June 1989, Reid feared al-Bashir was about to shut down Operation Lifeline.

Stern and speaking decent English, he told them that he knew what they were doing, he was aware of the relief campaign. He asked if it was worth all of the effort, and if it really did anything for the country, according to Reid.

Grant's response was to make the same pitch he had made to rebel leader John Garang.

"Mr. President, how many children do you have?"

It is unclear how, or even whether, al-Bashir answered.

Grant provided one for him, saying something like: "You have millions of children! You have become the father of all the children in Sudan."

Al-Bashir's elbows were resting on the arms of his chair, recalls Reid, and he shifted his position after Grant's proclamation. He looked uncomfortable.

"He was completely stupefied," says Rahman. "Here is this general right from the bush who had a coup that very day and was probably totally bewildered."

Grant asked al-Bashir for his commitment to Operation Lifeline Sudan.

Reid says now: "I think he was absorbing the meaning of it...He was used to barking things...he must have sensed that he was not in a barking circumstance with Mr. Grant."

Sudan's new president then told Grant that UNICEF was welcome to continue its work.

Operation Lifeline Sudan went on. By September, 110,000 tons of food had been delivered to the worst-hit areas, halting a gruesome famine many believed was inexorable. UNICEF later conducted a mortality survey in the south and found that the death rate had not increased at all. "It was a success," says Reid. If it hadn't succeeded, he adds, "it would have been a population extinction."

Less than a month after winning al-Bashir's cooperation in Sudan, Jim Grant prepared to make another proposition. The circumstances and setting were a little bit different. He stood in his suit on a pool patio in front of giant sunflowers in Croton-on-Hudson, New York. As his sons and daughters-in-law and grandchildren watched, he asked Ellan Young, Ethel's longtime friend, to be his wife.

Chapter 13
WE WILL HAVE OUR SUMMIT

Ellan Grant Young missed her shot.

Jim Grant's new wife had accompanied him on a field visit to Nepal, and they were flying in a UN plane past the immense, jagged, crumpled brow of Mount Everest. Ellan was a professional photographer, and she was furiously snapping pictures through the window as the great peak bobbed by on the left. As the mountain receded into the distance, she swiveled in her seat toward Jim.

"Jim, I missed a really nice shot," she said. "Do you think we could go back?"

Asking a UN pilot on an official mission to turn a plane around so you could take a personal photograph was cheeky — even though Ellan probably intended no offense. If you were on the ground, rolling past an ancient ruin in a UNICEF Land Cruiser, stopping for a picture was not that big of a deal (except if it was dark; UNICEF drivers kept off the roads at night).

Ellan Grant Young apparently thought nothing of it.

Grant considered his wife's awkward request.

"Hmm," he said. "Let me see."

According to Kul Gautam, who was then UNICEF's director of planning and coordination and was part of the delegation,
Grant got up and made his way toward the front of the small
plane. He spoke with the pilot and asked if they could make
another pass by Everest. His wife would like to take a picture,
he said. Soon the plane began to turn around, and she finally got
her shot.

He had known Ellan for nearly fifty years. She had gone to
UC Berkeley with Jim and Ethel and had become Ethel's lifelong friend. Her first marriage had ended in divorce; she was the
mother of three grown children. She was personable and capri-
cious and could be a lot of fun — a "free spirit" in Jim's words.
Her tousled hair was cropped short, and her youthful face would
shine with a winsome, slightly mischievous grin.

Many UNICEF staffers were surprised at how quickly it had
happened — she and Jim were married a little over a year after
Ethel's death. It was almost as though Grant were trying to fill
a crucial staff position as quickly as possible, one that was too
important to be vacant for long.

But Ellan was not interested in being the "first lady" of
UNICEF.

Ethel's dedication to Jim and UNICEF had been virtually
unqualified and had meant countless early mornings, long
nights, and routine personal sacrifice. She had entertained a
litany of luminaries, diplomats, and staff and hosted 6:30 a.m.
working breakfasts. She had packed Jim's bags (or rather bag) as

he rushed to get to the airport. She had also immersed herself in the issues that engrossed her husband and could speak fluently on any of them. She was his liaison, sounding board, barometer, and center of gravity.

"She was his partner in all of this, without whom he might not have succeeded," says UN veteran Mehr Khan Williams, who then served as UNICEF's director of communications. "It was as much her project as it was his."

In Ethel's jarring absence, he became unmoored and disoriented.

Maybe that was why he so quickly set his sights on his wife's good friend. Maybe he could infect her with his cause, sweep her up in his churning crusade.

Except that he couldn't.

In fairness to Ellan, this was an outsized expectation. It's a lot to ask someone to marry you *and* your job — especially when that job is a high-stakes, full-tilt race every single day. It was unlikely Jim Grant would ever find another partner like Ethel, who would so completely and selflessly embrace his mission. Such a relationship had also been obviously freighted by traditional gender stereotypes that were becoming less acceptable. And so he adapted.

His new wife helped him relax a bit more, and he would remark that she was "the most positive person I have ever met." The newlyweds were very much alike in one respect: they were both perennially late. Add to that Ellan's chronic disorganization, and the wrenching change of pace was even more profound. Jim found himself in the role Ethel had once played for him: packing Ellan's bags, keeping her on schedule, helping her get out the door.

Ellan liked to travel and she liked kids — she just didn't like the official stuff. During one trip to Cambodia, when she accompanied Jim, she sneaked out of a meeting. She corralled her friend, UN photographer John Isaac, to go exploring with her. Enough of these "boring meetings," she told him. "Let's go."

Isaac reluctantly joined her. "They freaked out, because she wasn't there," he recalls. "They didn't know where she had gone. There was a search party. I said, 'Ellan, you're going to get me in trouble.' She said, 'Ah, come on.'"

"She was a riot," adds Isaac.

This tectonic life shift came during what was probably the busiest, most fevered time in Jim Grant's career, when everything he had worked for over the last nine years was nearing fruition, when the child survival revolution was reaching its crescendo, and when the plight of millions of dying, impoverished children was finally — for the first time ever — beginning to get the kind of decisive attention that could make a lasting difference for generations to come.

But that attention was fickle, fleeting — unless he could sustain it. He could not allow himself to be distracted. He had to make sure he was heard over a screeching din, as the 1989 news cycle spun at warp speed, spitting out one momentous story after the other: Iran's Ayatollah Condemns Author Salman Rushdie to Death, Chinese Students Take Over Beijing's Tiananmen Square, Oliver North Convicted in Iran Contra Scandal, George Herbert Walker Bush Inaugurated as President of the

United States, Ruptured *Exxon Valdez* Tanker Leaks Millions of Gallons of Oil into Prince William Sound, San Francisco Earthquake Kills More Than 60 People, Berlin Wall Comes Tumbling Down (Bringing the Cold War With It), US Invades Panama. Grant watched all of this, calculating how he could advance the cause of children at a time of constant tumult, how he could keep child survival at the top of political and social agendas when old orders were crumbling and new ones arising.

The World Summit for Children was the key. The summit could deliver a resounding rebuke to the centuries of apathy and indifference to the welfare of children. It could cement the movement for child survival in history, make the whole world pause and pay attention — a conspicuous milestone by which subsequent achievements and/or failures could be judged.

Though probably the most effective children's advocate ever, Grant was not the first. In 1919 — shortly after World War I and twenty-seven years before Ludwik Rajchman spurred the founding of UNICEF — a British woman named Eglantyne Jebb was arrested in London's Trafalgar Square. She was protesting the Allied economic blockade of Germany and Austria-Hungary, which persisted for eight months after the armistice, and carrying leaflets showing emaciated children and bearing the headline: OUR BLOCKADE HAS CAUSED THIS — MILLIONS OF CHILDREN ARE STARVING TO DEATH. A fierce defender of the concept that all children deserve protection — no matter where they live or who their parents are — Jebb frequently wielded a potent George Bernard Shaw quote: "I have no enemies under the age of seven." She went on with her sister to found the Save the Children Fund, one of the first international development and relief agencies.

Seventy years later, Grant was trying to make it difficult, if not impossible, for anyone to reject or ignore Jebb's — and now his — plea: save the children, save them all.

The notion of a global meeting focused on children had been thumping around in his head for a while. Peter Adamson thinks the idea may have jelled when he and Grant were flying back from a vacation with their families in Montserrat in late 1987. They were sitting on the left side of the plane, sunburned and refreshed from days of swimming and walking on the verdant Caribbean island. But Grant was itching to get back to work.

He had never really stopped working.

"Jim could not quite grasp the concept of a holiday," says Adamson.

Over breakfast one morning, Grant had announced that, as long he was in Montserrat, he might as well meet with the head of state to see how many children were immunized. Adamson had been flummoxed. *This is a vacation*, he thought. Besides, Montserrat was tiny and "didn't have any particularly great problems," he says. This did not deter Grant, even when he learned that the head of state was away and that the only person available was the finance minister. Adamson accompanied him to the meeting, and Grant peppered the finance minister with question after question about child mortality and immunization. The minister sat there stiffly, repeatedly explaining that child health was not in his job purview — he simply did not have the answers. But Grant kept volleying questions. "He clearly thought [Jim] was mad," says Adamson, "and at that moment, I agreed with him."

On the plane home, as they hurtled toward a connecting flight in Miami, Grant's assiduous tempo only increased. How could UNICEF go even further, even faster? he asked. It wasn't about the money or the technology — it was, Grant kept saying, about that ephemeral commodity that Jon Rohde had named six years ago: political will. It was about homing in on what was doable, and what was unconscionable not to do.

Then he floated the idea: "We could hold a summit for children..."

Adamson wasn't sold.

"Outside the UN, people think of these things as talk shops," he told Grant. He added that such meetings had been held in the past — with government ministers or first ladies — and not much had come of them.

Then Adamson cast out a secondary argument, an off-the-cuff afterthought: "It would be a different thing," he said, "if you could actually get heads of state to come together, not health ministers or first ladies, but heads of government."

His tone conveyed another point: *But of course, that's not possible.*

As in earlier conversations, his attempt to dissuade Grant had the exact opposite effect. Adamson doesn't remember Grant's exact words, but he recalls the essence of his reaction: *Well then, that's exactly what we'll do.*

There had never been a global summit before, not on this scale. To get all of the heads of state from around the world in one room at the same time to talk about anything was a pipe dream, in the eyes of many. And to get them to talk about children—who would sign on for that? You might as well ask them to come together for a round of trust exercises and a group hug.

The idea of a global event highlighting children's welfare did have one precedent, of a sort: the International Year of the Child in 1979 (before Grant came to UNICEF). Championed by NGOs, the UN-backed occasion had raised a new level of awareness for children's issues. But its pizzazz quickly fizzled (though it did lend some impetus to creating what would become the Convention on the Rights of the Child).

What Grant was proposing was of an entirely different order of magnitude, and he knew the suggestion would be ridiculed—at first. He told Mary Cahill: "I'll be laughed out of town."

While representatives from several developing countries applauded the idea, wealthier countries were wary that it would become a "cheque-book conference," according to UNICEF historian Maggie Black's book *Children First: The Story of UNICEF.* Recalcitrance accrued.

Bangladeshi statesman Anwarul Chowdhury, who had chaired UNICEF's board in 1985 and 1986 (and who would later become president of the UN Security Council), loved Grant's proposal. He put out feelers to see what others at the UN thought about it and was surprised by the harsh reaction.

"Many told me that it was Jim's crazy idea—it will never happen," Chowdhury recalls. "The UN structure does not allow that to happen…They used to say Jim Grant can hype anything and get carried away by himself."

One day, Grant returned to UNICEF headquarters after a tense lunchtime meeting on the summit with some junior members of the UNICEF board — and he was visibly, uncharacteristically miffed. Jim Grant hardly ever got mad, so something must have really ticked him off. His face was tight, his lips pursed, his blue eyes burning fiercely. He walked up to a woman who was sitting at her desk and put his hand on her shoulder. "We will have our summit," he told her gruffly, "despite those damned idiots!"

The first big obstacle had been very basic: UNICEF did not have the authority to convene a global summit. It would have to be called by heads of state themselves. And so Grant courted six countries — Canada, Egypt, Mali, Mexico, Pakistan, and Sweden — and persuaded them to take ownership of the summit. Representing both the industrialized and developing worlds, they became the "initiators group" and were able to work outside the suffocating thicket of UN bureaucracy.

Grant and the initiators went about slowly amassing consensus for the global meeting, mortaring in support in one corner and then in the next. By now, he had an unmatched rapport with dozens of heads of state. It was not the executive director of UNICEF who was begging them for a favor — it was their friend Jim.

When he got a no, he would simply try again. Like a persistent teenage boy determined to score a date, he would not be chastened by numerous rejections. He would shamelessly chisel away, until the reluctance became thinner, weaker, and more likely to crumble.

"Jim knew how to move step by step," says Chowdhury. "He would not be disappointed by the first no. Not the second no. Not even the third no. Not even ten noes. With each no, he would advance one bit more."

As he hammered noes into maybes and maybes into yeses, other critical fronts demanded more and more of his energy — the Convention on the Rights of the Child, the education summit being organized by Dr. Nyi Nyi, and, of course, the campaign for universal childhood immunization. He did not let up on any of them. He saw each one as a make-or-break chance to shred the aura of inevitability that shrouded lethal poverty.

One of Grant's favorite lines around this time was a moral jab, courtesy of Peter Adamson: "Morality must march with capacity." In other words, if we can save children and don't — if we have the vaccines and medicines but choose not to use them — we are morally accountable.

Another, which Grant attributed to British historian Arnold Toynbee, was dropped into dozens of speeches and articles: "Our age is the first generation since the dawn of history in which mankind dared to believe it practical to make the benefits of civilization available to the whole human race." The Toynbee citation (a fairly close paraphrase of the actual quote) probably summed up Grant's personal philosophy more aptly than anything he ever said or wrote himself. He used it so much that it sometimes sent eyes rolling.

Though he was nudging the whole world to pick up its pace, two countries were far more important than any others: China and India. Without these behemoths, universal childhood immunization could simply not be achieved. And so Grant inundated them with copious praise and attention.

During a visit to India, he told several staff members that he wasn't as worried about China achieving the goal. He knew China would reach the target — it was, after all, an autocratic, one-party state. But India was a democracy — and a messy one at that — and India would have to try harder. And so would all UNICEF India staff.

But by 1988 India was trailing badly. According to WHO estimates, coverage for the third dose of the diphtheria, pertussis, and tetanus vaccine (DPT3) was 40 percent. The other vaccines were even worse: 37 percent for the polio, 32 percent for measles, and 23 percent for tuberculosis. The numbers were low, but just a few years earlier, they had been a lot lower; in 1980 India's immunization coverage was 6 percent for DPT3 and 2 percent for polio (it had not even provided vaccines for measles or tuberculosis). The vast country had come a long way but was still woefully off target.

Another nail-biter was India's neighbor Bangladesh, which had made only minimal progress. The country's DPT3 estimate had clambered from no coverage at all in 1980 to just 16 percent in 1988 (polio and measles rates were similar). The tuberculosis figure was slightly better, going from no coverage in 1980 to 26 percent in 1988. Overall, the results were dispiriting. For Bangladesh to reach 80 percent in any of the four categories would take a miracle. Hardly anyone expected that to happen. But Bangladesh would soon surprise everybody.

China's progress, as of 1988, was simply epic, according to WHO estimates. The mammoth Communist nation had, in fact, already exceeded the 80 percent universal childhood immunization target in all categories. Two years before the deadline, it had reached an astonishing 95 percent coverage for the DPT3, 96 percent for polio, 98 percent for tuberculosis, and 95 percent for measles. Even more extraordinary: in 1980, there was no coverage for any of the vaccines. Clearly, the notoriously repressive state had done something right. It had all begun with a prod from China's pushy native son, Jim Grant.

"China had the commitment to do it, not because they want to please UNICEF, but because they are proud," says Dr. Nyi Nyi. "What you do is you play up that ego. Both Jim and I, whenever we see Chinese leaders, we always say, 'You are the largest country in the world. And you have to show the way'... The Chinese, you don't have to tell them how to achieve it, they will achieve it, by hook or by crook."

China's smashing immunization success coincided with perhaps the country's greatest crisis in a generation. On June 4, 1989 — while Grant was consumed by Operation Lifeline Sudan — the country was engulfed in chaos. After months of protests in Beijing's Tiananmen Square, Premier Li Peng ordered a ruthless military crackdown on unarmed civilians. Hundreds, possibly thousands, were killed. For many, it became the dividing line in modern Chinese history — everything was then "before" or "after" Tiananmen Square, despite the government's subsequent efforts to scrub the event out of memory and history books.

As for Grant, who considered China his "home country" and even occasionally referred to himself as Chinese, the event was a conundrum. How you do promote a country's immunization gains when its government is being roundly condemned for murdering its own citizens?

And so, as much of the rest of the world watched in horror and denounced the vicious actions of China's government, Grant kept quiet. Tiananmen Square was the news of the summer of 1989, bandied by lips across the globe—but not by his. Several staff members who worked in the UNICEF China office say that—whatever his views on the matter—he simply did not discuss it.

But what else could he do? If he joined the chorus of outrage—if he spoke about Tiananmen Square in even the vaguest way—he would alienate China's government. During the final crucial lap in the global immunization crusade, UNICEF's biggest success story so far would be clouded by violence. He also didn't want China to stop cooperating and stop immunizing—not that it necessarily would have done so. But the government's vindictive reputation was clear.

Tiananmen wasn't the only instance when he avoided criticizing China. In fact, he once offered effusive praise for the country's brutal "one-child" policy, which was adopted in 1979 and led to forced abortions, sterilizations, and female infanticides. In 1976, while president of the Overseas Development Council, Grant had written a letter to Chinese officials lauding several figures, including Mao Zedong—one of the twentieth century's biggest mass murderers—as "outstanding leaders."

He waited for the Tiananmen furor to subside. In October 1989, four months after the massacre, he flew to Beijing and met

with several Chinese officials. He had traveled to China frequently over the last decade, including to visit his second grandchild, a girl named Divindy, who was born in Beijing at the same
hospital where he himself had been born in 1922. (Divindy's
father and Grant's middle son, Jamie, was then teaching in Beijing as a Fulbright scholar.) Every time he visited, he got the red-
carpet treatment.

China's state-run news service, Xinhua, covered his October
1989 visit as though he were a head of state. During a reception
held by UNICEF, according to the Xinhua account, Grant noted
that his grandfather had come to China as a missionary exactly
one hundred years ago, adding, "At this moment, I have a feeling
of returning to my homeland." He then heralded China's immunization gains, noting that the country's vaccination coverage
was now better than Western Europe's and North America's.

In late 1989 and early 1990, Grant and the tenacious Dr.
Nyi Nyi carefully watched immunization results from around
the world, looking for bright spots and signs of trouble. Globally, the overall coverage level had by now reached about 70
percent — a staggering figure, when you consider that in 1980
it had ranged between 16 and 21 percent. The number of kids
getting immunized had more than tripled, but the gap was still
wide. They would need a lot of speed and faith to vault across
it. Nyi Nyi began to lean on UNICEF country representatives
even harder.

The pressure was crushing. No one wanted to be singled out
for not making the target — a fear that may have led to over-
optimistic projections. Buzzing around the reports from various

countries was a persnickety question: Could the numbers be trusted? If they made it, did they really make it?

As the deadline barreled at him, Grant never betrayed any nervousness or worry — at least not publicly. "He never had any doubt," says Nyi Nyi. "He never wavered."

Chapter 14
THE IMPOSSIBLE MADE POSSIBLE

In front of a wall of iconic green marble, flanked by two giant television screens, Jim Grant stood in the spot that had been occupied by the greatest and most reviled leaders in recent history — a grand pulpit for despots and freedom fighters, peacemakers and warmongers — and gazed somberly into the vast, vertiginous, domed cathedral of the UN General Assembly. Radiating out before him in curved row upon curved row of seats were the most powerful people in the world, fixing their attention on the earnest, amiable man in the blue suit, all waiting to hear what he would say. Many of them were here today because he had asked them to be, because this was one person they simply could not turn down. It was the pinnacle of Jim Grant's life — a moment many decades in the making, a personal and professional cross-roads. Here, at the largest gathering of world leaders ever held, was an unrivaled opportunity to plead his case.

At the helm of UNICEF for ten years now, he had aged. The toll of the last decade had deepened the lines on his face.

Small liver spots dotted his forehead. He was thinner, ever more slightly stooped. Bags the size of large garlic cloves bulged under his bright, narrow, almond-shaped eyes. Still, those eyes gleamed like urgent beacons, searching, imploring, defying. As he took in the scene before him, the rustling panoply of influence and prestige, the sixty-eight-year-old lawyer prepared to deliver the most important opening statement and/or closing argument he would ever make.

After nearly two years of planning, arm-twisting, and behind-the-scenes tussling, he had pulled it off: the World Summit for Children had finally materialized. In February 1990, UN secretary general Javier Pérez de Cuéllar had sent out invitations to all heads of state represented in the General Assembly (since the apartheid government of South Africa was not a member state, it was not invited). Speculation about attendance swirled — would anyone actually show up? If so, how many? Would it be a pathetic handful? Would any of the big countries show up? To tamp down the anxiety, Grant started a one-dollar office betting pool. He proffered the boldest guess, predicting fifty-three world leaders would come. All other bets were far lower. When the final tally came in, even Grant's expectations were shattered. A total of seventy-one heads of state had accepted, in addition to eighty-eight high-level representatives from other countries.

Grant had insisted on securing George H. W. Bush, saying that it would be a second-rate meeting without the US president. Bush's attendance seemed unlikely at first, and Grant asked Canadian prime minister Brian Mulroney if there was anything he could do to get him to come. Mulroney told UNICEF staff that Bush's advisers had discouraged him from attending, but that he would impress upon the American president how important it was for him to be there.

It was a turbulent international moment, when Bush was trying to stake his claim in the post–Cold War world; getting him to focus on the issue of saving children was like asking a cutthroat investment banker to spend some time in a soup kitchen. A few weeks before the summit, on September 11, 1990, Bush had addressed the US Congress about Iraq's recent invasion of Kuwait and called for a "new world order...in which nations recognize the shared responsibility for freedom and justice." He was beginning to make a case for US military involvement in the Persian Gulf.

Whether or not Bush would show up became an open spigot of anxious conjecture right up until a day or two before the meeting. "The Americans kept us in suspense," says Kul Gautam.

The brewing conflict in the Persian Gulf was also on Grant's mind — he was worried it would siphon media attention away from the summit. Fortunately, it didn't seem to have much of an effect. In the month before the meeting, interest in children's issues soared among journalists — fueling stories in news outlets all over the world, including, in the United States, the *New York Times*, *Time* magazine, and CBS's *60 Minutes*. Grant was suddenly a sought-after media guest and was featured as the Person of the Week on ABC's *World News Tonight*. A week before the meeting, candlelight vigils highlighting the needs of struggling children drew more than a million people all over the globe. The preventable plight of dying and suffering children was now in plain view before the eyes of the world, as never before. Grant wanted to keep it there for as long as possible.

The sense of urgency swirling around the summit was intensified by the immunization campaign's imminent deadline and by the recent entering into force of the "Magna Carta for Children." On September 2, 1990, the Convention on the Rights of the Child had snared the requisite twenty country ratifications to become officially activated; it had been adopted and opened for signature by the UN General Assembly on November 20, 1989. The convention's fifty-four articles — which afford children a set of basic rights — had, in fact, been ratified faster than any other human rights treaty. The treaty had languished for years — until Allegra Morelli and other UNICEF staffers finally persuaded Grant to back it. The great mesmerizer's involvement had, once again, proven decisive.

At 6:30 on Sunday morning, Grant and the UN secretary general, Javier Pérez de Cuéllar, had stood with several senior UNICEF officials at the entrance to the UN's North Delegates' Lounge — like an eager wedding party at the head of a monstrous receiving line — and greeted heads of state as they filtered in for a buffet breakfast. Voluble and grinning, Grant was given to guffaws of delight as he jostled hands. Pérez de Cuéllar was reserved and mild-mannered; he often wore heavy glasses and a slightly startled expression. When shaking the secretary general's hand, most heads of state addressed him formally, calling him "Mr. Secretary General." But when many of them saw Grant, according to Kul Gautam, their formality dissolved. They gripped his arm enthusiastically or hugged him, yelling out "Jim!" or "Jim, my friend!"

But Pérez de Cuéllar didn't seem to mind — Grant had charmed him, too. The Peruvian diplomat appreciated the glory the "Mad American" had brought to the UN and, in turn, gave him pretty much free rein. This would not be the case with his successor, Egyptian bureaucrat Boutros Boutros-Ghali, who would come to power in 1992 and would try to shorten Grant's leash.

Even with leaders he personally liked, Grant kept his greetings on the receiving line as brief as he could. He knew it would take at least two and a half hours to process all the heads of state, which meant they had about two minutes to welcome and escort each one inside (including their entourages and security details). They had to accommodate seventy-one motorcades in rapid succession (some of them with five cars each) and coordinate with UN security; the New York City Police Department; the US Coast Guard; the US Bureau of Alcohol, Tobacco, Firearms and Explosives; the US State Department; and the Secret Service. They then had to herd everyone out of the limos and into the buildings before the 9:30 a.m. start time. The logistical challenges were Byzantine and off-putting — nothing like this had ever been attempted before.

"It got messy," says UNICEF veteran Fouad Kronfol, who was in the greeting party. Traffic snarls snaked along First Avenue, and some leaders ended up getting out of their limos and walking. But everyone was a good sport about it, Kronfol adds. "They were gracious."

Another quandary: persuading some leaders to be the first to arrive. Not everyone could get there at 8:30 or 9:00 a.m. In an environment of rigid protocol in which every leader expects fawning treatment, how do you not cause offense by telling one prime minister that he needs to leave his hotel at 6:00 a.m., while another can lounge around till 8:00 a.m.? How do you soothe a bevy of bruised, overweening egos?

The solution: you convince one very important leader to be part of the sunrise crowd. British prime minister Margaret Thatcher was asked if she wouldn't mind coming at 6:30 a.m. — so that the other early birds wouldn't feel slighted. The Iron Lady agreed. A special "Breakfast with Maggie" was organized. Grant escorted Thatcher up to the lounge, and many leaders clamored for a chance to mingle with Maggie.

There were other hitches. In one heart-stopping moment, a bomb threat was intercepted by UN security. Carl Tinstman, who had been tapped by Grant to act as UNICEF's security point person, was in the security control room when the threat was phoned in. Panic locked him in its vise. "Racing through my mind is: *Do we go down and tell them?*" recalls Tinstman. "*Do we evacuate all seventy heads of state and government?...We certainly don't want to have a bomb go off and kill seventy heads of state!*"

It turned out to be a hoax. The meeting went on.

One of the most trying crises took root weeks before, when special agreements that would be signed by all participating leaders were being negotiated. Grant didn't want the summit to be another "talk shop" (as Adamson had named such ineffectual meetings). The meeting had cost close to $3 million to organize; an additional $2.1 million had been slated for "mobilization activities." He knew what critics were saying and needed to show the money was well-spent. He also knew a whiff of hypocrisy might cling to the rarefied air during this historic occasion: many of these leaders, including Thatcher, had cut funding for children's programs or had enacted policies contributing to the suffering of their youngest citizens. In many cases, they were very much part of the problem. Why give politicians who had essentially harmed children the chance to burnish their public image for all the world to see?

Because Grant wanted to goad them into changing their policies. He wanted the leaders to walk away with a promise in their pocket — a promise he would do his utmost to make them keep.

Two documents were drawn up to extract that promise. World leaders had agreed in advance to sign them when they attended the meeting, but only after a protracted and testy negotiation. The World Declaration on the Survival, Protection and Development of Children bound participants "to give every child a better future" and set out a program that included a pledge to promote ratification of the Convention on the Rights of the Child, to "work for a solid effort of national and international action to enhance children's health," and to "work for a global attack on poverty." The accompanying and bluntly named Plan of Action had the real muscle, calling on governments to do a series of very explicit things, all by the year 2000. Among them: cut child mortality by one-third, cut maternal mortality by half, cut child malnutrition by half, eliminate guinea worm disease, eradicate polio globally, eliminate neonatal tetanus by 1995, eliminate iodine deficiency disorders, eliminate vitamin A deficiency disorders, and provide universal access to safe drinking water and basic education. Altogether, there were twenty-seven summit goals. Achieving them, it was believed, could save fifty million children's lives over the next decade.

The goals covered a wide range of issues — Grant could certainly no longer be accused of a narrow, myopic focus. The near success of the immunization effort had proven that sweeping progress on a global scale was indeed "doable" and had justified a broader and bolder agenda. It was time for Jim Grant's phase two.

The UN wasn't used to meeting goals with such time-bound specificity, and they made people nervous. As the language of the declaration and Plan of Action was being considered in the weeks before the gathering, some members of the UNICEF board stubbornly fought it. In one case, a diplomat from the Netherlands spurned quantifiable targets as a bad idea. This man essentially held the whole process hostage, says Gautam, who was involved in drafting the documents.

So Grant did what he called an end run — he simply went over the Dutch diplomat's head. He called the government minister who oversaw development cooperation in the Netherlands and mentioned the diplomat's opposition. Soon, the man received a call from the Dutch government instructing him to drop his objections and clarifying that "our government from the highest level supports Mr. Grant's approach," recalls Gautam. "As you can imagine, this guy lost face."

The thorniest protest over language in the summit documents came from the Catholic Church. A number of European
and Asian countries had insisted that the issue of family planning be addressed in the summit declaration as a way to combat population growth (this did not refer to abortion, but rather
to "birth spacing"). The Vatican lodged a stern protest. While
it was not a member of the General Assembly, the Holy See
enjoyed "permanent observer status."

"Jim Grant wanted the Catholic Church to be on our side,"
says Gautam. "The only way we could have them on our side was
not to speak about family planning...But there were many countries who said we absolutely have to have it, so what do we do?"

The only way out, says Gautam, was "creative wordsmith-
ing." The phrase "family planning" was changed to "responsible
planning of family size."

That seemed to do the trick.

"It took weeks to agree to those three or four words," says
Gautam.

The crisis was seemingly averted — until it wasn't. On the
day of the summit, attendees were given big, bound copies of
the summit declaration and the Plan of Action, translated into
each of the six official UN languages. Everything looked okay
until a Vatican monsignor (the pope couldn't make it) noticed
that the French version of the declaration did not contain the
agreed-upon phrase. The words *planification familiale* leered
conspicuously from the page. Apparently, the UN Translations
Service had goofed. In the ultrasensitive milieu of the General
Assembly, it was a tiny ripple that could become a tsunami.

Gautam was standing on a balcony in the Economic and Social Council (ECOSOC) chamber when he got an urgent message from Grant, via a UN page. The diminutive Nepali raced downstairs to find his slightly agitated boss.

"What happened?" Grant demanded.

Gautam explained the error and said that the Holy See might not sign the declaration. Grant listened, whispered, "Do something!" and then whooshed off.

Gautam quickly consulted with UNICEF's Marco Vianello-Chiodo, the towering, bearded Italian who had earlier secured Italy's transformative $100 million contribution. The two men came up with a possible solution: ask the Vatican to sign the English text, with an addendum explaining that the signature applies to the English version only. UNICEF would ensure all other versions were corrected posthaste.

The Vatican balked at first. Gautam repeatedly assured the monsignor it would be okay. Eventually, he relented.

The galvanic atmosphere at the UN on the morning of September 30 crackled with an undeniable sense that something big was happening. More than three thousand journalists had converged on the General Assembly, and a scrum of celebrities — including UNICEF ambassadors Audrey Hepburn, Peter Ustinov, Harry Belafonte, and Liv Ullmann — lent the event the aura of a Hollywood movie premiere. Enormous photos of smiling children peered down from the walls of the General Assembly and ECOSOC chamber. And there were actual children, too.

Boys and girls from the attendees' respective countries, many wearing colorful traditional garb, escorted the leaders to their seats. Some of the children looked intimidated; others seemed excited, in awe of the spectacle unfolding all around them.

The city of New York had marked the occasion the night before by dimming lights at the Empire State Building, the Chrysler Building, the Pan Am Building, and the Pepsi sign on the East River (which Jim Grant used to see from his old office window). The Teenage Mutant Ninja Turtles concert at Radio City Music Hall honored the children of the world with a moment of silence, as did the Mets during a game at Shea Stadium.

Before the opening session, world leaders were asked to pose for a photo — all seventy-one of them. The photo shoot became a logistical feat of its own — how do you make sure no one is grimacing or squinting? A team from the Eastman Kodak company donated their services for this task. The result is a slightly stilted panoramic group shot, taken in front of a large blue curtain, which almost resembles a motley fifth-grade class picture: some leaders are smiling, some are not; some appear at ease, some do not; some seem happy to be there, some do not. It was nonetheless a fascinating snapshot of a pivotal moment. As one former UNICEF staffer derisively — and perhaps hyperbolically — quips: "Half the people in that photo are dictators."

One of those dictators was summit "co-chair" Moussa Traoré, the president of Mali. Wearing a big, blue, broad-shouldered robe and a neat, white, religious-looking cap, he stood out in a sea of muted suits and ties. A thuggish general who had taken power in a 1968 military coup, he oversaw a repressive and corrupt regime. This "president for life" would himself shortly be ousted in another coup after ordering soldiers to gun down unarmed, pro-democracy protesters in March 1991. But today, General Traoré got to play the part of a dignified statesman and had the honor of inaugurating one of the UN's most auspicious gatherings ever. Wearing glasses and speaking French in a soft, low voice, he announced: "I declare open the World Summit for Children."

The summit schedule, drawn up with military exactitude, allowed each head of state between three and five minutes to speak during the afternoon session. Anybody who overran their time would be chastised with a red flashing light and the slam of a gavel. Since he was not a head of state, Jim Grant had initially not been permitted to speak at all. When the possibility was broached during the planning process, several diplomats were adamant: Grant cannot speak. The man behind the summit would have to keep quiet. "This made many of us really sad," Gautam says.

After a concerted lobbying effort, resistance yielded: Grant would be given four minutes — the same amount of time allotted to some heads of state. But four minutes was only enough time for a quick exhortation; Grant wanted to make a case for investing in a range of specific opportunities to advance child survival. To buy more time, Adamson suggested including a fifteen-minute video, arguing that the meeting couldn't be all speeches. The summit organizers agreed but said it could run no longer than eleven minutes. "We stretched it," admits Adamson, who added one more minute to the film. Adamson purposefully wrote the video script and Grant's speech to comprise one continuous presentation. So now, Grant essentially had sixteen minutes, instead of four.

The video followed remarks by the secretary general, leaders of several of the "initiator" countries, and President George Bush. At the last minute, the State Department had confirmed Bush's attendance. But the US president would have to cut out early.

To the annoyance of many, Bush skipped the entire afternoon session, when most other leaders spoke and when substantive discussions took place. This compounded an already widespread frustration with the United States over its refusal to sign the Convention on the Rights of the Child (a position stemming, in part, from conservatives' fears that the treaty prohibited capital punishment for minors and that it might limit parents' disciplinary options). But Bush's brief appearance would do what Grant had hoped — bolster media attention for the summit and help convey the magnitude of the event. It did something else, too. According to the *New York Times*, his presence "forced the Bush administration to focus on the problems of children in a way that the United States Government has not done in a decade."

As his bespectacled image hovered on the two large television screens on either side of the stage, Bush reiterated his call for a "new world order" and for improving the well-being of children "who will live in and lead this new world." He was eloquent, but his words sounded pat and tailored for this audience.

After Bush's speech, the giant TV screens flashed a white title: *341: A Film for the World Summit for Children*. Photos of babies were accompanied by a few eerie, sparse piano notes. The babies' faces then morphed into the faces of leaders in the audience, including Bush. Then Peter Adamson's crisp, somber, British voice floated into the General Assembly Hall: "We were all children once…"

His narration continued: "But some children never grow up to their potential. And some never grow up at all."

Forty-five seconds into the video, as children's faces faded in and out, white numbers start flashing. With each number came a loud, clicking noise. The unmistakable sound of a clock ticking.

The meaning of the numbers was soon made brutally clear by Adamson's serene voice: "forty thousand a day…a quarter of a million a week…a child every two seconds."

Each of those white numbers was a tombstone, marking a child's death. And they kept flashing every two seconds, a jolting, flinch-inducing reminder. By the end of the film — which went on to explain how the deaths could be stopped — the grim counter had reached 341. Three hundred forty-one young lives extinguished just in the last twelve minutes.

As the video vanished from the two screens, Jim Grant prepared to start his speech. The grandiose congregation was silent as he began.

Your Excellencies, ladies and gentlemen, children…

Now we know why there is a Summit for Children.

One week ago, over a million candles were lit for the success of this Summit — each candle a prayer, in whatever religion, that today will be a turning point in the lives of children.

A turning point for children everywhere, but especially for the children of the quiet catastrophe.

Never before have these children taken center stage. Never before has their voice been heard in a forum such as this, but as the Executive Director of UNICEF, it is my prayer that, with this Summit, their time has come. It is a prayer that this Summit will make the 1990s into a decade of doing the doable for the world's children. And the new horizons of the doable are defined for us in the Declaration and Plan of Action we will be considering today.

It shows that child deaths can be cut by a third — and it shows how. It shows that child malnutrition can be cut by half — and it shows how. It shows that a better quality of life can be achieved for our children — and it shows how.

To lead this effort, we here today can raise a new standard for children of the years to come, and on that standard, on that banner, is writ large a principle — the principle of a first call for our children, the principle that children should be the first to benefit from mankind's successes and the last to suffer from its failures.

I want to thank the agencies of the United Nations family who have widened the horizons of the doable. I want to thank the thousands of nongovernmental organizations who have made this Summit of yours into a global mobilization. I want to thank the initiators who had the courage — I repeat, the courage — to call this. And on behalf of UNICEF and the world's children I also want to thank you — you who have found time for the important in the midst of the immediate, you who have made this the largest gathering of world leaders in history.

Your Excellencies, there could be no greater gathering, and there could be no greater cause. For we are confronted here today with the noblest goal which mankind could ever set for itself—protection for the lives and the normal growth of all the world's children. It is within the power of those gathered here to achieve that great goal in our time.

And it is within the power of those gathered here to make this Summit into a turning point, not only for the world's children, but truly for us all. For it is on how we bring up our children that our civilization is measured, our humanity is tested and our future is shaped.

[Source: Statements by Heads of State or Government at the World Summit for Children, United Nations, 29–30 September 1990]

The World Summit for Children is widely considered UNICEF's finest moment — a watermark in the history of the UN and international development. It landed in the *1992 Guinness Book of World Records* for being the "largest meeting of heads of state and heads of government" and spurred many other such global "summits" over the years. The gathering's time-bound, specific targets for fighting child mortality, poverty, and other ills set a new standard and would eventually inspire the creation of the UN's Millennium Development Goals (MDGs). These eight antipoverty benchmarks, which have accelerated progress in many areas of health and development, are also time-bound: on December 31, 2015, the world decides if they have been met.

Grant did not bask in the summit's glow for long. At a post-summit meeting with his staff, a beaming general congratulated his weary foot soldiers, telling them: "You should all feel very good...on a scale of one to ten, it was certainly an eleven!" He said the gathering's success had represented many "can't be dones...that were done." He then told them he was going to sleep more than he ever had since World War II.

After that brief respite, he would start pestering, pushing each leader who had signed the pledge to craft a "national plan to action." Over the next four years, he would meet with more than one hundred presidents and prime ministers to check on their progress. He wasn't about to let anyone wiggle out of anything.

By the summer of 1991, they finally had the numbers. And those numbers added up to more than 80 percent. Though WHO and UNICEF would not officially certify it until a few months later — at a strange, stilted UN ceremony hosted by Audrey Hepburn — Grant and Nyi Nyi were now confident that the world had achieved universal childhood immunization. They could now say they had done what so many had pronounced impossible.

A total of sixty-four developing countries had actually made the target, and many others had come close (though some in Africa still trailed badly behind). Among developing countries, it was reported, immunization coverage rose to 90 percent for tuberculosis, 85 percent for DPT, 83 percent for polio, and 80 percent for measles.

An estimated three million young lives were being saved each year through vaccines against six killer diseases and as many as one million more were being saved through the increased use of oral rehydration salts — four million lives that had once been considered dispensable, four million cataclysms of grief unnoticed by the Western world. But now, those deaths had been prevented, and many people had seen it happen. Once it was widely known that impoverished children did not have to die in mass numbers, it was a lot harder to ignore those children. It was a lot harder to duck behind the comfortable cloak of fatalism — that cloak was in tatters.

The summit may have been Grant's crowning accomplishment, but universal childhood immunization was, by far, his most significant triumph. He had sparked a movement involving millions of people in every corner of the world, mobilizing whole societies. He dubbed it "the largest single peacetime collaborative effort in world history."

His "grand alliance for children" had included governments, hundreds of NGOs (such as Fazle Abed's Bangladesh Rural Advancement Committee), other UN institutions (such as the World Health Organization and World Bank), relief organizations, development agencies (including USAID), a wide range of donors (governments, corporations, and others), foundations (most importantly the Rockefeller Foundation), and service organizations (like Rotary International). It also comprised churches, mosques, synagogues, schools, media organizations, parents, doctors, nurses, Boy Scouts, volunteers, police officers, soldiers, and trade unions. The imperturbable Dr. Bill

Foege — a former director of the US Centers for Disease Control and Prevention, who led the Atlanta-based Taskforce on Child Survival — had helped Grant secure and maintain critical links among many organizations and funders. The once recalcitrant World Health Organization had provided critical technical assistance, monitored results, ensured vaccine safety and quality, and dramatically improved cold chain technology. (The WHO's Ralph Henderson, who led its EPI program, deserves considerable credit, including for some of the initial gains made in the late 1970s and early 1980s before GOBI was launched.)

The "real heroes" — as Audrey Hepburn would later note during the immunization certification ceremony — were the government health workers and volunteers who administered the vaccines. Many had braved bombs and land mines, negotiated treacherous mountain passes, and risked the threat of gunfire and abduction. In Turkey, two government immunizers who had been traveling by donkey to remote, blizzard-prone areas to deliver vaccines had frozen to death.

In Grant's mind, the true significance of UCI went far beyond immunization, says Jon Rohde. "Jim really wasn't about immunization," he says. He "was about reaching everybody and then doing more."

Indeed, the immunization campaign marked the first time a basic lifesaving service had been made available to so many on such a wide scale. "Never before in history had something been done for everybody," Rohde says.

But they had to keep reaching everybody, year after year. They had made a ragged, breathless, flat-out sprint to the finish line — but now that they had crossed it, they couldn't stop running. And it wasn't just UNICEF staff — countries that had funneled resources and energy and manpower into breakneck immunization drives would have to keep doing it (and some simply weren't equipped to). How were they going to maintain all this? What was the next move?

Grant hoped the summit goals might help. Many staffers knew that the one thing, the only thing, that would keep everything moving was Jim Grant himself.

Another pesky fear pulled at the seams of the otherwise celebratory mood: Would the numbers hold up? Would the entire enterprise be called into question? Grant never gave voice to any of these concerns, though they quietly nibbled away at some other staffers. India was the biggest quandary. Without the vast country, of course, the global goal would not have been achieved. It was reported in the 1992 edition of *The State of the World's Children* that India had exceeded the 1990 target, reaching 97 percent coverage for the tuberculosis vaccine, 92 percent for DPT, 93 percent for polio, and 87 percent for measles. But many UNICEF staffers were suspicious. Those figures seemed stratospherically optimistic.

Dr. F. Marc LaForce, a revered global health pioneer and veteran of the smallpox effort who would later oversee a review of the UNICEF immunization campaign, thinks the India results were questionable. "C'mon, give me a break, Jim," LaForce says now with a chuckle, in reference to India's sky-high statistics. "What happened was, in the end, it was clear he wasn't going to be able to make it unless India came in at a pretty high number."

And if India didn't make it, then the world wouldn't make it either.

"I'm surprised more people didn't come out and pull the rug out from under him," says one former high-level UNICEF staffer. "Because...I don't think we really did reach 80 percent...I think we were talking about somewhere in the 70 to 80 percent range from most people, and they were trying hard."

UNICEF and WHO depend upon countries to supply them with immunization data, and all of these figures are estimates that are subject to error and manipulation. The data have improved significantly over the last two decades, and the two agencies have developed more comprehensive and rigorous ways of measuring it. In 1999, UNICEF and WHO harmonized their respective processes for collecting and analyzing immunization information, coming up with a joint reporting system. In 2000, they conducted a retrospective review of immunization estimates going back to 1980.

Not surprisingly, some figures changed.

So, based on the latest information, did UNICEF and its partners really achieve 80 percent child immunization in 1990?

No, but they came very close.

Globally, they reached 76 percent coverage for the third dose of DPT, 76 percent for polio, 73 percent for measles, and 81 percent for tuberculosis — so, overall, about 76.5 percent. That's up from between 16 and 21 percent in 1980. Among developing countries and countries "in transition," according to a recent WHO analysis, the rates were very similar: 74 percent for DPT, 74 percent for polio, 72 percent for measles, and 82 percent for tuberculosis.

The total result is still astounding, a near quadrupling of immunization coverage for children under age one in the span of ten years. And it happened despite a major global recession, despite a surging population, despite plunging incomes, despite wars, despite widespread cuts in health services.

The impact was simply colossal. The number of measles cases plummeted from 4,211,431 in 1980 to 1,374,083 in 1990 (even though the number of new births went up by fifteen million during the same period). Pertussis cases fell from nearly 2,000,000 to 476,374. The incidence of diphtheria was cut by two-thirds and polio by half (polio cases would ultimately drop by 99 percent). These ancient, fatal diseases had stalked children for thousands of years, routinely and relentlessly laying claim to the weakest and most vulnerable. The antidisease campaigns of the 1950s and 1960s had temporarily held off some of these pervasive scourges, but now, across the globe, they were being beaten back with overwhelming force.

The revised immunization numbers also show stunning progress during that period in individual countries, many of which — even if they didn't hit 80 percent — made huge, historic leaps. Bangladesh, once widely considered a development "basket case," did not provide any of the four vaccines in 1980. By 1988, coverage rates had not climbed very much, hovering between 13 and 26 percent. But by 1990, in the space of just two years, they all shot up to 65 percent or above; the tuberculosis immunization rate hit 86 percent. Bangladesh did not make 80 percent in total, but it does not seem to have fudged any numbers either.

And how did India fare in the new calculation?

India also pulled off a remarkable feat, pushing its estimated DPT3 coverage from 6 percent to 70 percent, its best-performing category. Tuberculosis and polio coverage both topped out at 66 percent, and measles made it to 56 percent. In each category, though, a glaring gap of 20 to 30 percentage points yawned between the old estimates and the new ones.

Grant can't be held accountable for the overall changing quality of data, of course. But what if he knew that some statistical corners were cut — and effectively let it happen? Nyi Nyi insists that he and Grant did not allow any tweaking of numbers, not on the part of UNICEF staff anyway (he notes that a few countries may have boosted their figures but that this was often out of UNICEF's control). The former UCI taskmaster says that the figures available at the time showed that the goal was indeed reached. "We would never cheat," he says. "We would never even dream of it just to say we have achieved it."

Several UNICEF staffers say they believe some finagling of data occurred, whether it was committed by the countries themselves, UNICEF staff, or both. Most people don't think it was widespread.

"There are two ways of looking at this," offers LaForce. "One way is to really shake your finger and say, 'tut, tut, tut'... I think Jim was way beyond that. Jim recognized the importance of that 80 percent in terms of opening up a whole new set of doors."

He adds that the indomitable UNICEF chief "has always been one of my heroes" and calls the immunization gains that were actually realized — even if they fell short of 80 percent — "absolutely astonishing...one hell of an achievement."

Whether or not the goal was met in full, it was important for Grant to be able to say he had made it. It was important for fund-raising. It was important for kindling political will. It was important for maintaining the morale of the millions of people around the world who had answered his call to put children first. By saying he had made it, he would save more lives, it was as simple as that. It was a moral and strategic consideration. The inveterate marketer in him knew he couldn't say, *We almost did it. We were this close!* It had to be: *We did it!*

Chapter 15
WHAT WOULD IT TAKE?

"That sounds like a rocket-propelled grenade."

On the outskirts of Sarajevo, sitting in the cramped confines of an armored personnel carrier, they listened as a firefight seethed around them. Jim Grant, Jon Rohde, Alan Court, and a few others were part of a UNICEF delegation visiting the former Yugoslavia as it fell into bitter, internecine violence. A French crew was manning the carrier, which was part of a larger convoy. Earlier, they had been able to pop their heads out of metal hatches and look around, but then the shooting began. Now the hatches were closed, and as the bulky vehicle lumbered along, the group couldn't see anything. They could hear bullets pinging off the sides of the carrier. Then came a sudden, screeching *whoosh!*

Grant was the one who identified the grenade's nerve-jangling sound, as though naming the song of some rare bird.

"Very good, sir!" said a French crew member. "You recognize it."

Court was impressed and puzzled. He leaned toward Grant. "How did you recognize it?" he asked.

"You forget," Grant replied, perhaps smiling and raising his eyebrows, "I used to be in the infantry in the Second World War. I recognize those sounds."

He then added that it looked like their current situation "could get a bit hairy."

The violence had erupted after four of Yugoslavia's six republics — Croatia, Slovenia, Macedonia, and Bosnia and Herzegovina — declared independence in 1991 and 1992. There were three main sides to the conflict: the Bosniaks, who were Muslims; the Croats, who were Catholics; and the Serbs, who were Orthodox Christians. In the Bosnian republic, a proudly multicultural society, all three groups had, until recently, lived in relative harmony for the past several decades. But Serbian nationalists, urged on by the vitriol of leaders Slobodan Milošević and Radovan Karadžić, wanted to prevent the breakup of the Serb-dominated Yugoslav federation and to create a "Greater Serbia." Fighting broke out in Slovenia and Croatia in 1991 and spread into Bosnia in 1992. Much better armed than any of the other factions and backed by the Yugoslav army, Serbs began taking over much of Bosnia, leaving a blood-soaked path in their wake. As the violence escalated — the worst in Europe since World War II — acts of revolting, confounding brutality were committed by all sides. Women and girls were systematically raped, families were herded into concentration camps, and children were mutilated and murdered in front of their helpless parents. Everyone suffered immeasurably, but it was the Bosnian Muslims who bore the unforgiving brunt of the mounting atrocities, as Serbian forces began a calculated campaign to expel and exterminate them. The Serbian leaders were bent on genocide, or, as it was euphemistically called, "ethnic cleansing."

The city of Sarajevo, a sweeping, pretty patchwork of red terra-cotta roofs, pointed minarets, and blocky modern buildings, lies in a basin ringed by the Dinaric Alps. The looming, knuckled mountains — once known for their beauty — became suddenly synonymous with doom. It was in those mountains that Serbian snipers took up their positions. During the medieval-like, nearly four-year siege of Sarajevo, which began in April 1992, the snipers deliberately targeted noncombatants, picking off children and women, killing people as they crossed the street or sat in their living rooms. Nowhere was safe. Death rained down not only in the form of bullets, but also mortar bombs, which were sent screaming into hospitals, schools, libraries, crowded squares. Many families holed up in their basements. The Serbs even shelled funerals held for their previous victims.

This purposeful slaughter was, shamefully, allowed to happen. No one did anything to stop it. When Grant and his convoy arrived in September 1992, the UN was already drawing criticism for not halting the sniper and mortar attacks. UN airlifts were bringing critical relief into the city and other areas, and many aid workers were heroically distributing it. The blue-helmeted UN peacekeepers protected aid convoys but did little else. The crux of it wasn't their fault — peacekeepers act at the behest of the UN Security Council, and the Security Council had set a very limited mandate and low troop levels for Bosnia. The troops were ordered not to take sides. UN peacekeepers were regularly fired on with apparent impunity, and by 1995, 167 of them would be killed. The residue of failure that clung to the peacekeeping operation would only grow thicker and would, many people believe, help pave the way for the shocking Srebrenica massacre in July 1995. Led by the "Butcher of Bosnia" — the deranged and sadistic military commander Ratko Mladić — Serbian forces would easily overrun a meager Dutch UN peacekeeping force in this so-called UN safe haven and proceed to methodically torture, kill, and maim more than eight thousand Muslim men and boys. The unadulterated horror of Srebrenica was an embarrassing low point for the UN: the world body's first of four principal aims forged in the ashes of World War II — to "save succeeding generations from the scourge of war" — suddenly seemed hollow and meaningless. It wasn't that they had tried and failed. They never really tried in the first place — they had been ordered not to. NATO air strikes would finally end the slaughter.

Even as early as the fall of 1992, the circumstances in Bosnia were numbingly grim. What could Jim Grant do? He had no say over peacekeeping or the anemic international response to the atrocities. But maybe — if only for a short time — he could get critical aid to more Bosnian children. In a vacuum of international apathy, maybe he could temporarily halt the bloodshed.

He wanted to reprise his Days of Tranquillity — the idea that had worked so well in El Salvador and Sudan (and had also been successfully applied, in different ways, in Lebanon, Uganda, Afghanistan, and Iraq). In 1991, UNICEF had even managed to arrange a water-based zone of tranquillity to facilitate the delivery of aid by boat to the nearby Croatian coastal town of Dubrovnik, then under heavy bombardment (the "siege of Dubrovnik" ended in May 1992; the Serbs would save most of their fury for Sarajevo).

Why shouldn't Grant give tranquillity a try throughout the disintegrating Yugoslavia? If he could get Omar al-Bashir — a pitiless megalomaniac — to agree to put down guns in Sudan, why couldn't he persuade the murderous Serbian president Slobodan Milošević to do the same in Sarajevo?

Many attempted ceasefires had failed in Bosnia. Grant thought his would be different, because it would be about children. As in other conflicts, children would foster a common cause. Children would be a "zone of peace." But there are some people in the world so heartless and so devoid of conscience that not even saving the lives of innocents will sway them. As a rash of post–Cold War conflicts in Somalia, the Persian Gulf, and other places hampered new hopes for peace, Bosnia would test Grant as never before.

The task was made all the more urgent by the creep of winter in a place where many had no heat or electricity. Grant's goal, as he described it to staff and reporters alike, was to "winterize" children through the battle-rent region.

His convoy made it through the firefight without incident and took the delegation to the fortresslike post office in downtown Sarajevo. It was here, in the center of this battered, blackened, smoking city, that they would stay.

As they were leaving the office of Bosnian president Alija Izetbegović, after quickly securing his cooperation for a cease-fire, Alan Court noticed sharpshooters perched on the roof of the presidential palace. They were firing into the mountains.

He pointed them out to Grant. "You see these shooters shooting out?" Court said. "And no firing coming in?"

Grant looked up. "What are they doing?"

"They're trying to attract artillery fire to impress you," Court said. "They do that for visitors."

Grant was flabbergasted. The returning artillery fire could kill people. He had been "very sympathetic" with the plight of the Bosnian Muslims, says Court, and believed unreservedly that they were "the good guys." He was disappointed to see Muslim soldiers firing their guns unprovoked — even worse, doing so for his benefit. The Bosnian Muslim cause was indeed a just one — they had every right to defend themselves from the threat of annihilation. These shooters seemed to make a mockery of that right, though all the factions were guilty of such behavior. "He was horrified when he saw that everybody was playing these games," Court recalls.

Grant had sent Court to the former Yugoslavia in August to figure out what UNICEF could do to help children there. Before Grant's trip in September, Court got a call from Mary Cahill. She told him that Jim, now seventy years old, was not feeling well. "Get him to take it easy," Cahill suggested. "You've got to be kidding!" Court replied with a chuckle, then added: "I'll do what I can."

The resourceful, gangly Briton had traveled throughout the region before Grant's visit. He told his boss he had found that most ordinary citizens — whether Muslims, Serbs, or Croats — were good; it was the leaders who were bad. He also knew from firsthand experience that the snipers were not exclusively Serbian. During one visit to a Serbian-held part of Sarajevo, he was standing on a dirt sidewalk near his unmarked car when — *Boof!* — the ground a few inches from his right foot exploded in a fist of dust. He froze. A sniper from somewhere had just tried to kill him.

"I was transfixed," he recalls. His driver, a Croat, bolted out of the car, grabbed Court, and stuffed him headfirst through the front passenger window (no easy task — Court is well over six feet tall). His body scraped the window frame. It hurt. But he wasn't about to complain. The driver then ran back around, jumped in, started the car, and floored the gas pedal. As the Volkswagen Golf sped away and Court tried to adjust himself in the seat, the driver explained: "Armor-piercing...every five round for standard Yugoslav Kalashnikov...armor-piercing."

The bullet that had punched into the dirt inches from Court's foot was an armor-piercing round. That was news to Court, but even more surprising was where the bullet had come from: the roof of the Bosnian presidential palace. It was a Bosnian Muslim sniper that had targeted him, not a Serb. He later told Grant that he had been shot at and shelled by everybody — Serbs, Croats, and Muslims — and, as a result, he was "violently neutral."

After their meeting with the Bosnian president — in the very building from which Court's would-be killer had fired his shot — Grant went to the UN's main base in the city center. He had a lunch date with a French general who led the peace-keeping operation. During the meeting, he was treated to yet another artillery show. A series of thundering booms punctuated the afternoon, and Grant again identified the sounds: mortars.

Like before, he learned, the volleys were outgoing, sent to attract Serbian fire — and to impress him.

When they saw that he was not impressed, says Court, the mortars stopped.

For the trip back to the post office, Court borrowed an unarmored UN Land Cruiser to transport himself, Grant, and two members of a film crew — a "stupid" decision, as he would soon realize.

To get back, they had to drive down Sarajevo's "Sniper Alley," an exposed, bullet-raked, bloodstained boulevard, where snipers routinely shot at cars and pedestrians. Court had never been fired upon while in a vehicle with the UNICEF insignia. But this one was a generic UN truck.

He drove fast. Then the bullets came, striking the car. Court doesn't think they were directly shot at — the bullets may have ricocheted off nearby cars, walls, or lampposts. Nonetheless, he wrenched the car left, then right, zigzagging down the street, trying not to be an easy target. Sitting in the back, the two film-makers were terrified. They "were pissing themselves," says Court. "It was scary."

But Grant, in the front passenger seat, was perfectly calm. He even cracked a joke. As Court gripped the wheel and stomped on the gas, and as the car lurched left and right, bullets glancing off it, Grant looked over at him.

"You're enjoying this, aren't you?" Grant quipped.

Keeping his eyes on the road, Court didn't reply at first.

Then Grant added: "It is exciting."

Finally, Court barked at him: "Shut *up*, Jim!"

Grant just laughed.

Grant wanted to meet the Serbs, which meant that Court would have to negotiate a brief ceasefire to allow the delegation to travel to Pale, the Serb mountain stronghold. On their first night at the post office in Sarajevo — while most everyone else slept in their clothes on top of desks, on the floor, or in chairs — Court shuttled back and forth between the Serbian and Muslim liaisons. Both sides had offices in the vast building. He made several visits to each and drank several helpings of fruit alcohol that was offered to him. "They didn't have plants that you could throw the alcohol into," he recalls. "It did require several visits to the loo."

At around one in the morning, he ran into Grant. His boss was wandering the halls after a trip to the bathroom.

"Alan, how's it going?"

"Slowly," he said. "I'm doing more damage to my liver than to Bosnia."

"Ah!" Grant guffawed. "You'll do fine... You think we'll come to an agreement?"

"I think so, but I don't know when."

"Ah, you'll do it," Grant said. "Don't worry."

Then he added: "I'm going back to sleep."

At four a.m., Court had his agreement. The ceasefire would take place between 9:00 and 9:30 that morning. It was a narrow window. He didn't bother going to sleep. At 6:00 a.m., he saw Grant again. The UNICEF head was awake and buoyant. Court told him they needed to be ready to move in three hours.

"All right," Grant said. "We have three hours to kill. It'd be nice to go and see Kosevo Hospital."

Sarajevo's main hospital stood on a hill over a cemetery, where bodies from its busy morgue were hastily buried. Nearby, on the city's southern edge, rose Mount Trebević, a hulking, menacing presence. From that mountain, the Serbs shelled the hospital mercilessly. Grant and his delegation arrived to a find a whole exterior wall of windows riddled with giant jagged holes, like an outsized and overused shooting range target.

Inside, it was far worse. There was no electricity or running water. The medical staff was scant — many doctors and nurses had fled. The flow of badly wounded patients arriving each day was unceasing. And the hospital itself wasn't safe. Children who had come to be treated for other injuries had been killed and injured anew by the shelling. One shell had landed in a children's ward. Those who had survived were transferred to another ward, a big austere room with no lights. They lay there listlessly, some with heads and arms bandaged, some with legs in traction. Some had lost limbs. They were quiet, recalls Jon Rohde. They did not cry. "They were in bad shape," he says.

Grant went to several bedsides to speak with children. He wanted to assure them they would be safe — but how could he?

He didn't voice it, but Rohde could tell his friend was angry, could tell from the stern aura he radiated. A deep frown etched Grant's face as he moved through the dim, dreary halls. Says Rohde: "I got the sense that he felt, *I can do something about this...I'm the spokesperson for children in the world, and I'm going to stop this.*"

In one room they saw a little girl with trichinosis. Maybe two years old, she sat by herself in a metal crib, wailing and hiding her face with a blanket. She wore pink tights and, for some reason, was tethered to the side of the crib. A nurse told them that the hospital didn't have enough drugs for cases like hers. Trichinosis can normally be treated, but if it is not, it can be fatal.

In the oncology ward, they met a small, frail, bald boy who had leukemia. He was drinking out of a tin cup. Hospital staff explained that without electricity, the boy could no longer receive treatment and that his life was in immediate danger. Grant stood there listening, his eyes blinking rapidly, as the boy's condition was described.

The group was led to a small lobby area where young orphans were camped out on chairs surrounding a small, low, round table, eating a breakfast of jam and bread. They were in their pajamas, smiling and giggling — like kids anywhere. One girl wore a pink bathrobe. One little boy had on a purple sleeper. A doting, smiling nurse sat and chatted with them. Despite their jovial appearance, these children were deeply traumatized, the group learned. Their parents were gone. They cried themselves to sleep every night.

Outside, returning to the armored personnel carrier, an unsmiling Grant was handed a flak jacket. He hoisted it on with a grunt. Then he said, "I'm looking forward to the day when we no longer need these."

Their next stop was a meeting with the people who were causing the misery they had just witnessed.

The man most responsible for the atrocities in Sarajevo — the bushy-maned, double-chinned psychiatrist turned rabid Serbian nationalist, Radovan Karadžić — was not available to meet Grant. But Grant could, he was told, have an audience with Karadžić's deputy, a woman known as Serbia's Iron Lady. Biljana Plavšić was a biologist and former professor at Sarajevo University. She also happened to be an enthusiastic supporter of "ethnic cleansing" and reportedly harbored views so extreme as to even unsettle Milošević. After the Dayton peace accords in 1995, Plavšić would become president of the Bosnian Serb Republic and would later plead guilty to crimes against humanity at the International Criminal Court in The Hague (she would receive an outrageously light sentence of eleven years, probably less than the punishment for stealing a bike in some countries).

They sat on a patio in an elaborate alpine resort that had helped play host to the 1984 Olympic Winter Games a mere eight years before. It was a bright, crisp, cold morning in Pale, the Serbs' mountain headquarters. The view was dramatic and tranquil — green, snowless ski slopes meandered amid rows of tall, serrated evergreen trees. If not for the circumstances, it would have been a moment of respite in the rejuvenating mountain air.

Turkish coffee was served in small white cups with red stripes. They gathered around a skinny wooden table that was barely wide enough to hold the cups and saucers. Rohde, Court, and most others, including two of Plavšić's aides, sat on a long bench. The haughty military leader sat with her guest, Jim Grant, on pillows on the edge of a stone wall opposite the bench. On the other side of the wall was a drop of maybe six feet.

Wearing red lipstick, a voluminous whorl of hair, and big sunglasses, Plavšić looked like a fussy, wealthy, high-maintenance eccentric — she did not look like a genocidal killer. Grant, who wore his trademark blue suit and a tie with little hearts on it, made an apparent attempt at small talk. He told her he had recently visited Somalia (another placed gripped by gruesome violence and famine). Her demeanor was cordial. She spoke English fluently and did not need an interpreter.

Then, says Court, ensued "a ninety-minute discussion between Plavšić and Grant, and I have never seen the like." Grant leaned forward and focused so intently on his host, "it was like Jon and I weren't there," Court adds.

When Plavšić began spewing bigoted bile, she spoke calmly. She did not yell or rant. She sipped coffee all the while.

She started telling Grant how dreadful the Muslims were, how they were completely undermining the Serbian way of life.

"They are like vermin," she announced. "And they need to be exterminated."

As if any UN official would ever agree with such a disgusting statement. She may not have been seeking his agreement; she may have been trying to rile him up, goad him into a confrontation. She went on verbally savaging Muslims, but Grant didn't bite — he knew that wouldn't achieve anything. It would do no good to tell her that she was a repellent troll. He just listened.

His objective was threefold: get her to stop shelling the hospital (she was the one directing fire into Sarajevo), persuade her to restore electricity and water in Sarajevo, and win her support for his proposed week of tranquillity.

Rohde recalls that Grant did gently jab her, telling her that whatever policy the Serbs were following — whatever was happening down there in Sarajevo — there was simply no excuse for targeting children. He likely smiled as he said this, making sure that he sounded friendly, that his voice had no edge.

Grant also made a quick reference to Plavšić's boss, Radovan Karadžić, according to Rohde. Karadžić was a psychiatrist, which means he was a medical doctor. Grant told Plavšić that he didn't see how a doctor — how someone bound by the Hippocratic oath — could ever put children in harm's way.

None of these statements seemed to sway a woman who, says Rohde, "could have bit nails and chewed them and spit them out."

What did sway her, says Court, was a question repeatedly posed by Grant: *What would it take?*

What would it take for you to stop shelling the hospital? What would it take for you to stop shooting the linemen repairing electrical lines? What would it take for you to restore gas and electricity?

In answer to the first version of the question, she said that the Muslims should stop using the hospital grounds for firing mortars at the Serbs (the mortar bombs may have been coming from a schoolyard next to the hospital). Based on that complaint, says Court, a rough deal was sketched out. The back-and-forth went something like this:

"They need to take those mortars away," she said emphatically. "Can you make sure those mortars leave?"

Grant pressed her: "Will that stop you shelling the hospital?"

"Yes."

Grant swiveled to Court. "You'll take care of this when you get back to Sarajevo, won't you, Alan?"

Court said he would.

Then he pivoted back toward Plavšić. "And then you'll stop immediately?"

"Yes."

"So you won't fire on the hospital, unless you're fired at from the hospital?"

"Yes."

They went through the same process of affirmation and reaffirmation on the other issues, with Grant carefully extracting yeses. He also secured her support for the week of tranquillity.

Reflecting on the exchange now, Court still marvels at how Grant toppled her obstinacy. "It was amazing," he says. "It was a master class in how you take somebody whose position is diametrically opposed to yours and find common ground…it was really finding the quid pro quo, the tit for tat."

Within a week, Court persuaded the Bosnian forces to stop shooting mortars from the hospital vicinity. And in turn, he says, the Serbs stopped shelling the hospital. But the resulting peace would not last long. The hospital would eventually again come under fire.

"A real dour son of a bitch."

That's how Alan Court describes Slobodan Milošević. After traveling to the Serbian capital, Belgrade, Grant and his delegation met the president in a large, ornate, ostensibly ancient room. Twenty people arrayed themselves around a massive table. At the head of it, like a statue — like a part of the room itself — brooded a man who had brought death to scores of innocents. He was stiff, blank-faced. Completely unreadable. What Rohde recalls most vividly was "the huge head this guy had."

The dynamics of the meeting were not favorable to Grant. He liked one-on-ones. He liked being able to lean toward a person, reel them in with his eyes, feel out their weak points. But Milošević was too far away. And he was surrounded by his stone-faced sentries.

"The whole meeting was tense in a way I don't know how to describe," says Court. "You came out of that meeting glad you were out of it."

They communicated through interpreters. Milošević said that Yugoslavia must remain united. It is a shame, he said, what is happening. For too long, he lamented, the Serbs have been under the yoke of the Croats. He said that Marshal Tito, the Communist founder of post–World War II Yugoslavia, was a Croat (Tito's father was from Croatia, but his mother was from Slovenia). Now, Milošević added, it is time to assert our national identity.

But the Serbian president wasn't speaking to Grant. It didn't seem to matter who sat across from him. "Milošević was talking to the air," says Court. "Talking to an audience."

Grant made a straightforward appeal. He told Milošević that his influence in Bosnia and his backing would be critical to the week of tranquillity. He explained what he had in mind — the principle of "not firing first."

"We want to help children get through the winter," Grant said earnestly. "We need to get clothes and food to them."

He made sure to clarify: "This is *all* children."

Appealing to Milošević's quietly fulminating ego, he lacquered on some flattery. He praised the Serbs for how they were handling refugees from Bosnia. ("Most of the refugees were probably Serbian," notes Court, "but that didn't matter — the point was, they were refugees.")

On behalf of the UN, he thanked the Serbs for taking care of refugees. Noting that the Serbs had integrated some refugees into towns and villages, rather than building big camps, he lauded their "excellent processing." (Praising the Serb leaders must have put a knot in his gut; but Grant would say what he had to say.)

When Grant finished, Court recalls that Milošević may have nodded once — just once. He then said simply: "We will support this."

Whether he could be trusted — whether his brusque assurance meant anything at all — was a big gamble.

Back at the hotel in Zagreb, Croatia, where they were all staying, Court went to Grant's room around one in the morning. He needed to discuss travel plans — Grant was due in Geneva the next day. He knocked on the door.

"Come in," Grant hollered. "I'm in the bathroom."

Court made his way to the bathroom. Jim Grant was standing there in a T-shirt and boxers. He was washing his blue suit in a big, broad sink. Most people would probably have asked a guest to come back in a few minutes while they got dressed. But Jim Grant was not like most people.

He began to talk about his plans for the next day in Geneva. Grant had already secured support for the week of tranquillity from all relevant leaders in the region, including the presidents of Croatia and Montenegro. Now he had two more people to convince: both of them high-level UN officials.

He asked Court to go with him to Geneva. He wanted all the help he could get.

"Well, how will I get back?" Court asked.

"We'll figure that out." Grant said.

At the Palais des Nations, the UN's sprawling compound near Lake Geneva, Grant and Court strode the halls until they came to Sadako Ogata's office. Ogata was the United Nations high commissioner for refugees. She was also a friend of Jim Grant's. Without her, in fact, he may have never gotten his job. The soft-spoken Japanese diplomat and academic had chaired the UNICEF board when Grant's nomination was up for consideration and helped break a political logjam that had stood in the way. They walked into Ogata's office. Court recounts the series of events that followed.

"Sadako! How are you, my old friend?"

"Jim, so nice to see you!"

Grant sat down. "Sadako," he said. "I don't know what you've heard, but I'm trying to push for this week of tranquillity for the first of November, and I'm wondering if I can get your support."

Ogata, wearing a green suit and pearl necklace, said she had already heard about it from her staff in Sarajevo. "It's a good idea," she said.

Grant must have known he already had her imprimatur in the bag. She didn't take any convincing. Then he asked for a second favor.

"I'm going to see Cyrus now and present this to him … why don't you come with me?"

Cyrus Vance was the secretary general's special envoy to Bosnia-Herzegovina. The former US secretary of state under President Jimmy Carter, he had also served in the Kennedy administration at the same time Grant had.

"No," Ogata said. "Jim, this is your idea. You go."

"No, Sadako," Grant quickly shot back. "I think it's better if it's *our* idea. Your people are doing such great work on the ground," he continued. "It's absolutely fabulous what your people are doing. You're keeping the thing going completely for the UN. I think we should do this together."

She demurred, but Grant wore her down. As Court recalls, he looked at her, his face at an angle — a slight, sidelong expression that conveyed a naked, heartfelt certainty and was somehow more potent than a straight-on stare.

"You must come, Sadako," he said. "Let's do this together."

She gave in. "Okay," she said. "Let's go."

They marched to Cyrus Vance's office.

When they burst in, Vance was behind his desk, piles of paper all around him. His discerning eyes floated over the rim of his half-glasses, measuring the clutch of people in his doorway. His hair was white, and his ears stuck out as noticeably as Grant's.

"Uh-oh," he said. "What have you guys cooked up?"

Grant spoke first. "Sadako, why don't you tell him?

"No, Jim," she said quickly. "It's your idea."

"Sadako, you're really behind this," Grant lied. "You tell Cyrus. I'll fill in later."

Put completely on the spot, Ogata began to explain the concept of the week of tranquillity to Vance. Grant said nothing.

Vance leaned back and took off his glasses. "You know, you guys have got something cooked up here," he said. "What can I do? I can only support you."

Later, walking in the hallway, Court asked why Grant had let Ogata pitch Vance. "Why didn't you do it?"

"You know," Grant said. "We're all good at trumpeting our own ideas, but it sounds so much better when other people do it for us."

Ogata had helped provide a facade of consensus. If he had walked into Vance's office alone, his idea would not have seemed as urgent or as good. How could Vance say no to both of them — especially when they both appeared so enthusiastic?

After days of meetings with politicians and murderers and diplomats, the week of tranquillity was a go.

One of the men Grant had been unable to meet — one of the worst killers of all — bumped into him in a corridor at the Palais des Nations. Radovan Karadžić, a burly, six-foot-four-inch behemoth with the girth of a walrus, greeted Grant with a wide smile.

But Grant was not smiling. In a photo of the encounter, Grant looks uncharacteristically stunned, stricken, as though he had found himself exchanging pleasantries with the mass murderer Jeffrey Dahmer (Karadžić was way worse, judged by body count). The two men stood side by side, posing for the camera. Karadžić, in his vast, loose gray suit, was grinning over the swell of his double chin. Grant's face was clenched, as if saying, *Please, just take the damn picture already.*

Grant was usually careful not to disparage leaders he met, even those who were unquestionably brutal and corrupt. But he made an exception for Karadžić. He told Mary Cahill that he refused to shake the man's hand (though, in one photo, Karadžić appears to be gripping Grant's hand; it's unclear if Grant is willingly reciprocating, but it's also hard to imagine the UNICEF chief would risk alienating someone who could torpedo his "week of tranquillity"). Cahill also heard her boss openly express his disgust for Sudan's Omar al-Bashir, calling him a "bastard." "We have to work with these bastards," he said of Karadžić and other Serbian leaders, his voice taut with contempt. "We have to go above them, around them, or beneath them — but we have to work with them."

The day before the week of tranquillity was set to begin, Serbian bombardment killed as many as twenty-nine people in Sarajevo and wounded as many as 119. Not a promising start. Bosnia would indeed be more daunting than El Salvador or Sudan.

Would the violence really cease within the next twenty-four hours? Could the Serbs be trusted to keep their word?

Not on the first day, no. As the deadline on Sunday, November 1, came and went, the sound of gunshots and shells delivered a mocking rebuke. The fighting flared unabated. Not only that — the convoy Grant was leading from Belgrade to Sarajevo got lost. "They managed to get drivers who didn't know the way to Sarajevo," Court recalls. "They kept driving west. They would have driven straight into Croatia" if others hadn't intervened and altered their course.

This was more of a PR debacle than a humanitarian headache. The convoy was largely symbolic — "the show part of it," says Court. Most of the relief — clothes, blankets, vaccines, and medicines — was distributed separately. Once he arrived in Sarajevo, Grant opened a children's art exhibit at a cultural center; during the event, gunshots rang out next door.

Grant was annoyed and disappointed. He complained to Court: "I thought we were going to stop this."

"Patience, Jim," Court said. "We will."

And later that day, says Court, they did stop the shooting.

Another snafu snarled part of the delivery in Sarajevo: a minister from the Muslim-led government initially rejected the winter clothing because it was manufactured in Serbia. He said it was insensitive and insulting to hand out Serbian goods to Muslim children. In the end, the goods were accepted.

As for the next six days, Grant would later describe the period as "a week of relative tranquillity," during which the death rate "dropped very sharply." According to press accounts, the week was anything but tranquil. On Wednesday, November 4, United Press International reported that Serbian artillery struck a cable-bearing pylon in Sarajevo, causing a complete blackout across the city. On Friday, November 6, the newswire described "sporadic small-arms and anti-aircraft fire around the city." Still, the violence was likely far less severe than it would have been without the ceasefire.

Despite the setbacks, UNICEF was able to provide as many as 200,000 children with blankets, clothes, medicines, and vaccines during the first week of November 1992. The distribution efforts continued throughout the rest of the month, according to an internal UNICEF assessment, during which the number of beneficiaries nearly doubled. UNICEF also arranged for the evacuation of several severely injured children and their families from Sarajevo, flying them to France for treatment.

The fighting would grow ever more ferocious. The week of tranquillity was, at best, a mixed and fleeting success — an evanescent trace of light in a deepening chasm of darkness.

UNICEF and the UN's refugee agency would go on delivering relief, under harrowing circumstances, and Grant would keep trying to coax and shame leaders into protecting children. After a mortar attack killed six children in Sarajevo in January 1994, according to the Associated Press, he would lament: "There is nothing to be gained militarily by the killing of babies."

But no one seemed to be listening.

Chapter 16
NOT A GOOD ONE

He was yellow. His skin was yellow. The whites of his eyes were yellow.

Jim Grant first noticed the jaundice when he and Ellan went on a ski trip to Colorado. It was early 1993, not too long after his annual, UN-mandated physical exam. UN medical staff had run a series of blood tests but had apparently given him no reason to worry. So what was this? Did they miss something? Why was he yellow?

As he would eventually discover, one of his test results had been highly unusual. Grant's alkaline phosphatase levels were "out-of-this-world abnormal," according to Jon Rohde, who learned about the results later. This can be a sign of liver disease — "a huge red flag," he says. But for some reason, this information was evidently not brought to anyone's immediate attention. Perhaps it was considered an aberration or a mistake.

So Jim kept working. Then he and Ellan went skiing. All the while, he lost precious time. Six weeks, maybe eight. Had he known sooner, "he could be alive today," Rohde says.

After the ski trip, he got more tests — and an answer.

He returned from a doctor's appointment one day and asked Mary Cahill to step inside his office. There were three doors to his office: one for the public, one that led to Mary's office, and one to his speechwriter Mike Shower's office. He closed all three.

"I've got bad news," he said. "I've been diagnosed with cancer."

Then he added: "It's not a good one."

He told Mary he had liver cancer.

Shocked and distraught, Mary did not know how to respond. She couldn't even remember Grant ever taking a sick day. In the eyes of many, he was unstoppable. Invincible. How could *he* have cancer?

Grant tried to put her at ease. "But Mary, I've had a marvelous life."

It was a rare moment of unvarnished honesty — he would tell other people that he was going to beat the cancer, or he would downplay it or simply not mention it at all. He publicly treated his illness as a nonissue — like a pesky auditor's report. Cahill thinks he only made this comment to "make me feel less bad about it."

The cancer, he soon learned, had started in a bile duct. It was called a cholangiocarcinoma, or a Klatskin's tumor, and was "about the size of small walnut," according to a scribbled note in one of Grant's little steno pads. On May 4, 1993, doctors at Memorial Sloan Kettering Cancer Center in Manhattan tried to remove the tumor. They took out a big part of his liver and got some of the tumor, but not all of it. They did manage to release the obstruction to his bile duct. The jaundice faded, and he felt better.

On January 20, 1993, around the time of Grant's UN checkup, Audrey Hepburn died. Grant had become intensely fond of her and had relied on her more and more. She had recently been operated on for colon cancer. She had pushed herself until the end, traveling to Somalia for UNICEF in September 1992; photos from the trip show a visibly gaunt Hepburn, who must have been in great discomfort (though she was not one to complain). She did not feel well after the visit and was diagnosed shortly thereafter. As the news of his own diagnosis seeped in, Grant may have wondered if her suffering was a preview of what he would face.

He did speak about his illness with his sons, Ellan, Jon Rohde, and his vociferous French stepmother, Denise. The former nurse had written him a slew of letters during his fourteen years at UNICEF, perhaps trying to fill a void left by the death of both his parents more than twenty years earlier (his father died in 1962, his mother in 1973). Her letters were frank, nosy, philosophical, and teeming with opinions — on how Christianity had hastened the collapse of imperial Rome, on whether Jim should sell the "roof house," on why he should try a "peak mattress pad" for his back pain, on why one of his sons did not yet have a wife. They also provided a steady source of parental encouragement — she wrote often of how much she admired him and how he reminded her of his father. Her letters usually ended with the words "Carpe Diem!"

Rohde interpreted medical information for his friend. After the operation, Rohde recalls that Grant asked his doctors how much time he had left but did not get a definitive answer.

Grant's main physician was Dr. Murray Brennan, the affable, New Zealand–born chairman of surgery at Sloan Kettering. On the crucial question of time, Dr. Brennan avoided a specific reply. "I wouldn't phrase it that way," he says now. What he told Grant was that his survival would be "measured in months and not years." Brennan recalls, "It was not a curable situation — he knew that."

He adds that Grant "viewed that in his indefatigable way: What do we do to maximize the time I have?"

Grant did not share this grim news, of course. Some people at UNICEF knew he had had surgery but did not know why. Judging from a letter he received from his old friend John Sewell on May 9, 1993 (three days before his seventy-first birthday), Grant painted a rosy sheen on the issue whenever it came up — as he did with so much else.

Sewell wrote that Grant's speechwriter and aide Mike Shower had "indicated that the prognosis was not as bad as we thought. In fact, he said you were raring to go!" Sewell added: "This was good news personally and professionally. You still have a lot of work to do, and these will be exciting times."

In a letter to Grant's sister Betty, sent after his death, a childhood friend from China named Eddie Hoo wrote that he had run into Grant in China at some point after his diagnosis. Grant had told Hoo that his cancer was cured. "I told him that cancer would come back," Hoo wrote, "and that he was committing suicide if he didn't stop working so hard; I told him to write a memoir. He just shrugged his shoulders."

Maybe Grant really did believe his cancer had been cured after his first surgery (though this was tantamount to announcing you had won the lottery when all you had done was buy a ticket). Or maybe he just wanted others to believe that. Maybe he knew that to get his job done — to consolidate all the progress he had achieved, to save even more lives — he had to make others believe he would be around for a while. Either way, he was determined not to let cancer get in his way or slow him down. It was one of those hurdles he would either vault over or simply knock down. In one of his notebooks, under a collection of Chinese fortunes, he taped a scrap of yellow paper with the typed words: "I have cancer, but cancer does not have me."

Says Rohde: "He never admitted it could be anything but curable."

But the unspoken knowledge that it almost certainly wasn't — whether he admitted it or not — threw gasoline on his blazing zeal. There was still so much to do. Now, he had maybe a year, possibly a little more, in which to do it — if he was lucky. As a result, says Rohde, "he just went flat out."

He worked harder, moved faster, stepped up his already frenetic pace. He lined up a torrent of trips and meetings. He pushed his staff more insistently. He fixed his attention on a question now imbued with a churning new urgency: Who was keeping their World Summit for Children promises, and who wasn't?

The "national plans of action" — countries' individual blue-prints for reducing child mortality and improving child health, stemming from the summit — were pegged to a year 2000 dead-line. But Grant would not have until 2000. He might not have until 1996. A series of ten "mid-decade goals," growing out of several regional government meetings in 1992 and 1993, were hitched to the year 1995; these were created, not to accommodate Grant's cancer, but to provide an incentive to political leaders whose terms might expire before 2000. Nonetheless, for Grant, they became the only goals that mattered — he focused all his energy, all his mania on 1995. The mid-decade goals were his ever-sharpening set of spurs, and he used them unrelentingly.

In August 1993, Gautam wrote Grant a confidential memo cautioning him to let up a bit. While most country represen-tatives had felt "challenged" by the 1990 immunization goals, Gautam wrote, they were now "overwhelmed" by the mid-decade goals. The quiet and brilliant Nepalese man stated that some staffers felt the goals were "unachievable and unsustain-able." Then he got to the uncomfortable crux of it: "The timing is not helpful in that many staff feel that the current relentless pursuit of goals may very well slacken in a year or two with the change of leadership of the organization." As a result, he predicted some staff would merely humor Grant, saying they would meet the targets, even though they had no intention of doing so. The potential consequence: "we might inadvertently plant the seeds of cynicism which undermine the end-decade goals and goal-oriented programming which have served UNICEF so well."

Gautam suggested making the goals adaptable to the realities of each country. Some African countries, he pointed out, faced a much steeper and more arduous climb than countries in Latin America. He also addressed a long-simmering source of resentment, noting that there is a "perception that Reps and advisers who tow the party line and are good salesmen of their achievements are forgiven for their managerial shortcomings and even misconduct." He urged Grant to reinforce the need for "high standards of personal conduct and organizational discipline."

Gautam's advice, particularly this last bit, would soon prove sadly prophetic. But Grant seems to have largely disregarded it.

He hurtled forward, gaining speed as his body began to betray him, and new and old crises — "loud emergencies" — vied for morsels of his coveted attention. A growing series of emergencies and violent conflicts — in Afghanistan, Angola, Haiti, Iraq, Liberia, Mozambique, Somalia, Sudan, the former Yugoslavia — persistently waylaid him. And the work of field staff in many of these places seemed to be getting more dangerous. At a UNICEF board meeting on May 7, 1993 (just days after Grant's operation), Karin Sham Poo, then deputy executive director for operations, noted that five UNICEF staff members had been killed within the last year alone and that one more was presumed dead. In the early 1990s, the blue halo that had once protected many peacekeepers and UN staff had, in many places, become a target — and UNICEF and other agencies were completely unprepared for it.

"We were caught with our pants down," says UNICEF veteran Fouad Kronfol, who then ran the personnel division.

"We didn't have security in place for this. It was a big shock to us — we had seen ourselves as Boy Scouts."

Kronfol had told Grant that UNICEF needed to do a better job of protecting staff. Grant "was very supportive" and backed measures to improve communications in the field and coordinate security with other agencies. UNICEF tried to evacuate staff from trouble spots, but for some, it was too late.

Former UNICEF Somalia representative David Bassiouni remembers Grant attending the New York funeral of Marta Pompalova, a UNICEF doctor shot dead while sitting at a café in Bosaso, Somalia, in January 1992. Grant had approached Pompalova's husband, hugged him, and said, "She died for the cause of children." A year later in January 1993, Grant would offer his condolences to the family of another UNICEF staff member brazenly executed in Somalia. Sean Devereux, a twenty-eight-year-old Briton, was shot in the back of the head in the southern port town of Kismayo as he walked near the UNICEF compound. "Sean did not die in vain!" Grant said at Devereux's memorial service in New York, according to his prepared remarks. The enthusiastic and personable young aid worker, a Salesian Catholic missionary, became known as "the saint in shirtsleeves." During the service, Grant called him "a frontline leader who toiled and died for a great cause."

The mounting staff deaths dismayed Grant, according to several staff members, and dug at his guilt — perhaps echoing the torment of sending Americans into harm's way during the Vietnam War in the late 1960s when he oversaw USAID's programs there. But he didn't hesitate to dispatch staff into war zones; not when children were in peril. The circumstances would only grow more dire — the most catastrophic loss of UNICEF staff in its history was yet to come.

Grant's portable pocket marketing arsenal — which usually included an ORS packet, a growth chart, maybe a syringe — gained a new prop later in his term. It was a small dropper filled with liquid. He used it at state dinners and formal functions. He would ask the president or prime minister to pass the salt. He would take a plate or a saucer and shake a little pile of salt into the middle of it. Then out came the dropper, fished from his coat pocket. As everyone around the table watched, Grant would raise it over the little pile of salt, squeeze out a few drops, and watch. If the salt turned blue, that meant that it contained iodine. If not, the sudden and stifling air of embarrassment was as conspicuous as a mariachi band at the opera.

Iodine is a natural chemical element, essential to human development. For children without enough iodine in their diet, the results can be calamitous and life-crushing: severe neuro-logical damage, impaired speech and hearing, cretinism and goiters. Iodine deficiency also causes stillbirths and miscar-riages and elevates the risk of child mortality. In the early 1990s, in remote mountain villages in Nepal and Bolivia and dozens of other countries, it was grotesquely distending children's necks and silently strangling their futures. One way to stop this per-vasive global plague was to put iodine in their salt (a remedy UNICEF had been promoting since the 1950s).

Mary Cahill was with Grant in Beijing when the Chinese premier Li Peng hosted a big dinner in Grant's honor in the early 1990s at the vast Great Hall of the People (adjacent to Tiananmen Square, where Li had ordered the infamous and ruthless military crackdown a few years earlier). During the dinner, Grant produced his salt-testing dropper and explained to his bespectacled, pudgy-faced, hard-line host what it was and how it worked. He may have said that a lack of iodine can shave precious points off a child's IQ, and that it can hobble an entire country's economic prospects. Stopping it costs just pennies. Then, in front of Li and other guests, he squeezed a few drops onto the salt on his plate. He examined it. Nothing happened — the salt did not turn blue. Grant then informed the premier that his salt was not iodized. "He would risk embarrassing the premier of China to make his point," Cahill says.

Known for his frequent scowl, Li immediately summoned his chefs from the kitchen. Cahill recalls that two or three of them promptly appeared, wearing white jackets and standing at attention. The premier ordered that, from now on, only iodized salt would be used. Shortly thereafter, China embarked on a nationwide effort to iodize its salt.

Grant would do his salt test more and more frequently, embarrassing elite dinner hosts on numerous occasions. It became another obsession — another quick, cheap, demonstrable way to help children. Universal salt iodization was a mid-decade goal, and UNICEF would soon team up with Kiwanis International, a volunteer service organization, to raise money and awareness to try to make it happen.

As Grant ever more aggressively flogged world leaders, donors, and his own staff to make children's health a priority, he shunted his own health aside. He saw his doctor and got radiation, but treated the appointments as a muddle of minor distractions — he would slosh through them and then shake them off his boots as quickly as possible. Adamson went with him once when he received radiation at Sloan Kettering. He was able to watch the procedure, as doctors marked his boss's abdomen with a small ink cross — the target for the radiation — and then lowered a giant X-ray machine over him. "What I remember most," he says, "is that both before and after, Jim was talking about work issues and planning and *The State of the World's Children*. [The radiation] was just an interruption. It wasn't the focus of his day."

One focus may well have been how to get more mileage out of *The State of the World's Children*, UNICEF's flagship report written by Adamson and released every December. Grant usually kicked off the report in a different country each year, and it always garnered a barrage of media attention. How could he outdo all past report launches? Where could he unveil it in December 1993 that would trump all other locations?

There was only one place: the White House. George H. W. Bush — the US president who had skipped out on most of the World Summit for Children and almost didn't show up in the first place — likely wouldn't have been very receptive to the idea. But America's affable new president, sworn in earlier that year, was. Bill Clinton warmed to Jim Grant instantly. In his first speech to the UN General Assembly on September 27, 1993, Clinton repeated some of Grant's talking points, noting that thirty thousand children die each day of disease and malnutrition. Then the president said: "Our UNICEF director, Jim Grant, has reminded me that each of those children had a name and a nationality, a family, a personality, and a potential. We are compelled to do better by the world's children."

Three months later, the president and the first lady stood next to Grant in the East Room of the White House, under a glittering Christmas tree, as he prepared to release the 1994 edition of *SOWC*. Most UN reports are usually released in obscurity and then quickly forgotten. It would be hard to ignore this one.

Grant stood to the side, clutching a copy of the report, grinning like a giddy kid, as Hillary Clinton introduced him.

"In Jim Grant's fifty years of international service, he has extended his passionate and infectious enthusiasm for children to every capital and corner of the globe," the first lady said. She drew laughs when she mentioned his penchant for brandishing packets of ORS. She then proclaimed that the earnest American head of UNICEF had "helped to redefine what we mean when we talk about global development, peace, and global prosperity."

Applause frothed around him as he took the podium. His face looked thinner, the skin on his cheeks and throat a little looser. He put up both hands and said crisply: "Please." He thanked the Clintons. He delivered a fairly smooth speech, not as riddled with awkward pauses as many previous addresses. He swayed from side to side as he spoke. At one point, when mentioning how many more lives could be saved with greater political leadership, he turned around and wagged his finger at the president (as though telling him, *The ball is now in your court — you better pick it up*). He closed with a direct appeal to Bill Clinton, stating his "hope that the advancement of the great goals for the children of the world will become one of the defining moments of your presidency."

When Bill Clinton came to the podium, a few people in the audience noticed something unusual: he was wearing Jim Grant's tie. It was a "Save the Children" tie with bright, smiling faces of cartoon children emblazoned across it. Grant was, in turn, wearing the president's dark, muted tie. Before they had walked on stage, the president had remarked how much he liked Grant's tie, according to several UNICEF staff members to whom Grant had described the encounter. Without hesitating, Grant said, "You can have it," and began to remove his tie. He and the president quickly swapped ties.

The story is a favorite of many UNICEF people; it shows, they say, how quick Grant was on his feet, how he never passed up an opportunity to make a connection.

Mary Cahill agrees but notes that she had bought Jim Grant that tie as a personal gift. And she was in the audience at the White House, when it suddenly appeared on the president of the United States. She says with a chuckle: "That was my twenty-two dollars!"

The symptoms became harder to ignore, but Grant ignored them anyway. He developed ascites, a buildup of fluid in the abdomen. His belly became bloated, and his feet and ankles started to swell. Fevers and chills sent him shuddering. Jaundice seeped back into his skin. His face grew gaunt and sunken — one staffer says he reminded her of photos from the Biafran famine in the late 1960s. But he kept going to work, even when many people were shocked at the sight of him and thought he should be in the hospital.

His eyes still sparkled with mirthful enthusiasm, especially when he sounded off on his favorite topics — immunization or iodine deficiency or the Green Revolution or, of course, the mid-decade goals. But his Teflon optimism took a concussive, cracking blow on April 8, 1994, when his longtime aide, speech-writer, and trusted confidant Mike Shower died. Shower, who was openly gay at a time when homophobia had much sharper teeth than it does now, had contracted AIDS and succumbed to it at the age of forty-four.

Thin, serious, and moody, he was at Grant's side during most board meetings, whispering counsel in his ear. A former congressional assistant, he was a key liaison between Grant and US lawmakers in Washington and had been heavily involved in organizing the World Summit for Children. Like Nyi Nyi and Cahill and Rohde and Gautam, he had become intensely protective of his boss and unconditionally committed to him. The two men were gravely ill at the same time, both struggling with exhaustion, both withered and pale, both driving themselves to keep working — in that way, they shared a wholly unique camaraderie. Several staff say Grant had come to see both Jon Rohde and Mike Shower as his other sons. He held a special "celebration of friendship" to honor Shower before his death, inviting Shower's parents and a host of other people to a ceremony at UNICEF House; in one photo from the event, Shower is standing snugly between Jim and Ellan, smiling and looking noticeably emaciated. At his memorial service on May 10, Grant told those gathered that he and Shower had both been "dreamers aspiring to be doers."

Not pausing, not allowing sadness or illness to get a grip, he barreled toward his next objective. He traveled incessantly. Over one two-week stretch in April (which included the day Shower died), he visited five countries — Colombia, Mexico, Ecuador, Switzerland, and France — and then returned to the States for a slew of meetings in Washington and New York.

In June came another jolt: Grant's stepmother, Denise, died. She was his last living link to his father and had been a unique and nearly constant source of solace and forceful advice for most of Grant's adult life. Over the following months, he neither slowed nor stopped; he met with more than forty leaders in his final year. Rohde, Jolly, Adamson, and Cahill begged him to slow down, but he didn't listen.

On a trip to Mongolia in July, a Cessna airplane took Grant and then UNICEF China representative Farid Rahman to a remote area. They stepped out of the plane and got into a jeep for a bumpy ride into the countryside. Grant sat silently in his seat, his body hunched slightly forward. "He was in great pain," says Rahman, "but he didn't show it." He didn't ask for any help. Whenever the jeep stopped in a village and they greeted residents, Grant straightened his body and "put on his charm and his smile."

A personal boost came on August 8 when President Clinton awarded Grant the Presidential Medal of Freedom — the country's highest civilian honor. It wasn't the Nobel Prize, but it was a nice moment of recognition. Cahill, who went with Grant to the ceremony, worried about her boss during the event. As he stood next to the president, who draped a medal around his neck, he was glaringly, unmistakably jaundiced.

There were several hospitalizations. Adamson accompanied him on one occasion when Grant tried to check into Sloan Kettering. On the ride to the hospital, he had drifted in and out of sleep. He had barely been able to get out of the car and could hardly stand. But in the lobby of Sloan Kettering he was made to wait for half an hour or more. There was some problem with his American Express credit card, and the receptionists at the front desk were looking into whether his last bill had been paid (he had checked out only a few days earlier). Adamson thinks that Grant may have been given a wheelchair, but he needed a bed — he was about to fall over.

The experience enraged the cordial, normally unruffled Briton. "When you're more concerned about some past bill than an ill person standing in front of you who needs help, it's wrong," he says now. At that moment, standing there with his gravely sick boss, waiting for the credit card to clear, Adamson thought, *For all we grumble about our national health service in the UK, this would never happen.*

As Grant continually scurried to recover, to get back to work, a horrendous tragedy of unprecedented magnitude was unfurling across Rwanda, pitting the country's two main groups — Hutus and Tutsis — against one another. In April 1994, after a plane carrying the country's Hutu president was shot down, Hutu extremists used the incident as a pretext to start slaughtering Tutsis. Over the next one hundred days, political leaders and elements of the Hutu-led government carried out a dizzyingly swift and coordinated campaign of genocide. As many as one million Tutsis and moderate Hutus were killed. The death toll included an estimated 300,000 children. Many of the killings were done with machetes. The speed and scale of the violence dwarfed even the horror of Bosnia. And as in Bosnia, the UN peacekeeping response was shameful. In January 1994, the UN's peacekeeping commander, Canadian general Romeo Dallaire, had warned UN headquarters that Hutu forces might be planning massacres. But he was ignored. As the violence began, he begged for more troops. He was rebuffed and ordered to withdraw. Though many others left, Dallaire bravely disobeyed his orders. Remaining with a small, ill-equipped contingent of troops, he tried to save as many lives as possible. The United States was one of the strongest voices urging a pullout of peacekeeping troops; reeling from the recent "Black Hawk Down" episode in Somalia, it did not want to get involved. The world turned its back as the bodies precipitously piled up. The genocide ended in July, after the Tutsi-led Rwandan Patriotic Front defeated the Hutu militias and took control of the country. The international community's stubborn indifference in the face of such monstrous butchery was an irredeemable disgrace — and one of the UN's most spectacular failures.

But not every part of the UN abandoned Rwanda. Local UNICEF and World Food Program staff continued to provide relief during the genocide despite grave and constant risk. Though UNICEF was able to evacuate some of its staff, fourteen of its employees were killed — the highest number of UNICEF deaths at any one time. Many who survived suffered unspeakable losses. A UNICEF communications officer found out that all five of his children had been murdered. His wife had survived, but all the kids were gone, just like that. Astoundingly, instead of collapsing in grief, he went back to work. Maybe he could help other children who were still alive.

In the aftermath, UNICEF reestablished a full presence, providing a lifeline for survivors — clean water, vaccines, medical supplies, oral rehydration salts, high-protein biscuits, health kits, education kits, and cooking equipment. It eventually helped get 250,000 kids back into school (one pressing task was to make sure schools weren't mined) and helped to restore Kigali's electrical grid and water treatment plants. Perhaps its biggest challenge was caring for a sudden surge of unaccompanied children, who were wandering around alone, sometimes gathering in small groups on street corners and under trees. Attached to each one was a stark question: Was this child an orphan? Or was there a parent or aunt or uncle or grandparent somewhere out there? UNICEF staff developed what it called a "family tracing" program to answer that question and to connect children with surviving relatives (if there were any). They fanned out across the country, taking pictures of every kid they came across and assigning each one a reference number. The photos and reference numbers were posted all over Rwanda on big billboards. As a result, tens of thousands of children would be reunited with family members. The program became a model for similar efforts over the next several decades, including in Haiti after the 2010 earthquake.

In September, two months after the end of the genocide, Grant decided to go to Rwanda. Several staff members pleaded with him not to make the trip. He ignored them. He wanted to see for himself what was going on and try to lift the spirits of a battered and traumatized staff. During the killing spree, he had publicly pleaded with the Hutu militias to "spare the children" — to no avail. He largely kept his views on the political situation to himself, avoiding criticizing the UN or any country that could be a donor. But he privately vented to UNICEF staffer Abdul Mohammed, telling him: "We let them down...we let them down."

On the plane flying into the capital, Kigali, he breezily chatted with other passengers, including freelance photographer Betty Press. He mentioned that he had recently undergone an operation and, as a result, his body wasn't working the way it used to. Then he joked: "So I might have gas."

"He did it in such a lighthearted way," Press recalls. "He was always conscious of the other people around him and very much thinking of other people, even in those situations."

Also on the plane was Nigel Fisher, a slim, sanguine emergency operations guru, who looked a little like a bespectacled Scott Glenn. He had ably led UNICEF's response to the Gulf

War, and Grant had tasked him with getting the Rwanda office up to speed. When Fisher had arrived in Kigali in late June 1994, "the smell of death was everywhere." Bodies were strewn in fields and inside empty buildings. UNICEF had one jeep with sixty bullet holes in it, and the front door to the UNICEF office had been booby-trapped. Through a window, Fisher had glimpsed trip wires connected to grenades. Fortunately, he already knew it was a trap; General Dallaire had warned him, bluntly advising, "Don't go there!" The enterprising Canadian quickly realized that he had to improvise. He headed over to the abandoned World Bank office, which did not seem to be booby-trapped. He smashed a window, climbed in, and quickly set up shop there. The World Bank didn't seem to mind. "I called them and said, 'I've just liberated your office — can I keep it?' They said yes." Fisher and his team had to remove a body from the basement before they started working. With permission from the mayor, he and a few other international staff took up residence in the vacated homes of French dignitaries (France had supported the Hutu-led government). Australian UNICEF staffer Ian MacLeod moved into the house of the French cultural attaché. It was weird, he says — there were still dirty dishes in the sink. The former occupants had obviously left in a hurry.

Fisher had sent a message to Grant — he needed a lot more resources if he was going to get this off the ground. He said that unless he received more people, supplies, and logistical support, he would have to close the whole thing down.

Grant responded quickly. "The next thing I knew, Jim just said, 'Give Nigel what he wants now!'"

As Fisher built up and reassembled his staff, the atmosphere in the office became charged with tension and raw emotion. Many staff members were still in shock over losing loved ones and witnessing horrific acts of brutality. Fisher helped some locate the remains of relatives and arrange for proper burials. There were both Tutsis and Hutus in the office, and they were all bound by their commitment to UNICEF. But to remind them of that and make sure no animosity materialized, Fisher assembled everyone one day and told them: "When you walk through the doors of UNICEF every day, there is no Hutu, there is no Tutsi, there is no Rwandan, there is no foreigner. We are all UNICEF staff working for kids."

When Grant arrived in Kigali on Friday, September 9, 1994, the office was bustling. Fisher told the ailing executive director that he had been asked by headquarters to treat Grant gently. And no wonder — Grant looked awful. He was pale, his hair was thinning, his body had shrunk, and his bones protruded through his clothes; his suit was loose and seemed way too big, as though hanging on a mannequin made of wire. Fisher showed him the ambitious itinerary for the next few days, which included visits to massacre sites and refugee camps, and suggested scaling it back a bit. Grant wouldn't budge. "Nigel," he said, "let's go ahead."

Grant spoke with staff members individually and asked how they were coping. "He was very gentle," Fisher recalls. At a staff meeting in the office conference room, packed with about eighty people, the UNICEF chief said that the work everyone was doing now was the best memorial for friends and family who had been lost.

"That's our role at UNICEF," Grant told the mix of Tutsis, Hutus, and foreigners. "To be there for kids, especially at times like this. I know you have suffered, but what you can do for those you have lost is help the kids who are still surviving to have a future."

One of the first stops on the itinerary was the town of Nyamata on the outskirts of Kigali. During the helicopter ride, Grant took a catnap. "He was clearly really straining his resources," says Fisher, "but just kept going."

They visited a Catholic church where thousands of people had been killed. Bones still lay scattered inside. The brick walls were smeared with blood; the white altar cloth was soiled brownish red. Grant walked in and stood there silently for a moment. It was "the closest I ever saw him come to tears," says Fisher.

At a nearby UNICEF-supported center, they met children whose parents had been hacked to death in the church. Grant bent down to talk to them. One little boy, about eighteen months old, snared his attention. He was slight but seemed resilient, with big eyes and a shy smile. He wore shorts and a hoodie. Grant picked him up, cradling him in his pale, bony arms. A caretaker told him that the boy's name was Joseph, and that all of his family members had been killed. The boy grabbed Grant's finger with a tiny hand. Grant hugged him, pressing Joseph's cheek to his own grinning, sunken, wizened face.

While in Nyamata, he was treated to a performance of sorts — a reenactment of the genocide by children. The boys and girls — who had fashioned makeshift guns from sticks and bits of metal, rubber, and cloth and who split up into different sides — acted out the killings they had witnessed as a form of therapy. In a photo of the event, Grant appears to have waded into the throng of children with their toy guns, and he is bending down slightly, talking to a boy and inspecting his weapon. Betty Press, who took this picture, found the performance bizarre and somewhat troubling. "I was terribly affected by that," she says. "I don't know what the kids took from it, supposedly that was their way to get past it. To me, it was like, *Oh my goodness*, this is like reliving it…man, I had a hard time dealing with that."

She recalls Grant asking the interpreter about the event. "He wasn't content to just watch it," says Press. "He wanted to find out if it was helping."

The hectic, three-day schedule shepherded Grant through a series of meetings, including one with Rwanda's new president, Pasteur Bizimungu. It also included visits to nearby Burundi and Zaire (now the Democratic Republic of the Congo). "We were pushing him," says Fisher. "I remember telling him several times, 'We can slow down.'"

But Grant didn't want to slow down. "No," he said. "Let's keep going."

The most intense moment came during a stop at a squalid refugee camp near Bukavu, in neighboring Zaire. The camp, called Panzi, had become home to thousands of Hutu soldiers who had fled Rwanda. Many of them had committed terrible atrocities. And yet they were still armed, and many openly toted automatic rifles — as if daring someone to try and take them away. Panzi was a lawless, barren, and unpredictable place, with just a few scant services. Many people slept on the ground. Food was scarce, and cholera and dysentery stalked the inhabitants. On the day before Grant's visit, the Associated Press ran a story describing the scene at Panzi: "Teenagers sprawl on the ground in fatigues, playing cards and swearing. They bum cigarettes and beer from the soldiers and paw the breasts of passing girls." These boys and the girls they harassed were the reason UNICEF was interested in Panzi — among this crowd of killers and *geno-cidaires* were about a thousand children, many of whom had been abducted from their families. Some had been forced to do horrible things. Considered a lost cause by many, they were still children. They were UNICEF's constituents, and they did not belong in this bleak place.

In a series of negotiations preceding Grant's trip, UNICEF staff had persuaded Hutu authorities to free and "demobilize" the children and allow them to be transferred to UNICEF-supported centers, where they could resume their schooling and receive psychological counseling. It was decided that Grant would preside over a ceremony in which the adolescent and prepubescent fighters would remove their military jackets and symbolically cast off their association with war. Afterward, they and the other children would essentially be transferred into the custody of UNICEF.

Early on the morning of the ceremony, UNICEF's Abdul Mohammed went to Grant's Kigali hotel room to check on him. Knowing how ill he was, he wanted to make sure he was awake and had time to get ready. When he approached the door, he noticed it was already open. And he could hear a voice, ostensibly reciting something, perhaps ticking off items on a mental checklist. When Mohammed entered the room, he found Grant standing at a sink, washing his underwear and talking to himself. He was rattling off the day's itinerary, seemingly psyching himself up for what he had to do.

When they reached the camp, it was hot and dusty and bright, and the shadows were long and deep. Men with guns glared at them. Mohammed walked with Grant and stuck close to his side. He did not like the way the men were looking at him. "It was one of the scariest moments for me," says the mustachioed, professorial Ethiopian. "They thought I was a Tutsi."

He feared the Hutu soldiers might seize him and haul him away. There was nothing or no one to stop them — except Jim Grant. "I just hung to him," he says.

Grant noticed the stares, Mohammed says. He made sure to keep Mohammed at his side and to keep a car running nearby — in case they needed to get out of there.

As Grant and Mohammed and a few others walked to the site of the planned ceremony, where some five hundred children were gathered, Grant had some trouble, says Mohammed. He stumbled once but did not fall. Several people helped him along.

They arrived at the designated spot — a wide dirt clearing — and the children were waiting. A few dozen girls, some in brightly colored dresses, sat in rows on the red dirt at his feet. Beyond them radiated a rustling crowd of older kids, mostly boys, many in olive green military fatigues. Some were singing, Mohammed recalls, and a festive mood was percolating. In the distance, beyond the fidgeting assembly, a rusted tin roof glinted. Above it, on a bare ridge, stood a line of spindly, raggedy trees. The sun lacquered everything in viscous, pasty heat.

Grant wore a striped white dress shirt, the sleeves rolled up. His chest pocket bulged, perhaps stuffed with ORS packets and his tiny steno notebooks. He looked at his audience. Some were twelve and older; others looked about five, six, seven years old. A woman stood nearby ready to translate his words into Kinyarwanda. His voice was faint and thin, but he still spoke clearly and forcefully. Mohammed remembers a brief, potent pep talk: "You are children, and you don't belong here. You don't belong in war ... War is bad ... war should be avoided. War is not natural ... War is not for children."

Then, says Mohammed, Grant told them that it was time to move forward. It was time for them to go back to being children, to go back to school. UNICEF, he explained, would help them do that. Grant may have asked how many of them did not know where their parents were. A flock of hands likely shot up. He then may have said that UNICEF would try to connect them with their families. Right now, he needed to ask them to do something very important, both physically and symbolically. He announced that he had brought them some new clothes. But first, before he handed them out, he needed them to give up their military uniforms.

The next part was planned in advance, yet it became something more than what was scripted. Whether the kids had been told beforehand what was expected of them is unclear. But they indeed began to remove their olive green coats. The interpreter was enthusiastically yelling "Throw out your clothes! Throw out your clothes!" Coats became airborne, sailing into the bright white afternoon. The kids were howling, smiling, and whooping — and Grant was egging them on. He started throwing up his arms like an orchestra conductor, cheering and scooping the air with big sweeping motions, as more and more kids ripped off their uniforms and tossed them into the sky. The mood became that of a rollicking celebration, a rite of passage, a stark sort of graduation ceremony — a graduation from death and fear and the enforced thirst for blood.

Grant then made his way into the crowd of hopping, jostling kids. They were dancing now. They treated the frail UNICEF chief like a rock star who had just jumped off the stage. They hugged him, reached out for him, looked at him in stunned awe. He greeted them and began collecting their old clothes, clutching bundles of grubby coats and handing them off to staff members. A huge pile of coats and shirts steadily grew on the edge of the clearing.

Betty Press was snapping away, trying to capture the magnetic feeling that eddied around Grant. "It was the most incredible scene," she says.

Grant's face exuded complete, unalloyed elation. Says Mohammed: "He no more looked like a sick man."

After the festivities had subsided, and after Grant and his staff members had handed out hundreds of sets of new clothes and shoes, Mohammed was standing next to his boss.

"That makes your day," he said.

Grant looked at him. Then he replied, "You betcha!"

Chapter 17
A BIGGER MISSION

If you needed to spend money you didn't have, hire emergency staff at a moment's notice, buy a fleet of Land Rovers to help forestall a famine, play hopscotch with your budget lines, break a rule or ignore one — Jim Grant had your back.

If it could save a kid, he would tell you, then do it. Let him worry about the bureaucrats in New York. No matter how high the stakes, everyone knew that results trumped risks. The bigger picture also eclipsed the smaller one. Grant would advise: "Don't bend down to pick up paper clips."

For the most part, this empowering, permissive strategy returned breathtaking dividends, saved countless lives, and strengthened UNICEF's field operations.

It may also have helped spawn the biggest financial scandal in the organization's history. In November 1994, as Jim Grant's health precipitously eroded, UNICEF auditors uncovered serious irregularities in the Kenya office — and it was more than a few scattered paper clips.

As news of the shenanigans in Nairobi trickled out, questions swirled: Was this a result of Jim Grant–inspired risktaking? Was it the honest product of staff breaking rules to save kids and reach the mid-decade goals? Or was it deliberate malfeasance and abuse? Or a mix of both? How bad was it, and who was responsible?

The debacle's full scale — which wasn't officially revealed until after Grant's death — was potentially disastrous. Auditors would eventually determine that a total of $1 million had been lost to outright fraud, and another $9 million misused due to "alleged gross mismanagement." A total of twenty-four employees were involved, including several senior officials. According to the auditors' findings, there were payments to fictitious companies, falsified expense reports and medical insurance claims, and personal bills paid with UNICEF funds. The internal audit report determined that "inadequate oversight and supervision contributed to the late discovery of the irregularities." A report by the UN Advisory Committee on Administrative and Budgetary Questions concluded that "obvious indicators of irregularities were ignored or not effectively followed up by UNICEF headquarters."

The feared fallout, in terms of damage to UNICEF's fundraising ability, was a nauseating prospect.

Grant couldn't be held responsible for policing all 144 country operations. Budgetary problems routinely bobbed up in country offices all over the world — how could he be expected to tend to them all? Other people were supposed to do that for him. As for the crisis in Kenya, someone was clearly not minding the store there closely enough.

Still, some senior staffers felt Grant should have paid more attention to the initial signs of trouble in Kenya — this case was one of real malfeasance involving a lot of money. A few of them confronted him during a meeting when the irregularities first emerged, according to a staff member who was present. They told Grant this matter demanded his personal attention. This time, he needed to be directly involved.

Grant listened. Then, according to the staff member, he demurred. He said, "There is a bigger mission I'm concerned about."

Grant wasn't saying he would hinder the investigation or stand in its way or hush it up. Two of his deputy executive directors, Richard Jolly and Karin Sham Poo, insist he cooperated fully with auditors and that he wanted them to get to the bottom of it. He simply didn't want to deal with it himself. Many of the mid-decade goals hung tantalizingly close, and, as his time rapidly melted away, he simply wouldn't pay attention to much else. In his mind, the choice may have seemed as stark as it had always been: save lives or push paper — though one might argue that, in a case like Kenya, neglect of the latter could seriously crimp the former. Had he focused more on Kenya, would the outcome have been different? Could some of the damage have been checked? Maybe.

What really happened in Nairobi is still debated. Some former staffers believe it was not as clear or as damning as the auditors indicated. A major repercussion, some felt, was that the scandal gave Grant's successor, Carol Bellamy, a pretext to fundamentally alter UNICEF's management structure, placing an excessive emphasis on budgets and administration and undermining its decentralized way of operating. In fairness to Bellamy, Kenya could have done even more harm to UNICEF's reputation had she not contained it. Inheriting the mess from Grant, she ultimately restored a sense of confidence in UNICEF's management procedures that had clearly eroded.

Press accounts of the Kenya scandal, which came out several months after Grant's death, emphasized the shocking loss of $10 million, money that should have gone to help children. But the figure was somewhat misleading, says Richard Jolly. He acknowledges that up to $1 million "had been used totally corruptly, totally inappropriately." But the much larger balance — $9 million — was not stolen. These funds, Jolly explains, "had been used for buying pharmaceuticals without three competitive bids." If so, "gross mismanagement" may have been an overstatement. Still, $1 million in filched funds was a deeply troubling fumble.

Whatever happened in Kenya, the episode draped UNICEF in an acrid haze. It was one of "a series of shocks" — as one staff member put it — that afflicted Grant in his final days. Another one he knew was coming: a "management study" conducted by consulting firm Booz Allen Hamilton. The UNICEF board had requested the study, and Grant had balked. "He was dragging his feet," says Fouad Kronfol.

But eventually, the UNICEF chief gave in and pledged his cooperation. He had no choice.

The results, based on a survey of seven hundred and fifty staff members (and interviews with three hundred and fifty) were shared with Grant and others as early as October and formally released in December. While lauding UNICEF for its considerable achievements, the three-hundred-page report noted a "value system that staff renounce" and "personnel processes that have lost credibility." It cited complaints about global goals, concerns about accountability, and a perceived lack of transparency in financial management. It also concluded that the organization "does not have substantial experience" with important issues central to its mission, including child abuse and exploitation. Also pointing out "unusual hostilities" between the board and UNICEF leadership, Booz Allen called for major reforms.

Several Grant loyalists dismiss the Booz Allen report as a vindictive move by some board members to rein in a man they could never really control or understand — one whose unrivaled triumphs had stirred pungent feelings of jealousy and resentment. The study amounted to a betrayal, says Gourisankar Ghosh, whom Grant had recruited from the government of India to run UNICEF's water programs. "It was very unfair to him...I felt very, very sad the way he was treated toward the end."

Others see value in some of Booz Allen's recommendations, which included appointing a special "associate executive director" to handle day-to-day management issues that Grant clearly eschewed. Some of the problems cited in the report were valid criticisms, and they certainly needed to be addressed. Grant had pushed staff members past their limits, ignored unpleasant realities, blatantly favored some field operatives, hired and promoted people according to his own close-to-the-vest set of criteria, and upset an established system of career advancement. All of that was true. But Booz Allen did not seem to appreciate the context in which much of this had happened or the momentous change that had accompanied it. The firm did not seem to get who Jim Grant was or what he and UNICEF had done.

The tensions cited by the consulting company stemmed, in part, from friction between Grant and wealthy donor countries represented on the board, especially European ones. Some felt the UNICEF chief cared too much about child survival to the detriment of other issues and that he did not listen enough to UNICEF's principal funders. Grant's primary support on the board — and the reason he had been able to weather all the criticism for so long — came from the developing countries. They had always been in his corner, because he had always been in theirs. He had grown up in a developing country, after all, and his sympathies were far more attuned to the plight of the poor than most "first world" UN officials. The child survival revolution had focused on children in the poorest countries (where the most were dying) and directed a current of resources to their governments. Grant and Richard Jolly had openly challenged the World Bank and IMF for structural adjustment policies that unduly punished developing countries. Grant also repeatedly championed debt relief for strapped governments of poorer nations. And he often pointed out that, in terms of according priority to children, some developing countries had done a better job than their

richer peers; immunization rates in some cities in the developing world, he would joyfully note, were higher than in New
York City and Washington, DC. As the well-being of children
improved during the 1980s in some of the world's poorest
pockets, the situation of children in Grant's own country, the
United States, deteriorated — this sad truth, he would say, was
"my greatest disappointment."

"Jim became a hero to the developing countries," says Joe
Judd, an American who worked for UNICEF in Bangladesh,
China, Indonesia, and the Philippines. In return, he adds, they
"were not going to let Jim sink."

But at the very end, he was sinking a little bit anyway. Over
the course of fifteen years, he had defied every doubter in the
most extraordinary way. He had tapped the potential of the UN
as no one else ever had. He had unlocked a whole new realm
of possibility in health and international development. He had
shown that poor children did not have to die in mass numbers.
He had mobilized the entire world to take better care of its
young citizens. Now, after all that, his tenure was ending on a
stubbornly sour note.

As Grant's condition worsened, a small circle of friends, family, and staff kept gently pushing a harsh, unvarnished piece of
advice: quit. For his sake, and for UNICEF's, it would be best,
they told him, for him to step down now.

But he wouldn't. If he resigned, he was done — invisible,

insignificant, denuded of power. He was going to keep moving until he dropped.

Though he mentioned it to almost no one, Grant had been struggling for some time with the prospect of a post–Jim Grant UNICEF and a post-UNICEF Jim Grant. At some point within his last six months, likely before he became gravely ill, he had asked his senior adviser Jim Sherry to meet him at the Cosmos Club in Washington, DC, to discuss his future and his options. Charming, raspy-voiced, and politically astute (he was the former chief of staff for Congressman Sandy Levin), Sherry was an American doctor who had become part of Grant's inner circle.

He met Grant in the evening at the genteel private social club housed in a Beaux Arts mansion near Dupont Circle. Grant had been a member of both the Cosmos Club and Metropolitan Club for decades. The stately, stuffy bastions of male power in Washington had stirred controversy in the 1960s for denying membership to women and minorities. Though this had changed by 1994, they were still exclusive and reeked of elitism. As unfussy as he was, Grant still seemed to relish some trappings of prestige. But the main reason he belonged to the clubs, according to his son Bill, was that "they were the right places to meet the right people."

As Sherry listened, Grant talked about Halfdan Mahler, the legendary former WHO director general who had been both his adversary and his collaborator. Grant was fixated on what happened to him after he left WHO in 1988.

"It was as if he disappeared from the scene," Grant told Sherry.

They talked for a long time, but Sherry knew that Grant had another appointment — a very important one. He was supposed to see his eldest son John's family, including his grandsons. They lived nearby. And he was late.

"Jim, you gotta get going," Sherry said.

"Okay, okay, okay," Grant said. He seemed distracted.

At some point, Grant's son John called him (likely on a Cosmos Club phone) and asked him where he was.

"Okay, yeah, I'll get out of here right away," Grant said. "I'm a little delayed."

But Grant wanted to keep talking to Sherry. Sherry reluctantly agreed. He says now: "When he had an issue, he didn't let it go."

Jim Grant loved his family deeply. His sons Bill and Jamie say he was an excellent, caring, attentive father, husband, and grandfather (John Grant died of a stroke in 2000 at the age of forty-eight). But as several staff members have suggested, the children of the world came first — before anyone or anything else. The mission of child survival had progressively possessed Jim Grant, pervaded his soul — now perhaps more than ever.

He had not always been like this. His now near mythic persona had evolved, and he had evolved with it. "He wasn't 'Jim Grant' when he started at UNICEF," Sherry notes. "He was 'Jim Grant' when he left UNICEF."

And, as his days dwindled, his mission only grew more urgent.

On November 11, 1994, he gave what would be his last speech. Several people advised him not to appear, to skip this one. He was in "terrible shape," says Mary Cahill. "It looked like he could expire at any moment."

His jaundice was full-blown. His voice was light and wheezy and breathless. He was haggard and bony and short of breath. His discomfort was total. Sitting down for long periods tortured him — at least the speech would give him a chance to stand up and move around.

He spoke at the Third Committee of the Forty-ninth General Assembly of the United Nations. Though nominally about "child rights," this address covered a host of issues — his final laundry list of asks for the governments of the world. He plugged the Convention on the Rights of the Child and mid-decade goals. He urged the UN member states to keep children where he had put them — at the "very center of development strategy." He argued for a ban on land mines, a crackdown on child labor and child trafficking, greater protection for children trapped by war, and the humanizing of economic sanctions to make them less harmful to children.

As though anticipating that the unprecedented concern for children shown in recent years might evaporate as soon as he stepped away from the podium for the last time, he made a bald plea: "A child has only one chance to develop, and the protection of that one chance therefore demands the kind of commitment that will not be superseded by other priorities. There will always be something more immediate; there will never be anything more important."

Shortly after this speech — Mary Cahill thinks it was later that same afternoon — he left UNICEF House for the last time. Word zipped through the corridors that this might be the final chance to see the "Mad American," and a throng of people massed in the lobby and spilled onto the narrow Manhattan street outside. Traffic stopped. Grant carefully made his way through the lobby and past the UNICEF card and gift shop. The crowd parted, allowing him a path of about six feet. He did not rush, but he was determined to make it out. People reached out to try to touch him, shake his hand, and he greeted them. He stopped to hug them and to thank them. "He was saying goodbye with his eyes," says Judd. "Those eyes could communicate so much."

Staff members were crying and cheering and applauding for him as he walked by. Many could not believe the man who had made UNICEF what it was, who in some cases had made them who they were, who had galvanized the entire world, was now slowly shuffling off the stage. A palpable feeling of dread spread from the lobby through the crowd on Forty-fourth Street. How could UNICEF possibly go on without him?

"Everyone was really shell-shocked," recalls Judd. "It was an incredible spontaneous outpouring...He went out like the true showman he was."

A few days later, he slipped into a coma and was hospitalized again. Dr. Brennan performed another procedure, this one purely palliative. It was far too late to stop the cancer — that tumor had taken over most of his liver by now. But the surgeon was able to allow his bile to drain better and alleviate the jaundice and the bloating.

Cole Dodge remembers visiting him in his hospital room. Dodge, then the regional director for eastern and southern Africa, was in New York at Grant's request. Before he left Nairobi, he had bumped into the film director and UNICEF ambassador Richard Attenborough, who had given him four tickets for the New York premiere of his new film, a remake of *Miracle on 34th Street* (Attenborough was starring in it). The premiere was at Radio City Music Hall on November 15, the day of Grant's surgery.

When Grant found out Dodge had the tickets, he insisted that Dodge round up Ellan and Jon Rohde and take them to the premiere with him. "I don't want anybody around this hospital room," Grant instructed. "You just do it."

Dodge did as he was instructed.

A knotty question grew more cumbersome with each passing day: Who would succeed Grant after he died? Another question was tied to it: Would Jim Grant have a say in the matter?

He knew whom he wanted as his successor: his friend Dr. Bill Foege. A figurative and literal giant at six feet seven, Foege approached NBA altitude. His influence was even bigger. A former director of the US Centers for Disease Control, he had played a pivotal role in the eradication of smallpox in the 1970s. He was well known and well liked by virtually everyone in the universe of global health. As the chair of the Atlanta-based Child Survival Taskforce — a consensus-building group formed in the wake of the launching of GOBI — Foege had deftly sewn together cooperation from many disparate actors (including WHO, the United Nations Development Program, the World Bank, and the Rockefeller Foundation). Deliberate and unflappable, he had been able to soothe egos Grant had trodden upon.

Foege understood and wholeheartedly supported Grant's child survival revolution and was trusted by many at UNICEF. And more importantly, he shared Grant's zeal. To ensure that zeal — or some variety of it anyway — continued, there was simply no better choice than Bill Foege. Rohde and many others agreed.

The UN secretary general appoints the executive director of UNICEF, but there is always a secretive, behind-the-scenes tussle that sways the decision. The Europeans would undoubtedly front a candidate or two. Pressure was also building to appoint a woman to lead UNICEF. There was no guarantee that Grant's wish would be honored.

But Jon Rohde believed that, given Grant's near epic stature, there was no one who could say no to him — as long as he was still alive. Grant would have a much better chance of getting Foege installed, Rohde felt, if he stepped down now and made a forceful case for the transition.

Rohde wrote his friend a letter urging him to do just that. "I felt I owed it to him," the blunt pediatrician says. "He didn't have long."

No one can ignore you, Rohde wrote. No one will deny you your wish, your pick for the next executive director, as long as you are still breathing. But you have to resign in enough time to make it happen.

Grant disregarded the letter.

"He did not come to grips with his own mortality very well," says Rohde. He describes Grant's attitude: "I've got too much to do to die."

His denial edged into delusion. Instead of focusing on his successor and other important matters, Grant was concerned about getting his carpet cleaned. He wanted to get his apartment ready so he could entertain guests once he was better. He bought tickets for him and Ellan for a cruise along the Alaskan Inside Passage that he would never be able to use. Even when it was clear his cancer was inoperable and that his days were preciously finite, part of him never accepted it. He somehow believed he was going to resume his life and his mission. He was determined to "bulldoze reality," says Cahill.

Yet he made some concessions to reality. During his last few weeks, he called Foege numerous times. "He would call me at ten or eleven at night with an idea," Foege recalls, "and he would say, 'I just don't want this idea to be ignored.'"

Rohde and Adamson made an in-person appeal to urge Grant to devote his remaining energy to the matter of his successor. They went up to Ellan Young's house on Croton-on-Hudson, known as Camp Young, where Grant was living and receiving hospice care. He worked there as well. They sat in wicker chairs on a deck overlooking a pond. Grant faced the pond and Rohde and Adamson faced Grant. It was an unusually warm winter day. Grant was wrapped in a blanket. He needed to sleep a lot and had just woken up from a nap.

In all fairness, it was, of course, not in Grant's control to name his successor. Adamson and Rohde knew that. But they believed, recalls Adamson, "that if he put his mind to it, he'd find some way of end-running this one, too."

They also knew that Grant had become ever more determined to meet the mid-decade goals, and nothing — not Kenya, not Booz Allen, not his successor — was going to shunt his attention away from them.

But that's exactly what they were asking him to do.

Whatever capacity and energy and time and imagination and vision you have to change things in this world, they told him, all of it is now best directed at ensuring the right person succeeds you, a person who will carry on all that you are trying to do.

Grant's face registered a familiar expression, tight-lipped, stubborn, and slightly closed off. It was a look Adamson instantly recognized — it meant Grant didn't want to have this conversation. "He had the same reaction to a number of topics that he had some aversion to," says Adamson. "He never wanted to talk about AIDS, he never wanted to talk about contraception."

And so he turned them down.

Not only did he refuse to think about resigning, his term was extended into 1995, though it was wretchedly clear he would never complete it (part of this may have grown out of the UN secretary general's delay in appointing a successor).

Grant's personal notebooks from around this time show a blizzard of musings — medical concerns, his thoughts on

executive board meetings, personal issues, immunization figures. His handwriting was tiny, a frenzied cursive, each word
marching headlong into the next. On several pages, under the
heading "Castles in the Sky," he seemed to have listed some of
his many accomplishments, dating back to his college years.
Stuck throughout the pads were layer upon layer of Post-it
notes, adhered in stacks of ten and twenty. One of the notes
tracked his temperature and medications over the last several
months. Another contained a dense flurry of stats about Ethiopia's progress on a host of issues.

On December 19, he wrote a "New Year's memo" to staff
and noted that he was "thankful for the two extensions I've
been given — one by the secretary general and another by my
doctor." He then used the occasion of New Year's to nudge his
staff to work harder. "My number one new year's resolution
this year is to go all out, to give my best energies, for achievement of the goals," he wrote. "I sincerely hope that this will be
at the top of your action agenda, too." And he layered on an
exhortation that must have seemed like overkill: "We owe it to
the 2.5 million additional children whose lives will be saved if
the goals are reached."

About a week later, Grant drifted into another coma for about
eighteen hours and nearly died. Shortly afterward, he started
working again. He also resumed an extended interview session
being conducted at his bedside by Jon Rohde, Richard Jolly, and
his son Jamie; they were attempting to assemble his oral history.
They asked him about his philosophy, his influences, and his
upbringing, and he answered, at times, lucidly and at length. His

interviewers pushed him on several topics but not too hard, distinctly aware of how weak he was. It was a frenzied, valiant, yet incomplete effort that probably should have taken place much earlier — but Grant never would have offered them the time.

He officially resigned on Monday, January 23. He was seventy-two. After another bout of unconsciousness, he was hospitalized again. His small room at the Northern Westchester Hospital in Mount Kisco, New York, became filled with letters and expressions of gratitude from leaders all over the world. A huge, four-foot-tall card signed by hundreds of people from UNICEF was propped at the foot of his bed. Friends from numerous countries had sent him various miracle cures and homeopathic remedies, including an envelope of ginger roots from China. He had tried them all. His son Jamie, who was a teacher of Transcendental Meditation and who had his father's open, earnest face, thought meditation could help. Grant tried that, too. (He had, in fact, been meditating for over a year and had had some "excellent experiences," Jamie recalls.)

There was a small button he could press with his thumb to give himself a dose of morphine. When Adamson was visiting, he held up the morphine button and boasted, "I've hardly used any of this." On another occasion, when Rohde was in the room, Grant excitedly proclaimed: "You see this button? I can give myself a shot!" Rohde recalls that the nurses took away the intravenous morphine because Grant had been using it too much. They came in and asked him if he was in a lot of pain, and he said no.

"Well, you've been pressing this button quite a lot," one nurse said, adding, "You're supposed to press it when you have pain."

"Oh," Grant said. "It makes me feel really good."

He never stopped working. He even used one of the letters that had arrived in his room as a final and powerful point of leverage. It was a short note from President Clinton, thanking Grant for everything he had done for the children of the world. He received it on Thursday, January 26. Grant knew the letter gave him a fleeting opportunity born out of his impending death. On Friday, he insisted a response be sent to Clinton. He wanted to ask the president to sign the Convention on the Rights of the Child. The United States was, embarrassingly, one of the few holdouts to not endorse the landmark treaty guaranteeing children's basic rights. And Grant wanted the president to know that this was his last official act — his final request. How could the president of the United States refuse a dying man? Mary Cahill faxed the letter to the White House on Friday afternoon.

On Saturday morning, a nurse came into Grant's room and asked how he was doing. Gaunt, weak, wheezy, barely able to speak, Grant answered: "Full of enthusiasm!" He then raised his frail, sinewy fist in the air and said, "Fight, fight, fight!"

And on his last day, he proceeded to do just that. Adamson wrote in the anthology about Grant published by UNICEF: "It sounds like an over-dramatic figure of speech to say someone fights for a cause until the last breath in his body. In Jim's case, it was quite literally true."

Mary Cahill was alone with him on Saturday for about forty-five minutes. She had arranged for him to make a few calls to friends and staff members, a few last goodbyes. As he drifted in and out of consciousness, he murmured how important it was for UNICEF to continue its policies. She told him that, in his absence, Richard Jolly (who was the acting executive director) had said during meetings that everyone must go on pursuing Jim's vision and work. He muttered, "Good, good, good." He then added that both Kul Gautam and Nyi Nyi were also key people in keeping the cause alive.

At some point, he asked her to pass him his razor and a handheld mirror. As he shaved in his bed, he said to her: "Today is a very important day for me, Mary."

Then he looked toward the window to the left of his bed, as if something had suddenly drawn his attention.

"The light coming in the window is bright, isn't it?" he said.

Cahill peered at the window. She did not see a bright light. It was a dull, gray, January day outside. But she agreed: "Oh, yes, it is bright."

His sons Jamie and John were soon at his bedside; Grant's youngest son Bill was en route, in a plane. In case he didn't arrive in time, he called the hospital room and was able to speak to his father over the phone. Ellan was not there.

Grant was semiconscious and hallucinating. He seemed to think that he was in a UNICEF board meeting, and that he was addressing his directors. At one point, as his son John later recalled, he blurted out: "And I wrote it myself!"

Within the last forty-eight hours, he had told Jamie that he still thought he could conquer the cancer. "There has to be a way I can beat this," he had insisted in his now whistle-high voice. "There is always a solution."

Grant was determined to "end-run" his own death.

As his life separated itself from him, as he sank deeper into unconsciousness, his last moments seemed fixed not on his family or his wife or Ethel or his childhood or the epic sweep of his own time on this earth — but on UNICEF, on the cause, on the children whose fight he never surrendered.

Grant told those in the room he wanted his death to be an inspiration to others at UNICEF to meet the mid-decade and year 2000 goals. With faint, slurred speech, he asked them to carry on his work for children and to continue to improve the United Nations.

He died quietly in his sleep at around one in the afternoon of January 28, 1995.

On that day, in jungle hamlets and mountain villages, in cacophonous slums and sprawling refugee camps, on worn concrete floors and under roofs thatched of rice straw and banana leaves, in clay brick homes, on rutted, red dirt roads, and on scorching swaths of sand, children cried and screamed and sang and giggled and toddled and ran and fell and got back up and climbed on their mothers' laps and pulled their siblings' hair and gazed out in wonder at the big, bright world that swirled around them. Millions of boys and girls whose lives were reclaimed, whose stories were allowed to continue, who were not mourned or grieved or buried, but instead were loved and held and fretted over and scolded and prepared for the challenges of living, of surviving, all because of a man they had never met and whose name they would likely never know.

They filed in from the cold, in heavy coats and gloves and scarves, stepping into the cavernous, resonant, Gothic Cathedral Church of St. John the Divine on Amsterdam Avenue in northern Manhattan. They hugged each other briefly, shook hands, and quickly found their seats. A neat procession led by white-robed priests wended past the tall, intricately carved marble pulpit, as organ music blared against the soaring stone pillars and blue stained-glass windows. In the procession were Grant's family, friends, top advisers (including Adamson and Jolly), and at the end, a special guest, first lady Hillary Clinton. On February 10, 1995, about 2,500 people — dignitaries, celebrities, politicians, UN staff — had come to honor a man who, in many cases, had wooed them and challenged them and pestered them to take up his fight.

His death had drawn tributes and condolences from ambassadors and leaders the world over — Nelson Mandela, Li Peng, Jimmy Carter, Queen Noor, Jacques Chirac, Yoweri Museveni, and many, many others — but the upbeat lawyer in the wash-and-wear blue suit who had made the world care for its children as never before was unknown to most people. He had never won the level of recognition he had sought — the Nobel Peace Prize had eluded him (to the great disappointment of many UNICEF staff, one of whom grumbled that Grant deserved the award far more than the 2001 Nobel laureate, UN secretary general Kofi Annan). Grant's passing registered a few faint blips on the American media's radar. One of his admirers, activist and consumer advocate Ralph Nader, penned a column noting that Grant's obituary in the *New York Times* was short and buried deep in the paper; a few days later, the *Times* devoted a major front-page story and editorial to the passing of playwright George Abbott (Abbot's obituary was 2,427 words long; Grant's was 497 words). Wrote Nader: "The message from *The New York Times* in late January was: if you wish to be commemorated for a productive life, be a famous writer, producer and director of plays and not a person who is most responsible for saving the lives of 3 million children in the world every year." Nader also mentioned that major television networks, then in the thrall of the O. J. Simpson trial, "couldn't spare one minute for this great man's work." One network, NBC, did actually devote a few minutes for a special tribute by news anchor Tom Brokaw, who noted that Grant was survived by "his wife, Ellan, three children of his own, and millions of children around the world."

Grant's work was celebrated at quiet, candlelit memorial services in dozens of developing countries — from Bhutan to Ethiopia to the Philippines — and inside the immense stone sanctuary in New York City. One of the speakers at the Cathedral of St. John the Divine was Grant's longtime friend and confidant, Father Ted Hesburgh. The avuncular priest and president of Notre Dame University, clad in long red robes with his white hair swept to the right, told the crowd: "I always had the impression that he was my conscience when justice was needed in this great unjust world of ours." Hesburgh recounted how, sixteen years earlier, Grant had strong-armed him into raising awareness and funds to help those suffering in the wake of the Cambodian genocide. He claimed this effort saved the lives of one million people, adding that it "would not have happened without" Grant. "He got all of us to do things we didn't really want to do, because we were too busy or because the problem was too complicated or because we didn't have his enormous energy."

After UN secretary general Boutros Boutros-Ghali's remarks, Hilary Clinton ascended the pulpit (the Secret Service had inspected the venue and had required everyone in the first several rows to obtain a special pass). Clinton was wearing a dark dress, earrings, and a sparkling broach, and her long hair was pulled back with a headband. "I consider Jim Grant to be one of the great Americans of this century," she said into the microphone, her voice echoing in the immense, murky space. She recounted how when she first met the UNICEF chief, he had pulled out a packet "that looked like this." She held up a small, white packet of oral rehydration salts, as camera flashes popped around her. Grant had berated her about how easily and cheaply this packet could save lives.

Then the first lady surprised everyone. She mentioned that one of Grant's "greatest hopes" was that the UN treaty on children's rights "would serve as a standard of principle that would guide us into the next century." She paused and then continued: "Therefore…I am pleased to announce that the United States will sign the United Nations Convention on the Rights of the Child."

Sudden applause rippled through the cathedral. Smiles tugged on solemn faces as astonishment radiated through the crowd. Some people swiveled in their seats, whispering to those sitting next to them, perhaps saying, *Can you believe it? Can you believe it?*

Grant's last request had been answered.

Epilogue
WHAT IF?

Taking the full measure of Jim Grant's legacy is like trying to wrap your arms around a redwood tree — you can grip parts of it, but you'll never grasp the whole thing. UNICEF has estimated that his child survival revolution saved 25 million children's lives during the fifteen years he ran the organization. But the policies and programs he spawned — at UNICEF and in governments throughout the world — continued to reap lifesaving rewards long after his death, helping to steadily drive down child mortality.

Between 1980 and 2013, the global mortality rate for children under age five plummeted from 117 deaths per 1,000 live births to 46 deaths, according to estimates from the UN's Interagency Group for Child Mortality Estimation. During that time, the number of child deaths fell from 13.9 million per year to 6.3 million. And this occurred despite a huge increase in population. The group also calculated that since 1990, almost 100 million children's lives have been saved by the worldwide effort to combat child deaths (though it overlaps by five years with the 25 million figure cited above, this estimate cannot be compared or added to the earlier figure; the numbers are likely based on different data and methods of calculation). These successes reflect the work of many people and span more than eighteen years after Grant's ashes were scattered on a California mountain, but his influence is indelibly stitched into them. Much of the overall recent progress in international development and global health also bears his fingerprints.

But that progress is not as robust as it could be. After Grant's death, the historic, high-octane momentum he created began to fumble and falter. Immunization rates stagnated, and the decline in child mortality slowed. There were many reasons for this: the merciless and growing toll of the AIDS epidemic, donor fatigue, a slackening in the investment of national governments, and cutbacks in services spurred by structural adjustment programs. But many feel that the overwhelming factor was the stark lack of a bold, unifying voice.

UNICEF's public profile has also diminished considerably since Grant — its annual flagship report, *The State of the World's Children*, garners a fraction of the attention that it received during his tenure.

"UNICEF, very specifically after Jim, took a nosedive in its leadership," says Robert Black, chairman of international health at the Johns Hopkins Bloomberg School of Public Health. No subsequent executive director, he adds, has brought the energy or clarity of vision provided by Grant.

Black was one of the authors of an influential 2003 series in the British medical journal the *Lancet*, which found that attention to and investment in child survival programs had slumped during the late 1990s and which called for a renewed commitment to carry on the work Jim Grant had started. The following year, the *Lancet's* editor, Richard Horton, wrote a blistering editorial charging that UNICEF had "lost its way" under Grant's immediate successor, Carol Bellamy. By focusing too much on the matter of "child rights," Bellamy had essentially dropped the ball on child survival, according to Horton. "This rights-based approach to the future of children fits well with the zeitgeist of international development policy," he wrote. "But a preoccupation with rights ignores the fact that children will have no opportunity for development at all unless they survive. The language of rights means little to a child stillborn, an infant dying in pain from pneumonia, or a child dessicated by famine. The most fundamental right of all is the right to survive." Horton asserted that "child survival must sit at the core of UNICEF's advocacy and country work. Currently, and shamefully, it does not."

Black claims that immunization programs became a lower priority during Bellamy's tenure, which he calls "criminal." "It was so irresponsible," he says. "With Bellamy, the medical approach was out and it was not really her priority. She could have just as well focused on human rights and continued some of the things, but this was a political regime that came in and rejected the previous one."

Bellamy sees this a little differently. The former head of the US Peace Corps, who had served as the president of the New York City Council in the late 1970s and early 1980s and had also worked as an investment banker, was known for her toughness and short temper. She was nominated to succeed Grant by President Bill Clinton. Clinton had initially supported Grant's choice, Bill Foege. But, after Grant's death, the president was forced to drop Foege in light of UN secretary general Boutros Boutros-Ghali's insistence that the next head of UNICEF be a woman (Grant was obviously no longer around to say anything about it).

To Bellamy's credit, she did give priority to important issues that some feel Grant had neglected, including child protection and HIV/AIDS. She flatly denies that she rejected Grant's regime and speaks of her predecessor in the most glowing terms. "It's much harder following a God," she says, "than following somebody who hasn't been that highly regarded."

Bellamy insists that immunization and child health programs remained significant priorities during her administration — she simply wanted to tackle other problems as well. "I suppose it is correct that there is less attention, but there was still attention to child survival," she says. "The attention...I believe, correctly broadened to include other critical issues that were confronting children." Some former UNICEF staff members feel that the *Lancet* editorial was unfair and praise Bellamy for tightening UNICEF's management systems, strengthening its support for education, promoting the advancement of girls, enhancing its emergency response programs, and, in 1997, for successfully resisting an ill-advised and potentially disastrous plan to merge UNICEF with other UN development operations.

Regardless of Bellamy's accomplishments — and many were considerable — it is indisputable that UNICEF lost its place at the vanguard of child survival during her tenure. She didn't abandon the issue entirely, but she did relinquish the organization's role as the leader of the child survival revolution. To this day, no one has reclaimed it.

Some blame Grant himself for part of this. One of the biggest criticisms leveled against him — in addition to his avoidance of administrative and budgetary issues he considered unpleasant — was that he left UNICEF in a compromised position. He took the agency to unimagined heights, but he also ran it ragged. His blind spot for ethically deficient employees effectively allowed some unsavory staff members to injure his agency and his mission. He also exalted the all-or-nothing pursuit of goals over everything else.

His loyalists point out that none of this was ever about trying to enrich himself or advance his own position — it was always about the mission. Even so, the lapses contributed to credibility problems and opened the door for his successor to make major changes. He did not plan for a UNICEF that outlasted him — even though he knew it would — and the organization suffered as a result.

Several former UNICEF staffers also believe that some of the unparalleled feats he set in motion were hasty and unsustainable — too focused on the quick fix, the dramatic marketing message, the "doable" success story. Many wonder if his legacy would be even stronger had he been more careful.

A year after Grant's death, a committee of outside experts convened by UNICEF issued a detailed report on the strengths and shortcomings of the universal child immunization campaign. Chaired by Dr. F. Marc LaForce, the committee lauded UNICEF and its partners for putting children's health in the "public and political eye" and for undertaking an effort that "prevented a remarkable amount of disease and death in children." But LaForce and his team also concluded that the historic global endeavor had excessively focused on short-term goals to the detriment of long-term sustainability. According to their report, funding for immunization programs in some countries had actually started declining in the early 1990s after the excitement of the 1990 deadline had worn off. The mad dash to meet immunization targets by 1990, they claimed, may have siphoned resources from other important programs, led to "shortsighted" decisions, encouraged the manipulation of data for political benefit, and made some countries too dependent on external sources of funding that would eventually dry up. After interviewing 150 people at UNICEF, WHO, government ministries, and NGOs, the committee found that "reports of problems with campaigns generally outweighed reports of advantages."

The committee offered valuable recommendations for improving UNICEF's immunization work and raised valid questions. And yet — despite the swarm of concerns about sustainability and waning commitment and overambitious goals and shortsighted decisions — the UCI gains *have* largely been sustained. According to WHO estimates, global coverage levels achieved in 1990 did not go up much over the following decade — but they didn't go down much either. With some declines here and there, they basically held firm, saving as many as three million children's lives year after year. Some countries did experience major drops throughout the 1990s (particularly in sub-Saharan Africa), but the rates did not generally fall to 1980 levels. Had Grant been more cautious, had he taken the time to focus more on long-term planning and sustainability, would he have accomplished as much? His approach was a calculated gamble that could have failed. But it worked.

Sustainability is important, but it can also be a synonym for complacency, says Kul Gautam. Being bold and pushing hard for huge leaps in immunization coverage will make much more of an impact than carefully maintaining minor increases, he says. "If you go from 20 [percent] to 70, and then somehow go down to 60, that is not a disaster," he explains. "It is still better than the so-called sustainable way that many people were pushing, [people] who were too easily satisfied with modest gains."

Starting in 2000, after the Gates Foundation funded the creation of the Global Alliance on Vaccines and Immunization (GAVI), the stagnant rates started to go up again.

Grant's greatest weapon — the reason he was able to essentially get four-fifths of the world's children immunized and spark a global movement involving millions of people — was the children themselves. As he often said, "Who can say no to children?"

But a few people did say no. A total of 195 nations have ratified the Convention on the Rights of the Child, but the

United States is not one of them. While President Bill Clinton's administration did sign the treaty — as Hillary Clinton had promised — the US Senate needs to ratify it for it to take effect. As of this book's first printing, it has not done so. The only other holdout is the newly created nation of South Sudan (the lawless state of Somalia ratified the treaty in January 2015). Some of the reasons cited for US recalcitrance over the years: the treaty prohibits the death penalty for minors (this is now moot; the US Supreme Court abolished juvenile executions in 2005), it does not expressly oppose abortion, and it limits parents' ability to discipline their kids. All are ludicrous, born mostly of conservative fear mongering.

What of Grant's mid-decade goals — the grand aspirations that stubbornly gripped his thoughts even in his final moments? As of July 1996, a year and a half after his death, a report by UN secretary general Boutros Boutros-Ghali found that most countries were on track to achieve most of the mid-decade targets. Ghali's study said the World Summit for Children goal process had unleashed "an extraordinary mobilizing power, generating a renewed level of activity on behalf of children around the world and creating new partnerships between Governments, NGOs, donors, the media, civil society and international organizations in pursuit of a common purpose." The report cited "striking progress" on immunization coverage, diarrheal diseases, polio, guinea worm, iodine deficiency disorders, access to safe drinking water, and breast-feeding promotion. The secretary general also noted that fifteen countries had incorporated the principles of the Convention on the Rights of the Child into their constitutions and that more than thirty-five had passed new laws to bring them in line with the convention. A few areas, including primary education and malnutrition, showed little progress. Sub-Saharan Africa and South Asia were also trailing behind other regions (as Gautam and others had warned they would, if the goals were not customized for each country).

Five years later, the new secretary general, Kofi Annan, released an update on the year 2000 summit goals — and this one was not as rosy. Some goals, he said, had sparked major gains since 1990: 1.5 billion people using iodized salt, sixty countries achieving a one-third reduction in child mortality, 175 countries now polio-free, one million fewer diarrhea deaths, a 40 percent decrease in the incidence of measles, a 50 percent reduction in neonatal tetanus deaths. Even with so many triumphs, Annan announced, most of the summit targets had not been reached. He attempted to explain why: "We have fallen short largely because the needed investments for children were not made." Both donor and developing countries had simply not set aside enough money. He cited other impediments: the widening gulf between rich and poor, the punishing burden of debt, the increase of conflict, the scourge of AIDS.

Another possible reason Annan did not mention: the absence of Jim Grant (and his stalwarts who had departed UNICEF, like Nyi Nyi).

The pest, the nudge, the unstoppable irritant was simply no longer there to whisper in countries' ears: *You've got to do more! And you've got to do it now!*

But the promise of the summit goals did not die when they expired in 2000. The time-bound, audacious yardsticks — perhaps too audacious in some cases — spurred the creation of the UN's Millennium Development Goals (MDGs). These eight bold, quantifiable targets, established in 2000, have catalyzed the most concerted effort ever undertaken to fight the worst aspects of poverty. The deadline is December 31, 2015. Each MDG contains several subgoals, some of which have already been met or are getting close. The world reached the MDG water subgoal of giving some 2.3 billion people access to clean drinking water since 1990. It also beat the poverty subgoal five years ahead of schedule, helping 700 million people escape the desolation of extreme poverty by 2010. Even if most are not met by the end of 2015 (and it looks like many will not be), the activity and resources mustered by the goals are aiding billions of people. These advances cannot be solely attributed to Grant and the MDGs, of course — the blossoming of democracy, the march of economic progress, the benefits of foreign aid, and the gain in living standards in many countries all undoubtedly played a role (though in many countries, these developments are likely linked to the goals). Perhaps the most important result is a radically changed set of expectations — before the MDGs, and before Grant, the world was not keeping track of the fight against poverty with much rigor or precision. It's hard to be motivated to do better when you don't really know where you've been. By demonstrating the power of measurable, time-bound goals — with clear plans of action to achieve them — Grant changed the modus operandi of the United Nations and numerous organizations and donors now working to enhance global health and development.

The child survival revolution continues today, even without a galvanizing leader. There are many organizations and individuals — including the staff of UNICEF and its vast network of national committees and on-the-ground NGO and community partners — who work assiduously to save and protect the youngest inhabitants of our planet. Donors and volunteers and governments across the globe steadfastly support this critical effort. In recent years, the rate of decline for child mortality has, in fact, accelerated. UNICEF has recently made the issue more of a priority, and donor and partner interest has been somewhat reignited. Amid copious stories of waste and scandal and corruption in the UN system and a miasma of skepticism about foreign aid and development, the campaign against child mortality stands out as one of the world body's most striking successes.

The most important people in all this, of course, are children and their parents. A lesson Grant's father, John Black Grant, instilled in many of his medical students and in his own son: any effort to help people must grow out of their community and involve their participation — or it will not work. Jim Grant was erroneously accused of being "top-down" and of callously telling parents what they should do and how they should do it. But his ultimate aim was not to impose his or anyone else's will on mothers and fathers in the developing world — it was, quite simply, to empower them to save their own sons and daughters. Regardless of "top-down" or "bottom-up," all parents — no matter where they live — want the same thing: for their children to survive and grow up and have a decent shot at life. Why should this be denied to any parent? Such an assurance doesn't seem like too much to ask, yet for millions of families beyond the reach of vaccines, clean water, education, and the most basic health care, it still is.

The road toward human progress runs through a clamoring gauntlet of skeptics. Some will say that international development is a flawed process, riddled with failure and conflicting agendas. Many past efforts have done more harm than good. Aid fosters dependency. Top-down prescriptions risk unseen perils (especially without local buy-in). Poverty cannot be fixed or solved. It is not like putting a man on the moon. All of that, to some extent, is true. But complexity can also be a cop-out. As Peter Adamson points out, the child survival revolution is really about "taking up the slack." There is no good reason that any child anywhere should die of a preventable disease or grow up illiterate or be physically and mentally stunted for lack of proper nourishment. There are ills in this world that can be stamped out, that *can* be fixed — Jim Grant proved it. His grasp of international aid and poverty was extensive, but his most basic belief — the belief that fueled nearly everything he did — was a simple one: the benefits of science and society should be made available to the many, not just the few.

One question that quivers on the lips of several former UNICEF staff: What if Jim Grant had lived another ten or fifteen years? He was in the midst of his crusade when cancer took him — he had many other plans. What else would have been achieved had he been allowed to carry on? A few have suggested that polio would now be eradicated, measles consigned to history books, child mortality reduced to an even lower rate than it is now. Maybe the world would have already met the fourth Millennium Development Goal — to reduce child mortality by two-thirds, based on 1990 levels (we are currently not on track to reach the target, despite recent gains). All speculation, of course, but it's impossible not to wonder about the what-ifs. Another question that has been bandied about: What would Jim Grant say now?

Jon Rohde attempted to answer this during a lecture he gave at George Washington University in March 2010. Somewhat indignant, his speech was also defiantly optimistic. He told the audience who Grant was, what he had done, and what lessons we could all learn from him — among them: bureaucracies can't replace visionary leaders; precise, "doable," time-bound goals are essential; be persistent — don't abandon a valid program at the first sign of donor fatigue; good governance is key — Grant made children the "proof" of good governance. Then the brusque, insistent doctor told everyone what he thought Grant would be doing today. He would, said Rohde, "focus on those most left behind in the progress of the last decades...transform UNICEF back into the agency it was when he joined — known for field presence...defend the right to child survival with the same intensity we defend civil and political rights...strengthen UNICEF support for education, especially of girls."

He would also "forge an alliance among partners" and would make "children the integrating catalyst." Then with a jolt of incredulity, Rohde added: "What political leader today consistently stands high to speak for children — their needs, rights and futures? . . . Where do we see that today? Why have they forgotten such a basic lesson? Jim would put children back on the political agenda."

Indeed, were he here, Jim Grant would likely be decrying the continuing global scandal that still takes place every single day — 17,000 children under age five dying needlessly today, tomorrow, and the day after that. Dying even though the vaccines and medicines and other means to protect them readily exist. That number is less than half of what it was when Grant took the helm of UNICEF in 1980. But in the twenty-first century, that's not good enough. It's a statistic of shame. We should no longer be keeping tabs on the number of children who die each day because we have not bothered to save them.

"Jim was a phenomenon," says Dr. Bill Foege. "Now we take it for granted that the number of child deaths under age five has come down dramatically — it's still far too high, and it's still obscene, but it's come down so much in the last few decades. Who thanks Jim Grant for that? But they should."

Acknowledgments

This book would not have happened without the generosity and commitment of a large number of people.

My wife, Kathy, urged me to pursue this idea and has steadfastly supported me from the beginning. For several years, she put up with my ridiculous schedule and took care of our young kids on countless nights and weekends to give me time (and on some weekends took our son and daughter to her father's place). I certainly would not have seen it through without her. I am also grateful for the warm encouragement provided by my parents and father-in-law.

My agents, Larry Weissman and Sascha Alper, believed in this book, and they believed in me. They guided me as I wrote my proposal and stuck with me throughout the entire process. I could not have asked for better or more devoted advocates.

Judith Gurewich, of Other Press, immediately understood the importance of this book and put her publishing house firmly behind it. Her passion and vision—and incisive editing—have made the book stronger and more nuanced. I feel deeply fortunate to have a publisher who is so personally invested in my project. I have also been lucky to work with a top-notch staff at Other Press, including Marjorie DeWitt, Lauren Shekari, Jessica Greer, Terrie Akers, and Yvonne Cárdenas.

I interviewed eighty-six people in the course of my reporting, many of whom proved pivotal. I am particularly grateful for the time and attention of Mary Cahill, Jon Rohde, Peter Adamson, Kul Gautam, Richard Reid, Cole Dodge, Alan Court, Abdul Mohammed, Dr. Nyi Nyi, Richard Jolly, Sheila Barry, Fouad Kronfol, Manou Assadi, John and Mehr Kahn Williams, Yohannes Tsadik, Agop Kayayan, David Haxton, Ulf Kristoffersson, and not least, Jamie and Bill Grant. The assistance offered by Ted Thomas, Marea Hatziolos, Warren Unna, and Melissa and Sarah Young was also extremely helpful.

Mary Cahill truly went above and beyond, time and again providing me with important information and connecting me with dozens of Jim Grant's colleagues and friends; probably a third of the people I interviewed were referred by Mary. She was also a wonderful source, who helped me understand her extraordinary and indefatigable former boss. Jon Rohde, Peter Adamson, and Grant's sons, Bill and Jamie, were all very gracious, indulging numerous interview requests and e-mails; each also read a draft of the book and provided useful and meaningful feedback.

Many other sources were hugely helpful as well, and I apologize for not mentioning them all here.

It was a great privilege to tell this story. Thank you to everyone who enabled me to do so.

A Note on Sources

Most of the information in this book is based on interviews I conducted with Jim Grant's colleagues, friends, family members, and others. Altogether I interviewed eighty-six people, many of them multiple times. I also relied upon a wide array of original material: internal and external UNICEF reports on numerous topics; official UNICEF board records; UN and UNICEF audits; memos; schedules; trip logs; press releases; Jim Grant's oral history; John Black Grant's oral history; UNICEF staff oral histories; UNICEF historical accounts; speeches; correspondence; Telexes; video footage; photos; Grant's academic, military, and citizenship documents; and his personal letters, files, and notebooks. I acquired these items from a range of sources, including the UNICEF archives, the UNICEF Web site, the UN's online document system, and Grant's family members (John Black Grant's oral history was obtained from the Columbia University Center for Oral History).

UNICEF's annual flagship publication, *The State of the World's Children* (which Grant launched with Peter Adamson), was a significant source of information, particularly for the early years of Grant's tenure. I also relied upon facts, figures, and additional information from many other UNICEF publications, including *1946–2006: Sixty Years for Children*; *America's Partnership with UNICEF: A Report to the United States on the Impact of Its Contribution to UNICEF from 1985 to 1995*; *Promises Kept: James Grant in South Asia*; the *UNICEF Annual Report* (numerous years); and *UNICEF Staff News* (the organization's regular internal newsletter). Immunization coverage figures were provided by the World Health Organization.

Selected Bibliography

I found many books, scholarly works, news articles, and other published accounts useful in researching this book, and I have listed here those that were especially helpful. Published works that I quote directly are attributed in the body of the text. Three books were especially important: *Jim Grant: UNICEF Visionary*, edited by Richard Jolly and published by UNICEF; and Maggie Black's two volumes on UNICEF history (titles provided below). I would encourage anyone who wants to learn more about UNICEF and/or aspects of the Jim Grant period not covered in these pages to read them.

BOOKS

Anderson, G. Norman. *Sudan in Crisis: The Failure of Democracy.* Gainesville: University Press of Florida, 1999.

Balinska, Marta A. *For the Good of Humanity: Ludwik Rajchman, Medical Statesman.* Budapest: Central European University Press, 1995.

Becker, Jasper. *City of Heavenly Tranquility: Beijing in the History of China.* Oxford, UK: Oxford University Press, 2008.

Black, Maggie. *The Children and the Nations: The Story of Unicef.* New York: UNICEF, 1984.

———. *Children First: The Story of Unicef, Past and Present.* New York: Oxford University Press, 1996.

———. *The No-Nonsense Guide to International Development.* Oxford, UK: New Internationalist Publications, 2007.

Bornstein, David. *How to Change the World: Social Entrepreneurs and the Power of New Ideas.* New York: Oxford University Press, 2004.

Broz, Svetlana. *Good People in an Evil Time: Portraits of Complicity and Resistance in the Bosnian War.* New York: Other Press, 2005.

Bullock, Mary Brown. *An American Transplant: The Rockefeller Foundation & Peking Union Medical College.* Berkeley: University of California Press, 1980.

Cash, Richard, Gerald T. Keusch, and Joel Lamstein. *Child Health & Survival: The UNICEF GOBI-FFF Program.* London: Croom Helm, 1987.

Chang, Iris. *The Rape of Nanking: The Forgotten Holocaust of World War II.* New York: Basic Books, 1997.

Cornia, Giovanni Andrea, Richard Jolly, and Frances Stewart. *Adjustment with a Human Face.* Vol. 1, *Protecting the Vulnerable and Promoting Growth.* Oxford, UK: Clarendon Press, 1987.

Dodge, Cole P., and Magne Raundalen. *Reaching Children in War: Sudan, Uganda and Mozambique.* Sweden: Sigma Forlag, with the Scandinavian Institute of African Studies, 1991.

Dodge, Marilyn S. *The Way It Was: Connections with Hope.* Lexington, KY: CreateSpace Independent Publishing Platform, 2013.

Duarte, José Napoleón, with Diana Page. *Duarte: My Story.* New York: Putnam, 1986.

Farmer, Paul, Jim Yong Kim, Arthur Kleinman, and Matthew Basilico. *Reimagining Global Health: An Introduction.* Berkeley: University of California Press, 2013.

Fisher, Roger, and William Ury. *Getting to Yes: Negotiating Agreement without Giving In.* Boston: Houghton Mifflin, 1981.

Goodfield, June. *The Planned Miracle.* London: Cardinal, 1991.

Grant, John B. *Health Care for the Community: Selected Papers of Dr. John B. Grant,* edited by Conrad Seipp. Baltimore: Johns Hopkins University Press, 1963.

Huq, Mujibul. *Near Miracle in Bangladesh.* Bangladesh: University Press Limited, 1991.

Jolly, Richard. *UNICEF (United Nations Children's Fund): Global Governance That Works.* London: Routledge, 2014.

——, ed. *Jim Grant: UNICEF Visionary.* Florence, Italy: UNICEF Innocenti Research Centre, 2001.

Kamm, Henry. *Cambodia: Report from a Stricken Land.* New York: Arcade Publishing, 1998.

Knowles, Elizabeth M. *Oxford Dictionary of Quotations.* Oxford, UK: Oxford University Press, 1999.

Koivusalo, Meri, and Eeva Ollila. *Making a Healthy World: Agencies, Actors and Policies in International Health.* London: Zed Books, 1997.

Minear, Larry. *Humanitarianism Under Siege: A Critical Review of Operation Lifeline Sudan.* Trenton, NJ: Red Sea Press, 1991.

Mukerjee, Madhusree. *Churchill's Secret War: The British Empire and the Ravaging of India During World War II.* New York: Basic Books, 2010.

Offit, Paul A. *The Cutter Incident: How America's First Polio Vaccine Led to the Growing Vaccine Crisis.* New Haven: Yale University Press, 2005.

Oshinsky, David M. *Polio: An American Story.* Oxford, UK: Oxford University Press, 2005.

Rieff, David. *Slaughterhouse: Bosnia and the Failure of the West.* New York: Touchstone, 1995.

Sen, Amartya. *Development as Freedom*. New York: Anchor Books, 1995.

Shawcross, William. *The Quality of Mercy: Cambodia, Holocaust and Modern Conscience*. Glasgow: Fontana/Collins, 1985.

Shirer, William L. *The Rise and Fall of the Third Reich: A History of Nazi Germany*. New York: Fawcett Crest, 1962.

Spence, John D. *The Search for Modern China*. New York: Norton, 1990.

Vianello-Chiodo, Marco. *Under-Soldier*. Bloomington, IN: Author-House, 2012.

JOURNAL ARTICLES AND LECTURES

Bellagio Study Group on Child Survival, "Knowledge into Action on Child Survival," *Lancet* 362, no. 9380 (July 26, 2003): 323–27.

Black, Robert E., Jennifer Bryce, and Saul S. Morris. "Where and Why Are 10 Million Children Dying Every Year?" *Lancet* 361, no. 9376 (June 28, 2003): 2226–34.

Cueto, Marcos. "The Origins of Primary Health Care and Selective Primary Health Care." *American Journal of Public Health* 94 (November 2004): 1864–74.

Duffy, Jim. "John Black Grant: A Revolutionary in China." *Johns Hopkins Public Health,* Spring 2005, 14–17.

Grant, James P. "A Fresh Approach to Meeting the Basic Needs of the World's Poorest Billion." *Internationales Asienforum* 9 (1978): 7–25.

———. "Jumpstarting Development." *Foreign Policy*, no. 91 (June 22, 1993): 124.

Gwatkin, Davidson R. "Why Bother? GOBI-FF, Population Growth, and Human Well-Being." Washington, DC: Overseas Development Council, 1983.

Horton, Richard. "UNICEF Leadership 2005–2015: A Call for Strategic Change." *Lancet* 364, no. 9451 (December 11, 2004): 2071–74.

Hulme, David. "Lessons from the Making of the MDGs: Human Development Meets Results-Based Management in an Unfair World." *IDS Bulletin* 41, no. 1 (January 2010): 15–25.

Litsios, Socrates. "John Black Grant — a 20th Century Public Health Giant." *Perspectives in Biology and Medicine* 54, no. 4 (2011): 532–49.

Newell, Kenneth. "Selective Primary Health Care: The Counter Revolution." *Social Science and Medicine* 26, no. 9 (1988): 903–6.

Pincock, Stephen. "Rajanikant Arole." *Lancet*, 378, no. 9785 (July 2, 2011): 24.

Quinley, John C., and Timothy D. Baker. "Lobbying for International Health: The Link between Good Ideas and Funded Programs: Bread for the World and the Agency for International Development." *American Journal of Public Health* 76, no. 7 (July 1986): 793–96.

Rohde, Jon E. "Why the Other Half Dies: The Science and Politics of Child Mortality in the Third World." Leonard Parsons Memorial Lecture. Birmingham, UK, March 15, 1982.

Sartorius, Rolf H., and Vernon W. Ruttan. "The Sources of the Basic Human Needs Mandate." *Journal of Developing Areas* 23 (April 1989): 331–62.

Sen, Amartya. "Mortality as an Indicator of Economic Success and Failure." Innocenti Lecture. Florence, Italy, March 3, 1995.

Snyder, Alison. "Carl E. Taylor." *Lancet*, 375, no. 9722 (April 10, 2010): 1248.

Wisner, Ben. "GOBI Versus PHC? Some Dangers of Selective Primary Health Care." *Social Science and Medicine* 26, no. 9 (1988): 963–69.

NEWS ARTICLES, COLUMNS, AND FEATURES

Abrams, Jim. "Marco Polo Bridge to Be Tourist Attraction: Chinese Spruce Up Landmark of War with Japanese." Associated Press, October 25, 1987.

Adamson, Peter. "Fighter for Children in the Third World." *Manchester Guardian Weekly*, February 12, 1995.

Anam, Mahfuz. "Interview with James P Grant: UN System's Moving Spirit." *Daily Star* (Bangladesh), February 1994.

Applebaum, Anne. "Where Economic Ambition Meets Reality-Rwanda." *Washington Post*, September 25, 2011.

Associated Press. "Man Is Found Liable in '80 Killing of Salvadoran Archbishop." September 4, 2004.

———. "New Chief Assumes Office in Colombia." August 8, 1982.

———. "Sixteen People Sentenced in Child Sex Scandal." March 7, 1988.

———. "Text of Bush's Speech: 'It Is Iraq Against the World.'" September 12, 1990.

———. "UNICEF Deplores Slaying of Six; Injured Youths Evacuated." January 24, 1994.

Baligh, Dalia. "In Famine's Grip: Hyenas Drag Corpses Away." Associated Press, October 24, 1988.

Barber, Tony. "The Bosnia Crisis: Serbs, Croats and Muslims: Who Hates Who and Why." *The Independent*, August 9, 1992.

BBC News. "UN Admits Failure in Rwanda." December 16, 1999.

———. "Biljana Plavšić: Serbian Iron Lady." February 27, 2003.

———. "Scarred by History: The Rape of Nanjing." April 12, 2005.

Becker, Elizabeth. "The Politics of Famine in Cambodia." *Washington Post*, November 18, 1979.

Beltrhan, Raul. "Undeclared Truce in El Salvador." United Press International, April 21, 1985.

Berger, Marilyn. "Cyrus R. Vance, a Confidant of Presidents, Is Dead at 84." *New York Times*, January 13, 2002.

Bernstein, Richard. "Lyrical Colombian Brings the U.N. to Its Feet." *New York Times*, October 6, 1983.

Biswas, Soutik. "How Churchill 'Starved' India." *BBC News*, October 28, 2010.

Bradley, Ed. "Michele." *60 Minutes*, CBS News, May 4, 1986.

Briscoe, David. "Immunizations Save Nearly 4 Million Children." Associated Press, December 21, 1993.

Brittain, Victoria. "SA Blamed for Child Deaths. UNICEF Report Shows Angola and Mozambique Have Highest Child Mortality Rates in the World." *The Guardian*, January 30, 1987.

Brody, Jane E. "UNICEF Urges Four Steps to Save Children's Lives" *New York Times*, December 17, 1982.

Brokaw, Tom. "An American Close-Up: Tribute to UNICEF Executive Director James Grant for His Unending Work Dedicated to Children." *NBC News*, February 3, 1995.

Brown, David. "Worldwide Vaccination Progresses; Protection Extended to 80% of Infants." *Washington Post*, October 9, 1991.

Buerk, Michael. Report from Korem camp in Ethiopia. *BBC News*, October 23, 1984. Accessed at: http://news.bbc.co.uk/2/hi/8315248.stm

Burns, John F. "The Dying City of Sarajevo." *New York Times*, July 26, 1992.

———. "A Sarajevo Hospital Works in 'Horror Beyond Anything.'" *New York Times*, October 18, 1992.

Cabrera, Annie. "Duarte Says Health Campaign Gave Country a Day of Peace." Associated Press, February 5, 1985.

Cassidy, Denis. "Remembering the 'Saint in Shirtsleeves.'" Independent.ie, December 12, 2013.

Chang, Gordon C. "Born of Struggle: 'Forgotten Ally' by Rana Mitter." *New York Times*, September 6, 2013.

Chavez, Lydia. "Duarte Not Planning an Inquiry on Nuns." *New York Times*, June 4, 1984.

———. "Duarte Vows to Crush Death Squads." *New York Times*, May 1, 1984.

Claiborne, William. "Angry Mobs Hunt Down Sikhs; Hindus Disregard Appeals for Calm." *Washington Post*, November 2, 1984.

Clancy, Joe. "Plavšić: The Iron Lady Who Turned," CNN.com, January 10, 2001.

CNN.com. "The Man Who Took on the Dissidents: Li Peng (1928–)." 2001. Accessed at: http://www.cnn.com/SPECIALS/1999/china.50/inside.china/profiles/li.peng/

Crosette, Barbara. "U.N. Details Its Failure to Stop '95 Bosnia Massacre." *New York Times*, November 16, 1999.

———. "UNICEF Says Third World Children Are Dying as Development Falters." *New York Times*, December 20, 1988.

C-SPAN. "1994 State of the World's Children." December 21, 1993.

Dahlburg, John-Thor. "Politics, World Crises Sap 'Child Survival' Funds." *Los Angeles Times*, December 4, 1995.

Danner, Mark. "To Haiti, With Love and Squalor." *New York Times*, Book Review Desk, August 11, 1991.

———. "The Truth of El Mozote." *New Yorker*, December 6, 1993, obtained from markdanner.com/articles/the-truth-of-el-mozote.

Davies, Karin. "Rwanda: Will Today's Children of War Be Tomorrow's Warriors?" Associated Press, September 10, 1994.

Deen, Thalif. "Population: Vatican Fails to Stop UNICEF Role in Family Planning." Inter Press Service, July 14, 1992.

———. "U.N.: U.S. Influence Seen Over Key U.N. Appointments." Inter Press Service, January 19, 2012.

Deng, Francis M. "In Sudan, Masses Die as Rebels, Government Use Food as a Weapon." *Los Angeles Times*, February 5, 1989.

Deutsche Presse-Agentur. "Casualties from Wartime Ordnance Increase in Cambodia." August 27, 2014.

Diebel, Linda. "Waiting for Aristide." *Montreal Gazette*, reprinted from *Toronto Star.* September 18, 1993.

Diplomatic World Bulletin. "U.S., U.K. Are Failing Their Children, UNICEF Reports." October 15, 1993.

Drudge, Michael. "Salvadoran Archbishop Reports 86 Deaths." United Press International, March 3, 1985.

Economist. "King Hassan of Morocco: Luck of the Devil." August 2, 2001.

Essoyan, Susan. "United Nations Begins New Year with Immunization Drive." Associated Press, October 26, 1985.

Faison, Seth. "The Persistent Mystery: How Many Died in 1989?" *New York Times*, June 4, 1999.

Fifield, Adam. "A Cruel Past Lingers: Genocide's Horrors Weigh on a New Generation." *Philadelphia Inquirer*, December 12, 2004.

Frazier, Joseph B. "Rebels, Government Hold Fire to Allow Doctors to Fight Disease." Associated Press, February 4, 1985.

Friedman, Josh. "Summit for the Children; 71 Leaders Vow to Save Sick, Hungry." *Newsday*, October 1, 1990.

Gettleman, Jeffrey. "Sudan's President, in Power since 1989, Won't Run Again." *New York Times*, February 21, 2011.

Globe and Mail. "Sudanese Complaints Halt Relief Train's Journey." May 15, 1989.

Golden, Tim. "Salvador Officers Named as Killers in U.N. Report." *New York Times*, March 15, 1993.

Grabar, Henry. "What the U.S. Bombing of Cambodia Tells Us About Obama's Drone Campaign." *The Atlantic*, February 14, 2013.

Grant, James. "Who Says the World Has Aid Fatigue?" Letter to the Editor, *New York Times*, June 6, 1986.

Gray, Denis D. "Relief Agencies Will End Food Aid to Pol Pot Areas." Associated Press, July 7, 1980.

Greenhouse, Steven. "Europeans Oppose American as Next Director of Unicef." *New York Times*, March 6, 1995.

Gregory, Joseph R. "Hassan II of Morocco Dies at 70; A Monarch Oriented to the West." *New York Times*, July 24, 1999.

Harley, Richard. "Cambodia Has Been Saved from a Holocaust by One of the Greatest International Aid Efforts in History." *Christian Science Monitor*, January 8, 1981.

Higgins, Alexander. "Two Nurses Killed in Shelling of Sarajevo's Main Hospital with PM-EC Yugoslavia-Peace Talks." Associated Press, December 1, 1993.

International Magazine of Peter Justesen, no. 3 (1985). "James P. Grant: Executive Director, United Nations Children's Fund — PJ Profiles."

Inter Press Service. "Children: Statistics of Shame Reveal Unfinished Business." December 15, 1994.

Irvin, Rebecca. "Saving the Children in Colombia." United Press International, September 3, 1984.

Izadi, Elahe. "Why It's Such a Big Deal that Oscar Romero Was Declared a Martyr by Pope Francis." *Washington Post*, February 5, 2015.

James, Caryn. "Audrey Hepburn, Actress, Is Dead at 63." *New York Times*, January 21, 1993.

James, Randy. "Sudanese President Omar Hassan al-Bashir." *Time*, March 5, 2009.

Jennings, Peter. "Person of the Week." *World News Tonight with Peter Jennings*, ABC News, September 28, 1990.

Jones, David W. "U.N. Officials Launch Massive Relief Effort." United Press International, April 1, 1989.

———. "Famine Relief Efforts in Africa Face Obstacles." United Press International, April 12, 1989.

——. "U.N. Officer Says Famine Relief Working in Sudan." United Press International, May 7, 1989.

Kifner, John. "Syria Said to Raze Part of Rebel City." *New York Times*, February 18, 1982.

Krebs, Albin. "Samora M. Machel, Man of Charisma." *New York Times*, October 21, 1986.

Landler, Mark. "Declassified U.N. Cables Reveal Turning Point in Rwanda Crisis of 1994." *New York Times*, June 3, 2014.

Landsberg, Michele. "1½ Million Babies Are Alive Because Jim Grant Cared." *Toronto Globe and Mail*, December 20, 1986.

Lazzaro, Joseph. "Bengal Famine of 1943 — a Man-Made Holocaust." *International Business Times*, February 22, 2013.

Lehrer, Jim, and Robert MacNeil. "India After Indira: Death of a Dynasty?" *The MacNeil/Lehrer NewsHour*, November 1, 1984.

——. "Report on Famine." *The MacNeil/Lehrer NewsHour*, November 9, 1984.

LeMoyne, James, and Patricia Sethi. "A Prince for Paupers." *Newsweek*, October 5, 1981.

Lewis, Paul. "Child Sex Scandal Roils UNICEF Unit." *New York Times*, June 25, 1987.

——. "First Convoy of Children's Aid Reaches Sarajevo." *New York Times*, November 2, 1992.

——. "Food Aid Seen as Averting Famine." *New York Times*, September 17, 1989.

——. "In War's Brutal Din, a 'Week of Tranquillity.'" *New York Times*, November 1, 1992.

——. "World Leaders Endorse Plan to Improve Lives of Children." *New York Times*, October 1, 1990.

——. "World Summit for Children: World's Leaders Gather at U.N. for Summit Meeting on Children." *New York Times*, September 30, 1990.

Los Angeles Times. "Hatchet Victims." Editorial Writers Desk, September 15, 1986.

Lyons, Christine. "He's a Cheerleader, Champion for Children." *USA Today*, September 1990.

MacArthur, Greg. "Agency Plan to Save Lives of 7 Million Children a Year." Associated Press, December 16, 1982.

Malkin, Elisabeth. "El Salvador Leader Apologizes for Archbishop's Assassination." *New York Times*, March 25, 2010.

Maykuth, Andrew, Sam Dillon, and *Miami Herald*. "José Napoleón Duarte, Salvadoran Leader, Dies." *Philadelphia Inquirer*, February 24, 1990.

"Military Overthrows Mali Dictator, Promises Democracy," Associated Press, March 26, 1991.

Mohammed, Abdul. "A Lifeline for Sudan." *Washington Post*, May 25, 1989.

Mouat, Lucia. "U.N. Takes Heat on Peacekeeping, Relief Effort in Bosnian Crisis." *Christian Science Monitor*, November 3, 1992.

Mulley, Clare. "The Woman Who Hated Children…and Saved Them." *Daily Express*, March 19, 2010.

Nader, Ralph. "*Memoriam: James Grant*," February 14, 1995; obtained from the "Nader Blog" at https://blog.nader.org/1995/02/14/memoriam-james-grant

Nasar, Sylvia. "The Conscience of a Dismal Science." *New York Times*, January 9, 1994.

Nelson, Harry. "UN Cites Children's Heavy Death Toll." *Los Angeles Times*, December 11, 1986.

New York Times. "Michael S. Shower, Unicef Adviser, 44." *New York Times*, April 10, 1994.

———. "The World's Best Shots." December 25, 1985.

———. "UNICEF Cites Success in 2 Child Health Programs." December 12, 1986.

New York Times News Service. "Famine Threatens Cambodia Again." March 22, 1980.

Newsweek. "Child Abuse Charges Rock UNICEF." July 6, 1987.

Nossiter, Bernard. "UNICEF, Going Against Trend, Plans Big Expansion." *New York Times,* June 7, 1981.

Oberdorfer, Don. "$69 Million Cambodian Aid Pledged." *Washington Post,* October 25, 1979.

Osman, Mohamed. "Convoy Pulls Out of Khartoum to Begin Massive Relief Effort." Associated Press, April 1, 1989.

Pace, Eric. "José Napoleón Duarte, Salvadoran Leader in Decade of War and Anguish, Dies at 64." *New York Times,* February 24, 1990.

Pandya, Haresh. "Sunil Janah, Who Chronicled India in Photographs, Dies at 94." *New York Times,* July 9, 2012.

Paulson, Tom. "Vaccine Program Hopes for Success Where Others Failed: Gains from Successful Immunization Campaigns Begun in the 1980s Were Being Lost by the Mid-'90s," *Seattle Post-Intelligencer,* March 22, 2001.

PBS's *FRONTLINE.* "Interview: General Romeo Dallaire." Fall, 2003.

Pear, Robert. "U.S. to Support U.N. on Children, But Money for Programs Is Scant." *New York Times,* September 26, 1990.

Perlez, Jane. "For Ethiopia, Catharsis Lies in Grim Truth." *New York Times,* January 19, 1992.

———. "Sudan, Racked by Famine, Agrees to $100 Million U.S. Food Airlift." *New York Times,* October 13, 1988.

Perlez, Jane, and Victoria Burnett. "Benazir Bhutto, 54, Lived in Eye of Pakistan Storm." *New York Times,* December 28, 2007.

Pinyan, Charles. "Geldof Announces Sport Aid." United Press International, March 5, 1986.

Platt, Stephen. "Opinion: Is China Ripe for a Revolution?" *New York Times,* February 9, 2012.

Press, Robert M. "World's Highest Rate Finally Falls." *Christian Science Monitor*, June 30, 1988.

Reuters. "Arturo Rivera Damas, 71, Dies; Outspoken Salvadoran Bishop." November 27, 1994.

———. "Rwandan Kid Soldiers Leave Army; UNICEF Wins Release of 8- to 12-Year-Olds." September 12, 1994.

———. "Sarajevo; 'Tranquility Week' Is Greeted by Machine-gun Fire." November 2, 1992.

———. "Strike Stops Sudan Trains." April 24, 1989.

———. "Sudan Train on Rebuilt Track Takes Food to Starving Town." January 13, 1989.

Robinson, Claude. "Ethiopia: U.N. Official Criticizes Slow Response to Famine." Inter Press Service, October 31, 1984.

———. "Starving the Children to Pay the Debts." Inter Press Service, April 18, 1985.

Robles, Frances. "For Haiti, No Payback after Duvalier's Regime." *Miami Herald*, January 26, 2011.

Rohde, David, and John F. Burns. "Executions Were Mladić's Signature, and Downfall." *New York Times*, May 26, 2011.

Rollnick, Roman. "Children Dying at High Rate in Mozambique, Angola." United Press International, January 29, 1987.

Rosenfeld, Stephen. "Billion-Dollar Bargain." *Washington Post*, December 21, 1982.

Rosenthal, Elisabeth. "Li Peng Retires, but His Infamy for Tiananmen Massacre Endures." *New York Times*, March 11, 2003.

Severo, Richard. "Roberto d'Aubuisson, 48, Far-Rightist in Salvador." *New York Times*, February 21, 1992.

Smith, Hedrick. "U.S. Confirms a Rightist Plot in El Salvador to Murder Envoy." *New York Times*, June 23, 1984.

Solomon, Stephen. "The Controversy over Infant Formula." *New York Times*, December 6, 1981.

Spielmann, Peter James. "U.N. Official Says Emergency Food Program Will Miss Target." Associated Press, April 26, 1989.

Stackhouse, John. "Putting a Head Count on Poverty: Development Agencies Sometimes Exaggerate — and Fabricate — the Statistics to Promote Their Worthy Causes. As with War, Truth Can Be the First Casualty of Aid." *Toronto Globe and Mail*, January 14, 1995.

Stanley, Alessandra. "World Summit for Children — Reporter's Notebook; A Protocol Nightmare: Silencing World Leaders." *New York Times*, September 30, 1990.

Steavenson, Wendell. "Assad's Hama Rules, Again." *New Yorker*, February 4, 2012.

Sullivan, Kevin. "Humanitarian Aid Convoy Turned Back." United Press International, November 6, 1992.

Swinton, Donald W. "Attorneys to Seek $504 Million from Duvalier in Europe, US." Associated Press, January 20, 1988.

Tamayo, Juan. "Betancur Takes Over in Colombia in Simple Rites Amid Nation's Woes." *Miami Herald*, August 8, 1982.

Tharoor, Shashi. "The Ugly Briton." *Time*, May 29, 2010.

Toynbee, Arnold J. "Not the Age of Atoms but of Welfare for All." *New York Times*, October 21, 1951.

United Press International. "Best of Times, Worst of Times for UNICEF." December 17, 1982.

———. "Relief Convoy Halted, U.N. Officials Robbed." May 22, 1989.

Usborne, David. "UN Pilloried for Failure over Rwanda." *Independent*, December 17, 1999.

Usher, John. "'Hidden Hunger' Kills 40,000 Children a Day." United Press International, December 17, 1982.

———. "UNICEF Report Says 100 People Dying Every Day in Ethiopia." United Press International, October 27, 1984.

Wechsberg, Joseph. "At the Heart of UNICEF." *New Yorker*, December 2, 1961.

Weisman, Steven R. "Reagan Criticized by Colombia Chief on Visit to New York." *New York Times*, December 4, 1982.

Williams, Ian. "Wherefore Romeo — Dallaire, That Is!" *Huffington Post*, November 11, 2013.

Williamson, Don. "A Grim Tour of Slaughter and Starvation." *Seattle Times*, November 3, 1992.

Winder, David. "United Nations Questions Its Ability to Keep the Peace while Social Programs such as UNICEF Wrack Up Impressive Records." *Christian Science Monitor*, December 31, 1982.

Wren, Christopher. "Ex-Bosnian Serb Chief Is Said to Surrender." *New York Times,* January 10, 2001.

———. "UNICEF Says Fraud Cost $10 Million." *New York Times*, May 26, 1995.

Xinhua General News Service. "China, U.N. Children's Fund Co-Operation Fruitful." October 16, 1989.

———. "UN Official Praises China's One-Child Family Drive." June 1982.

———. "UNICEF Executive Director Finds Dignity, Well Being amongst Chinese People." June 28, 1981.

REPORTS, STATEMENTS, AND MISCELLANEOUS ITEMS

1946–2006: Sixty Years for Children. New York: UNICEF, 2006.

America's Partnership with UNICEF: A Report to the United States on the Impact of Its Contribution to UNICEF from 1985 to 1995. New York: UNICEF, 1997.

Amnesty International Report 1984. London: Amnesty International, 1984.

Binet, Laurence. *Famine and Forced Relocations in Ethiopia, 1984–1986.* Paris: Médecins Sans Frontières, 2013.

De Waal, Alex. *Evil Days: 30 Years of War and Famine in Ethiopia.* An Africa Watch Report. New York: Human Rights Watch, 1991.

Department of Public Information, United Nations. "Former Yugoslavia — UNPROFOR: United Nations Protection Force." August 31, 1996. Accessed at: http://www.un.org/en/peacekeeping/missions/past/unprof_p.htm

Dolman, Anthony, Jan van Ettinger, and Jan Tinbergen. *Reshaping the International Order: A Report to the Club of Rome.* London: Hutchinson, 1976.

Evaluation and Research — Sustainability of Achievements: Lessons Learned from Universal Child Immunization. Report of a Steering Committee. New York: UNICEF, 1996.

Federal News Service. "Release of 1994 State of the World's Children Report, Main Lounge, National Press Club, Washington, DC, Tuesday, December 21, 1993, with James Grant, Executive Director of UNICEF." Major Leader Special Transcript. Washington, DC: December 21, 1993.

———. "'Spare the Children,' UNICEF Chief Pleads, Following Massacre of Orphans in Rwanda." May 4, 1994.

Forsyth, Justin. *Eglantyne Jebb: A True Children's Champion.* London: Save the Children, August 25, 2013. Accessed at: http://blogs.savethechildren.org.uk/2013/08/eglantyne-jebb-%E2%80%93-a-true-children%E2%80%99s-champion/.

The Fourth Ten Years of the World Health Organization, 1978–1987. Geneva: World Health Organization, 2011.

"From Madness to Hope: The 12-Year War in El Salvador." Report of the United Nations Commission on the Truth for El Salvador, S/2550, March 15, 1993, transmitted from the secretary general to the Security Council on April 1, 1993.

Gaud, William S. "The Green Revolution: Accomplishments and Apprehensions." Address to the Society for International

Development, Shoreham Hotel, Washington, DC, March 8, 1968. Accessed at www.agbioworld.org/biotech-info/topics/borlaug/borlaug-green.html

Gautam, Kul Chandra. "Marking Three Decades of Child Survival and Development Revolution and 30 Years of RESULTS: Contribution to Shaping Global Development Agenda." RESULTS International Conference, Washington, DC, June 21, 2010. Obtained from Gautam's Web site, www.kulgautam.org

———. "Ten Commandments of Jim Grant's Leadership for Development." June 20, 2001. Obtained from www.kulgautam.org

"Halfdan Mahler celebrates the Ottawa Charter for health promotion." Video accessed at: https://vimeo.com/51714332

Human Rights Watch. "Haiti: Prosecute Duvalier." News release, January 17, 2011. Accessed at: www.hrw.org/news/2011/01/17/haiti-prosecute-duvalier

———. *Human Rights Watch World Report 1989.* Section on Cambodia. New York, 1989.

"The Immunization Programme that Saved Millions of Lives." *Bulletin of the World Health Organization* 92, no. 5 (May 2014).

International Commission of Inquiry on Darfur: Report to the Secretary General. Geneva, January 25, 2005.

International Criminal Tribunal for the former Yugoslavia. "The Conflicts." Accessed at: http://www.icty.org/sid/322

Levels & Trends in Child Mortality: Report 2014 — Estimates Developed by the UN Inter-agency Group for Child Mortality Estimation. New York: UNICEF, World Health Organization, World Bank, and the United Nations, 2014.

Maier, Karl. "Conspicuous Destruction: War, Famine and the Reform Process in Mozambique," an Africa Watch Report (New York: Human Rights Watch, 1992).

Nyamata. Genocide Archive of Rwanda, Web site. Kigali, Rwanda.

Accessed at: http://www.genocidearchiverwanda.org.rw/index
.php/Nyamata

Peking Union Medical College Hospital: Twentieth Annual Report of the Medical Superintendent. Peking: P.U.M.C. Press, 1928.

"Primary Health Care Comes Full Circle: An Interview with Dr. Half-dan Mahler." *Bulletin of the World Health Organization* 86, no. 10 (October 2008).

Promises Kept: James Grant in South Asia. New Delhi, India: UNICEF, 1996.

"Progress at Mid-Decade on Implementation of General Assembly Resolution 45/217 on the World Summit for Children." Report of the UN Secretary-General, Fifty-first session of the General Assembly, A/51/256, July 24, 1996.

Reagan, Ronald. "Statement on the United Nations Children's Fund, April 18, 1983." Ronald Reagan Presidential Library. Accessed at www.reagan.utexas.edu/archives/speeches/1983/41883a.html

———. "United States Participation in the United Nations." Report by the President to the Congress for the year 1983. US Department of State.

"Robert Strange McNamara." World Bank online archives. Accessed at: http://web.worldbank.org/WBSITE/EXTERNAL/EXT ABOUTUS/EXTARCHIVES/0,,contentMDK:20502974~pagePK: 36726~piPK:437378~theSitePK:29506,00.html

Rotary International. "Ending Polio Timeline." Accessed at: http:// www.endpolio.org/about-polio

"Smallpox: Dispelling the Myths. An Interview with Donald Henderson." *Bulletin of the World Health Organization*, 86, no. 12 (December 2008).

The State of the World's Children. Published for UNICEF by Oxford University Press. New York: UNICEF, various years (1980–1995).

The State of the World's Refugees: Fifty Years of Humanitarian Action. Geneva: United Nations High Commissioner for Refugees, 2000.

Statements by Heads of State or Government at the World Summit for Children, United Nations, 29–30 September 1990. New York: UNICEF, 1990.

UA 111/91 — Mali: Extrajudicial Execution / Legal Concern: Bintou Maiga, Brehima Beridiogo and Over 20 Others Arrested and Over 150 People Killed. Index Number FR 37/003/1991. London: Amnesty International, March 25, 1991.

UNICEF Annual Report. New York: UNICEF, various years (1979–1996).

United Nations International Criminal Tribunal for Rwanda. "The Genocide." Accessed at: www.unictr.org/en/genocide

United States Holocaust Memorial Museum. "Genocide Fax: Part I." Accessed at: www.ushmm.org/confront-genocide/cases/rwanda/turning-points/genocide-fax-part-i

U.S. Agency for International Development. "The U.S. Government Special Advisor for Orphans and Vulnerable Children First Annual Report to Congress, August 2007 — Highly Vulnerable Children: Causes, Consequences and Actions." Washington, DC: August 2007.

U.S. Department of State. "Address by President Bill Clinton to the UN General Assembly." September 27, 1993. Accessed at: www.state.gov/p/io/potusunga/207375.htm

Vincent, George E. (president of the foundation). *The Rockefeller Foundation: A Review for 1921.* New York: Rockefeller Foundation, 1922. E-book obtained through Google Play.

We the Children: Meeting the Promises of the World Summit for Children. Report released by Kofi A. Annan, secretary general of the United Nations, prepared by the staff of UNICEF. New York, September 2001.

ADAM FIFIELD is a journalist whose work has appeared in the *New York Times, Washington Post, Christian Science Monitor, Chicago Sun-Times, Village Voice, Philadelphia Magazine,* and *Philadelphia Inquirer,* where he was a staff writer. He is also the author of *A Blessing Over Ashes* (William Morrow, 2000), a memoir about his Cambodian foster brother. From 2007 to 2013, he served as the Deputy Director of Editorial and Creative Services at the U.S. Fund for UNICEF.